I0752599

IMAGES
of America

Lānaʻi

ON THE COVER: *Paniolo* (cowboys) James Kauila (left) and Sam Koanui Piimoku were ready to move *pipi* (cattle) to another location on Lāna'i Ranch at Kō'ele. Bred on the ranch, the horses were noted for their endurance and ability to travel long distances between watering. The two men carry lariats for roping, but ranch manager George Munro discouraged roping pipi unless it was necessary in an emergency. (Hawaiian Pineapple Company collection.)

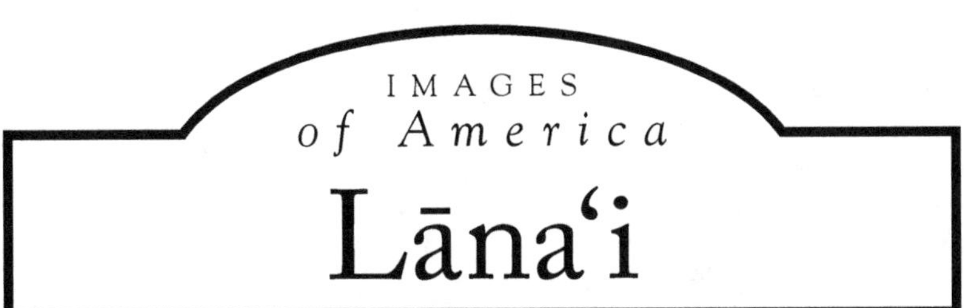

Alberta de Jetley

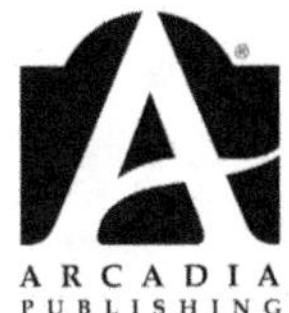

ISBN 978-1-5316-7831-9

Published by Arcadia Publishing
Charleston, South Carolina

Library of Congress Control Number: 2015936956

For all general information, please contact Arcadia Publishing:
Telephone 843-853-2070
Fax 843-853-0044
E-mail sales@arcadiapublishing.com
For customer service and orders:
Toll-Free 1-888-313-2665

Visit us on the Internet at www.arcadiapublishing.com

This book is dedicated to the memory of Ernest and Rebecca Richardson.
The memories they left us of Kōʻele will forever be in our hearts.

Contents

Acknowledgments

After I began to compile this book, I realized I had been collecting memories and photographs for it from the very first time I went to Kōʻele, the Lānaʻi Ranch's headquarters, in 1952. Our family was fortunate to be able to move into a ranch house previously occupied by the Forbes family during the ranching days. When we finished exploring our new home, Rebecca Richardson, our new neighbor, was there to greet us. She and her husband, Ernest, became our most beloved *hānai* (adopted) aunty and uncle. Mahalo to my parents, Richard and Anita Morita, my siblings, Marlene, Phyllis, Richard, Albert, Hermina, Gertrude, and Wallace, and our next-door neighbors, William and Eva (Kaopuiki) Kwon and their children for giving me a lifetime of memories of Kōʻele. Mahalo to Kepā Maly, Simon Tajiri, and Mikala Enfield at Lānaʻi Culture and Heritage Center (Lānaʻi CHC) for helping me search through their extensive archives for photographs used in this book, sharing their collective memories of people and places, and the cultural center's reference booklet *To Know Lānaʻi Once Again: A Historical Reference and Guide to the Island of Lānaʻi*, which was compiled by Kepā and Onaona Maly by Kumu Pono Associates; Dr. Kenneth Emory's collection of photographs (Emory collection) and information from his book *The Island of Lānaʻi, A Survey of Native Culture*; and Hawaiian Pineapple Company (HAPCo) and its newsletter, the *Pine Islander*. Providing me with insights into daily life on Lānaʻi were the books *True Stores of the Islands of Lānaʻi* by Lawrence Kainoahou Gay and *The Story of Lānaʻi* by George C. Munro. Mahalo to David H. Murdock of Castle and Cooke who published the *Lānaʻian* newsletter and hired me as its editor.

Special thanks go to Robin Kaye for scanning images from Lānaʻi CHC's collections. In addition to my own photographs, mahalo for photographs from the following sources in Lānaʻi CHC's archives and personal collections:

Henry Ahyin Kau Aki
Army Air Corps
Charlotte Babcock
Ray Jerome Baker
Belez family
A. Duane Black
Gregorio Cabusalay
Rosita Camero
Clarabal family
Russell de Jetley
Andrew dela Cruz
Aurelio Del Rosario
Adolph Desha
Fr. Gailen Everest
Richard Fuller
Chas. Gay
Cookie Hashimoto
Roberto Hera
Roberta Kauffman
Kepā Maly
Matsumoto family
Albert Morita
Richard Morita family
George Munro family
Tokumatsu Murayama
Frances Pagay
Clarence "Hoss" Richardson
Donald Rietow
Jack Ross
Simon Tajiri
Joana Varawa

INTRODUCTION

Without a written language, Hawai'i family genealogies and legends were shared orally through storytelling and chants. Separating fact from fiction is challenging, especially as stories may be embellished as they are retold and feature events that may have occurred centuries ago.

Māui, a demigod, pulled up the islands of Moloka'i, Lāna'i, and Maui while fishing with his brothers. He told them not to look behind them, but when they did, his line broke before he could pull out the entire land mass.

Lāna'ihale, Lāna'i's mountain range, rises to 3,370 feet above sea level. Although a wreath of white clouds crown its brow daily, its precious moisture has already been dropped onto the West Maui Mountains, leaving Lāna'i's slopes dry and barren of most vegetation except scrubby grass and low-lying trees. Slightly less than 14 miles wide and 13 miles long and with no rivers, streams, or lakes, Lāna'i was a formidable island to populate; but first, demon spirits had to be vanquished.

Lāna'i's legend of Kaululā'au tells how he tricked its evil demons and made it inhabitable for humans. Kaululā'au is the first in a line of strong men who carved their names into the island's soul, creating the home we cherish today. Archeological evidence show more than 6,000 natives may have lived on Lāna'i sustainably, using the ocean and land to gather and grow their own food more than 800 years ago. However, prior to the 1800s, war raged between the islands. In 1778, Kalani'ōpu'u, *mō'ī* (king) of Hawai'i Island, slaughtered many Lāna'i natives. One individual, Kini, jumped off a cliff at Kaunolū to escape from his captors. Time heals, and other natives settled here.

Natives had no resistance to Western diseases, and when missionaries and whaling ships arrived, Ma'i 'ōku'u, an epidemic believed to be Asiatic cholera, swept through the Hawaiian Islands in 1804 and 1805. More than 150,000 natives died, including 2,000 on Lāna'i. By 1825, four missionary schools were established, and in the 1840s, coral stone churches were being built at Maunalei and Kihamāniania. In 1848, Kamehameha III changed the way land was appropriated. The Great Māhele divided the kingdom's land between the government, chiefs, and people. Five of Lāna'i's 13 *ahupua'a* (land sections) were awarded to chiefs, eight were retained by the king and government, and natives were awarded 55 small house and planting sites. By 1850, Lāna'i's population dropped to 604. In 1854, Mormon elders leased land in the Pālāwai ahupua'a and formed a settlement they named Iosepa, City of Joseph. However, when their leaders were recalled to Utah, they abandoned it in 1857 due to the devastation of its crops by insects and drought conditions.

The most colorful person in Lāna'i's story is Walter Murray Gibson. Born on March 6, 1822, his history included possibly gun-running in the Caribbean, inspiring rebellion in the East Indies, and questionable land acquisitions in the Hawaiian kingdom. Gibson arrived in the Hawaiian Islands in 1861 and became a close confidant of King David Kalākaua. Gibson spoke Hawaiian fluently, and the natives embraced him as one of their own, especially when he became a citizen of the kingdom. He served as the king's prime minister in 1886 and also held the titles of minister of foreign affairs, health, and the interior.

Tasked by the Mormons in 1862 with purchasing land to reorganize their failed settlement in Pālāwai, Gibson purchased land from Chief Levi Ha'alelea for $3,000 but recorded the title in his own name. When

Mormon elders returned to the island in 1864, they charged him with misconduct and excommunicated him from the church. Gibson's hospitality and storytelling became legendary. He was also buying more land. The white foreign settlers in the kingdom derogatorily nicknamed him the "Shepherd of Lāna'i," as he had more than 40,000 sheep in addition to goats, cattle, and horses on his ranch. In the end, when he lost his political power in 1887, he left the islands and died in San Francisco on January 21, 1888. Frederick and Talula Hayselden, his son-in-law and daughter, inherited Gibson's estate, which included fee-simple ownership of five ahupua'a and leasehold rights on the eight others. After the Gibson estate was settled in 1893, the Hayseldens formed Lāna'i Land Development Company. In 1899, they incorporated Maunalei Sugar Company, built a village at Keōmoku, and hired 700 employees. In March 1901, it went bankrupt and closed.

Charles and Louisa Gay arrived on Lāna'i in 1902 from Ni'ihau, having purchased a part of the Gibson-Hayselden holdings, and began the ranch's transition from sheep to cattle. Gay's biggest accomplishment was the acquisition of all of Lāna'i's government lands in 1907. Gay's older relatives had purchased the island of Ni'ihau in 1864, making them the only family in Hawai'i's history to own two islands.

To satisfy some of their mortgage debts, in 1910 they sold some of their lands to Honolulu investors William G. Irwin, Robert W. Shingle, and Cecil Brown. The *hui* (group) formed Lāna'i Ranch Company and Lāna'i Ranch and sold both to Maui ranchers Frank and Harry Baldwin in 1917.

New Zealander George Munro was hired to manage Lāna'i Ranch in 1911. He recognized the importance of watershed management and began the reforestation of the island. In 1922, the Baldwin brothers sold their Lāna'i lands to James D. Dole for $1.1 million. Lāna'i Ranch continued to operate under the management of George Munro. In 1950, Lāna'i Ranch closed down, ending 40 years of ranching history.

James Dole's Hawaiian Pineapple Company turned Lāna'i into the world's largest pineapple plantation. It later became part of Castle & Cooke, a Hawai'i corporation started by missionary descendants. But, by 1985, worldwide competition from foreign markets was hurting Hawai'i's pineapple industry; its heyday as the island's economic engine was ending.

David H. Murdock, a self-made multimillionaire and real estate developer from California, purchased a majority share of Castle & Cooke in 1985. Hawaiian Pineapple Company became Dole Pineapple, a small part of Murdock's international food empire. Challenged to turn Lāna'i's economy around, between 1986 and 1991, he built the 102-room Lodge at Kō'ele, the Mānele Bay Hotel with 203 rooms, two golf courses, more than 300 homes, and three apartment complexes. He also planted hundreds of Cook Island pine trees along the main roads.

By 1997, Murdock had acquired more than 93 percent of Castle & Cooke's stock and returned the island to its previous status of being owned by one person. However, like many of Lāna'i's previous owners, after fighting through a worldwide recession during the 2000s and struggling to keep the island intact under one ownership, Murdock sold Lāna'i for an undisclosed sum to multibillionaire Larry Ellison, reputed to be the fifth-richest person in the world, ending his role in shaping 22 years of Lāna'i's history.

Lāna'ihale's clouds shroud the island's future—another chapter is beginning.

One

Legend or Fact

Kaululā'au Drives away Demons

'Ulu (breadfruit), a staple food for Polynesians, is what bought Kaululā'au to Lāna'i's shore. In some variations of the legend, he is described as the son of a Lāhainā chief. In others, he is just a youthful and rascally native who is banished to Lāna'i after he destroys 'ulu trees in Lāhainā.

When Kaululā'au is left on a Lāna'i beach, he is greeted by evil spirits who make it uninhabitable for humans. They welcome him warmly into their midst, but he knows that when night comes, they will search the island to kill him. Every day when they greet him, he lies about where he slept the previous night. One night, he tricks them into searching for him in surf pounding against the reef. Some of the spirits drown and enter the bodies of *weke* (red goatfish). To this day, weke may cause some people to have terrible nightmares.

Finally, only Pahulu, chief of the evil spirits, remained. Kaululā'au tricked him into looking at his own reflection in a pond by telling him he would sleep in its depths. When Pahulu peered over the pond's side, he saw Kaululā'au's image reflected beside him and jumped into the pond to grab him. However, Kaululā'au was standing behind the spirit. He hit Pahulu over the head with a rock, and one of Pahulu's eyes flew out of his head and landed at Kalaehī, a white coral knoll on the road to Keōmoku village, creating a hole. The spot is called Ka maka o Pahulu (the eye of Pahulu). A variation of the legend says that Pahulu fled to Kaho'olawe to live.

After Pahulu's demise, Kaululā'au lit a bonfire to signal villagers in Lāhainā. In the morning, they arrived to take him back to Maui, but Kaululā'au soon returned with others to form the first settlement on the island.

Archaeological evidence indicates Lāna'i was inhabited for close to 800 years, and as many as 6,000 natives may have lived here sustainably before Western contact. In the period prior to the 1800s, war between chiefs decimated the population. By the 1890s, only 175 natives remained on the island.

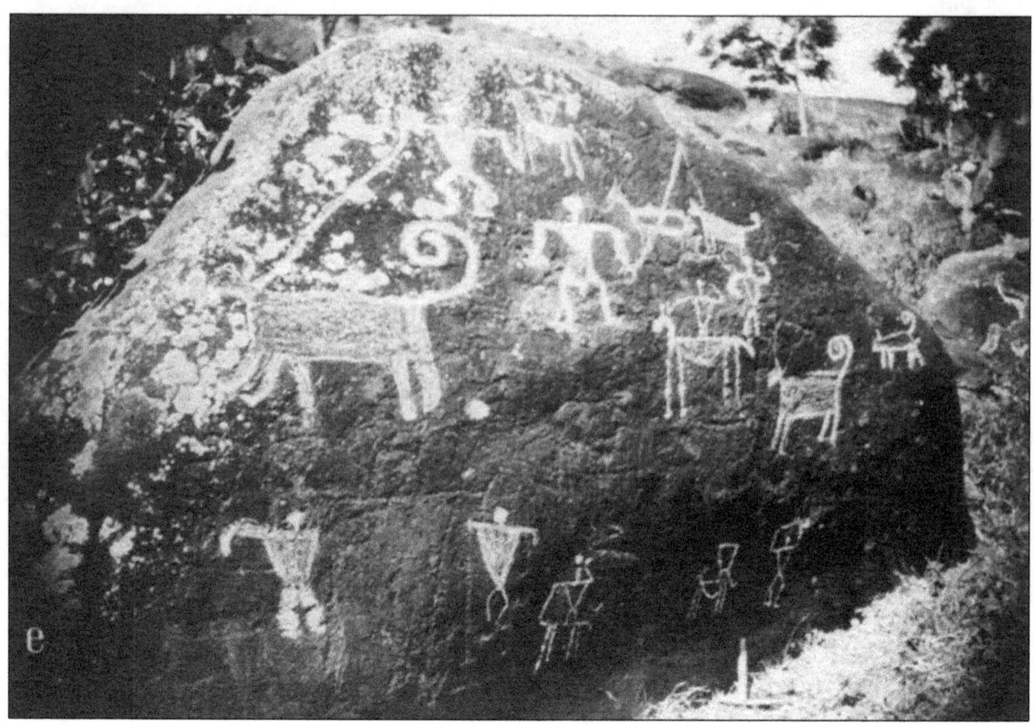

The field of petroglyphs at Luahiwa was surveyed by Dr. Kenneth P. Emory and recorded in his book *The Island of Lānaʻi, A Survey of Native Culture*, first printed in 1924 by the Bernice P. Bishop Museum. Petroglyphs found at Kahalu'u, Oʻahu, may date to 1600. Luahiwa's petroglyphs may date to the 1800s, but others at Kaunolū may have been made in the 1780s. (A. Duane Black collection.)

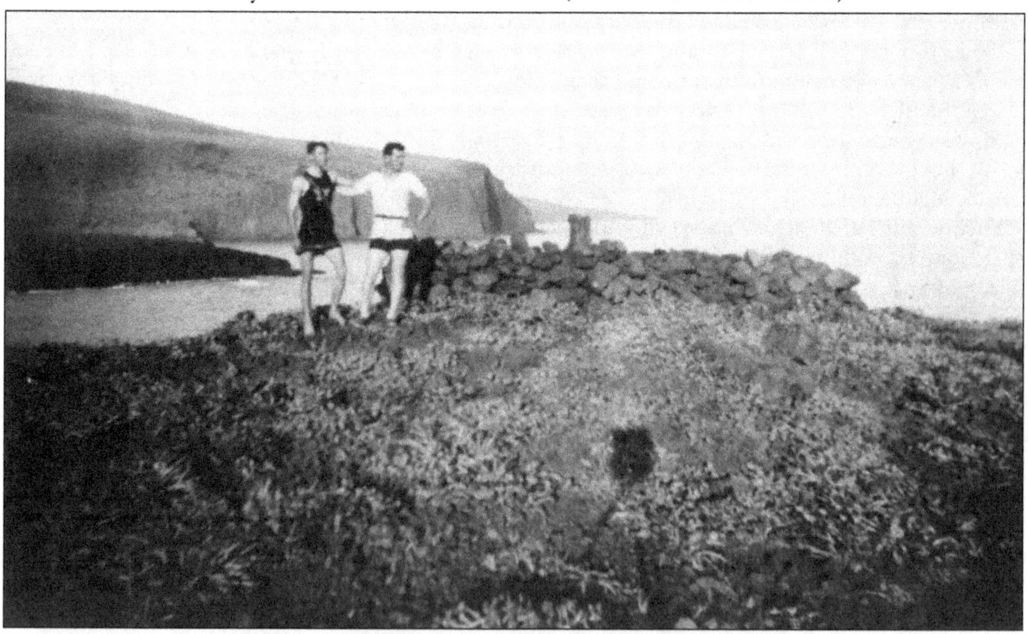

Accompanied by Hector Munro, the nephew of George Munro, Dr. Emory climbed to the top of Puʻupehe to survey it. This 1921 photograph clearly depicts the rock formation, which may be an ancient fishing shrine rather than the legendary grave of two lovers. (George Munro collection.)

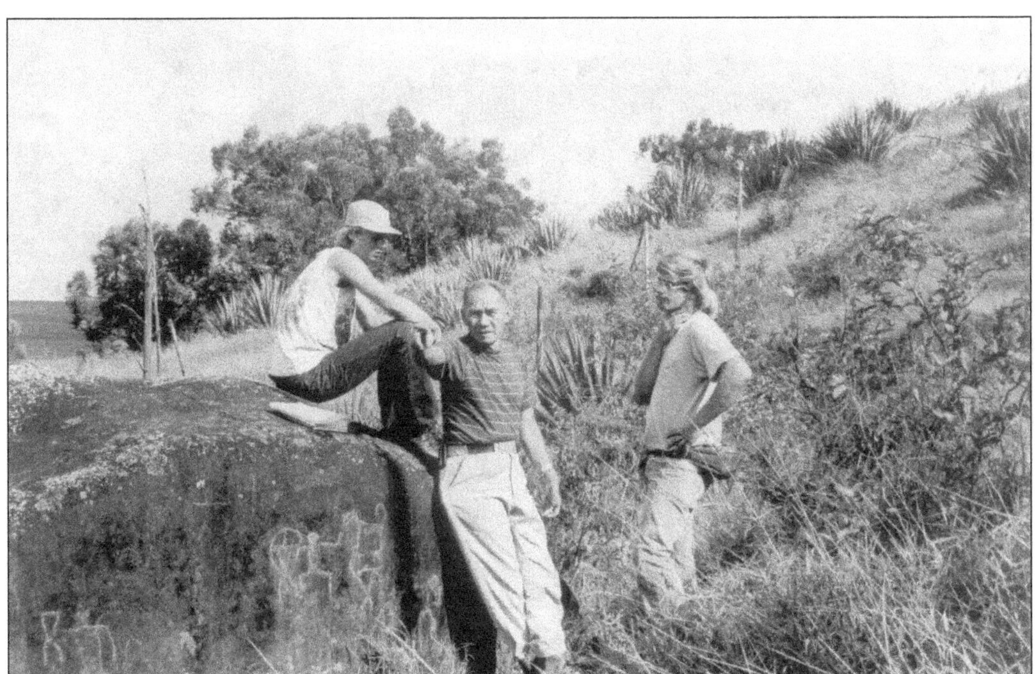

Lāna'i resident Lloyd Cockett points out landmarks to Dr. Emory's young helpers, Kepā Maly (standing) and Kamakaonaona Judd. Cockett is a descendant of families who lived in the Pālāwai on a land grant given to them during the time of the Great Māhele. He frequently joined Emory's excursions to study different sites. (A. Duane Black collection.)

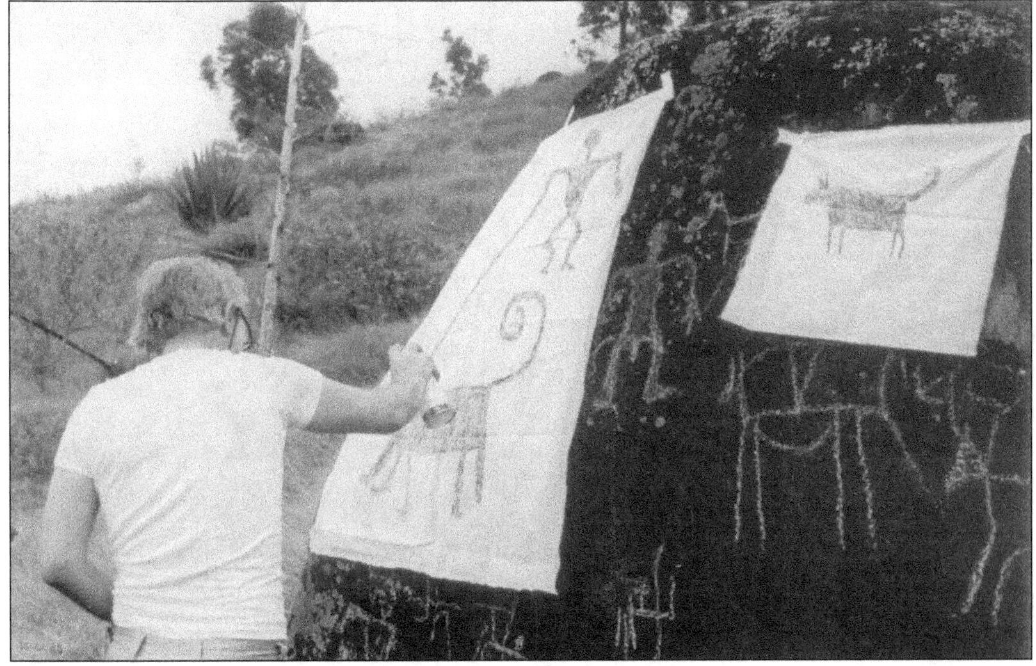

Bob Krauss sprays a fixative on a rubbing he has completed. Today, it is recommended visitors do not make rubbings or use chalk to outline the petroglyphs for photographs. Tall grass and the hillside's steepness make it difficult to access the Luahiwa site. (A. Duane Black collection.)

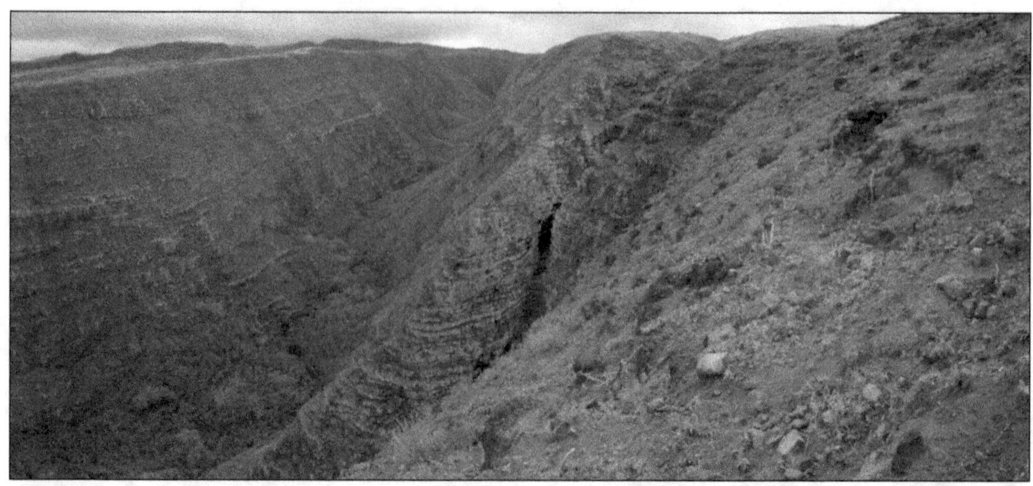

Maunalei's steep ridges ran red with blood in a fierce battle between Kalani'ōpu'u, mō'ī of the Big Island of Hawai'i, and Kahekili, mō'ī of Maui, in 1778. On the fortified ridge of Ho'okio, it was possible for warriors to sling rocks across to their enemies. However, it was a difficult place to defend, and all of the Lāna'i warriors were slaughtered without mercy. (Simon Tajiri collection.)

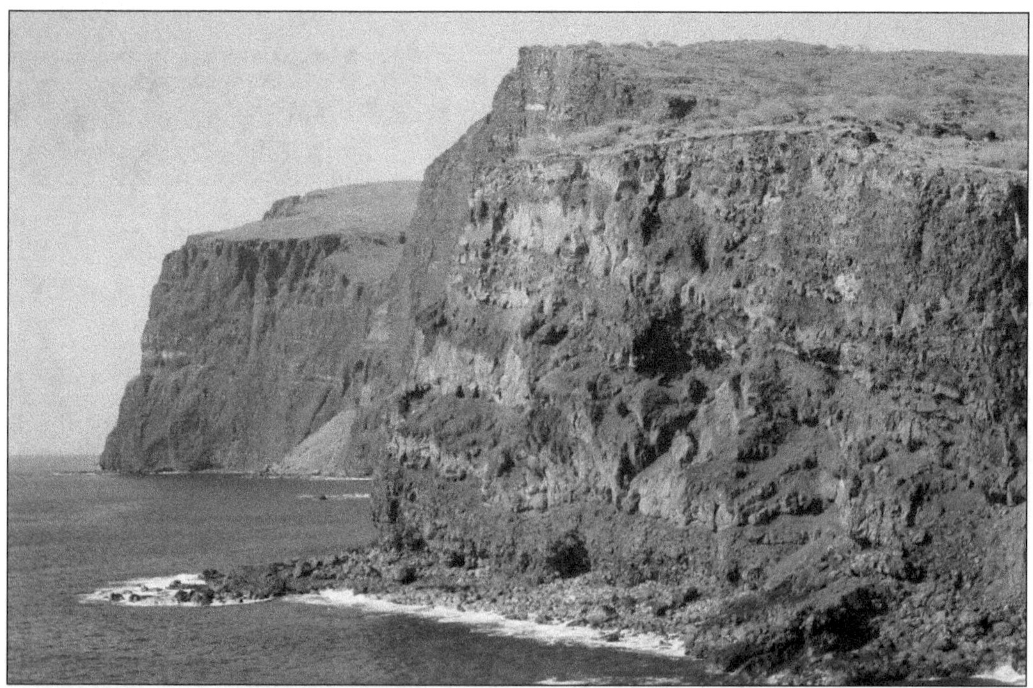

At Paoma'i, natives hid in the forest to escape Kalani'ōpu'u's wrath. Almost every living being was hunted down and slaughtered, except one person named Kini. Captured alive, Kini's hands were tied, and he was taken to Kanoulū to appear before Kalani'ōpu'u. Faking an illness, Kini's bonds were loosened, and he jumped off the cliffs and swam to safety. (Simon Tajiri collection.)

Two

War Rages on Mountain Ridges

Kalani'ōpu'u Conquers Lāna'i

Sailing canoes carrying fierce warriors journeyed between the islands to wage war, and Lāna'i was not exempt from their battles. Kalani'ōpu'u, mō'ī of Hawai'i Island, and Kahekili, mō'i of Maui, fought a huge battle on the sand hills of Waikapū on Maui in 1776. Kalani'ōpu'u was defeated; suing for peace, he retreated to the Big Island of Hawai'i to plan his retaliation. The following year, he attacked Maui again, raiding Kaupō on its eastern flank before retreating to Hawai'i Island. In 1778, he raided Kaho'olawe's natives. Confident he would succeed, he sailed into Lāhainā, Maui. Kahekili's warriors were able to defend their villages, and Kalani'ōpu'u sailed across 'Au'au, the nine-mile channel separating the islands, to Lāna'i.

Accompanied by the young warrior Kamehameha, Kalani'ōpu'u attacked natives who had gathered to defend themselves on the fortified ridge of Ho'okio, located on the upper section of Maunalei Gulch. Without mercy, Kalani'ōpu'u's warriors slaughtered them all. They proceeded to travel across the island killing almost every *kāne*, *wahine*, and *keiki* (man, woman, and child) in their path.

One man, Kini, survived their march across the land. Captured alive, they bound his hands and took him to Kalani'ōpu'u. When they approached the cliffs of Kaunolū, where Kalani'ōpu'u and Kamehameha had set up their command post, Kini asked his captors to loosen his bonds, saying he was suffering from dysentery and had to release his bowels.

Confident he could not escape, they loosened his bonds. Unbeknownst to them, Kini was famous for his cliff-jumping skills. As soon as they freed his hands, he ran to the edge of the cliff and plunged off it. From the cliff top, they watched Kini swim to safety.

When Kalani'ōpu'u and his warriors continued to stay on Lāna'i, they ran out of food. Reduced to eating roots, they became sick with dysentery. To this day, Kalani'ōpu'u's raid is referred to as "the battle of loose bowels" by the descendants of natives he murdered.

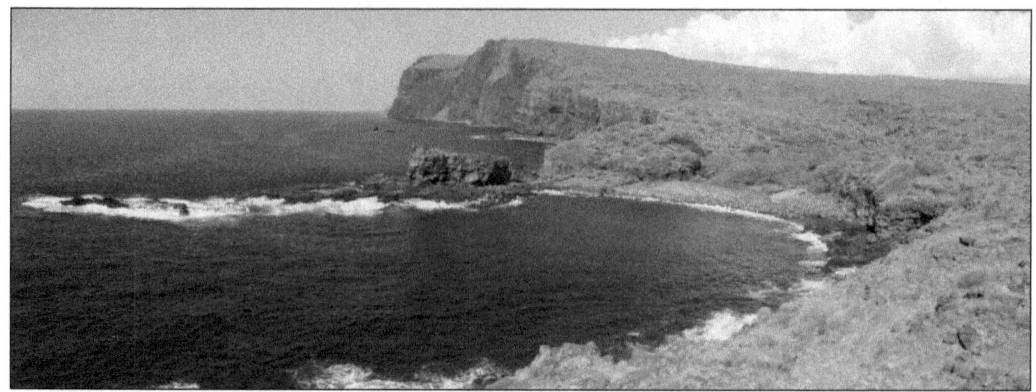

Kamehameha I was a young warrior of 42 when he accompanied Kalaniʻōpuʻu on his raid of Lānaʻi. In later years, he continued to return to Kaunolū to rest on his voyages between the islands. In 1868, his grandson Kamehameha V asked Pālāwai landowner Walter Murray Gibson to write down some of the stories of his grandfather's Lānaʻi exploits. (Simon Tajiri collection.)

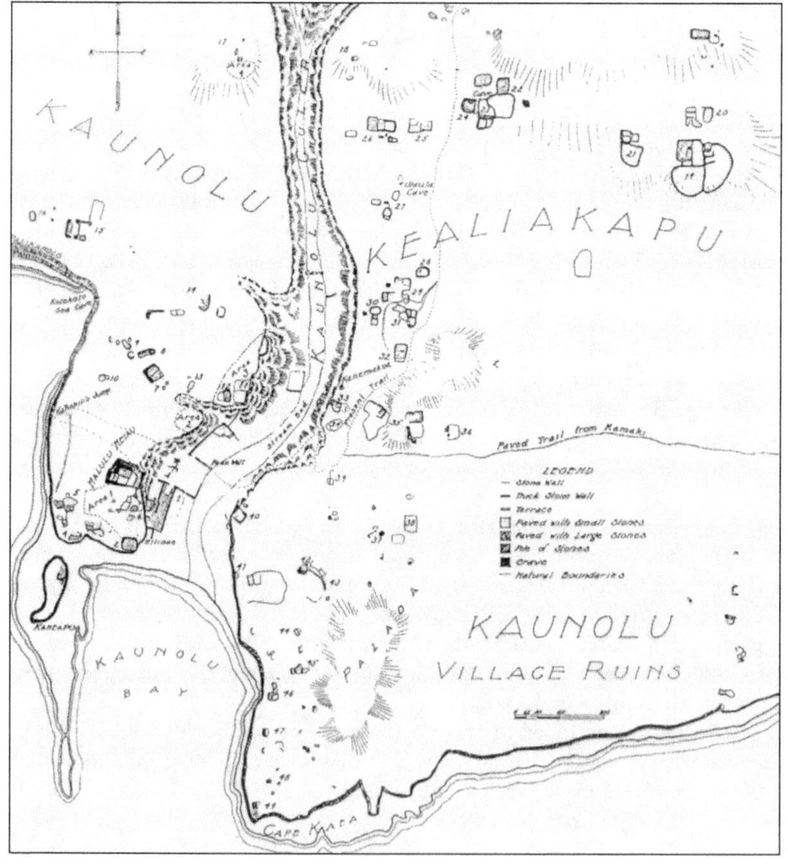

Dr. Emory drew this map of Kaunolū showing the village ruins he surveyed. Kamehameha the Great used this area as a resting place in his voyages between the Big Island and Oʻahu. (Emory collection.)

Three

Keōmoku Village and Pālāwai Basin

Living Mauka and Makai

Hawaiian natives lived sustainably off the *aina* (land) and traveled *mauka* (toward the mountain) to plant crops such as sweet potatoes, bananas, and taro. Going *makai* (toward the sea), they gathered a variety of food such as *limu* (seaweed), *'ōpihi* (limpets), *honu* (turtles), and fish. Remnants of their presence can still be seen today at village sites at Kaunolū, Mānele, and Maunalei.

Early archeological data show the island's population before Western contact may have exceeded 6,000. After a savage war in 1778 between island chiefs, only a few natives remained. Natives from Maui slowly repopulated the island, and by 1823, the population was estimated to be 3,000. However, by 1832, it dropped to 2,000, and by 1850, to 604.

Many of the original villages and isolated homesites appear to be far from water sources. Later accounts note mauka villagers collected dew from plants and water from natural depressions or shallow wells near Kaunolū and Kaumālapa'u. Some of the island's ravines show signs of having been deepened so rainwater could be collected and stored in them for later use. At Maunalei, a perennial stream was a reliable source of water; agricultural terraces following its path still remain. Along the coastline, wells with potable but brackish water were dug.

By 1893, Lāna'i was home to 200 people and 50,000 sheep. In 1899, the Maunalei Sugar Company established a village for 800 workers at Keōmoku. By 1901, the company closed; its wells drew water too brackish to irrigate sugarcane, and almost everyone left.

Kō'ele became the center of the island's population of less than 100 people with the economy focusing on ranching. Under the stewardship of its manager, George Munro, windblown land grazed down to rocks was slowly covered with grasses again. Bare mountain ridges were covered with trees, and the land began to heal. Although one or two families remained at Pālāwai, the last inhabitants of the Keōmoku moved to Kō'ele or the new Lāna'i City by 1951, leaving only their memories of it behind.

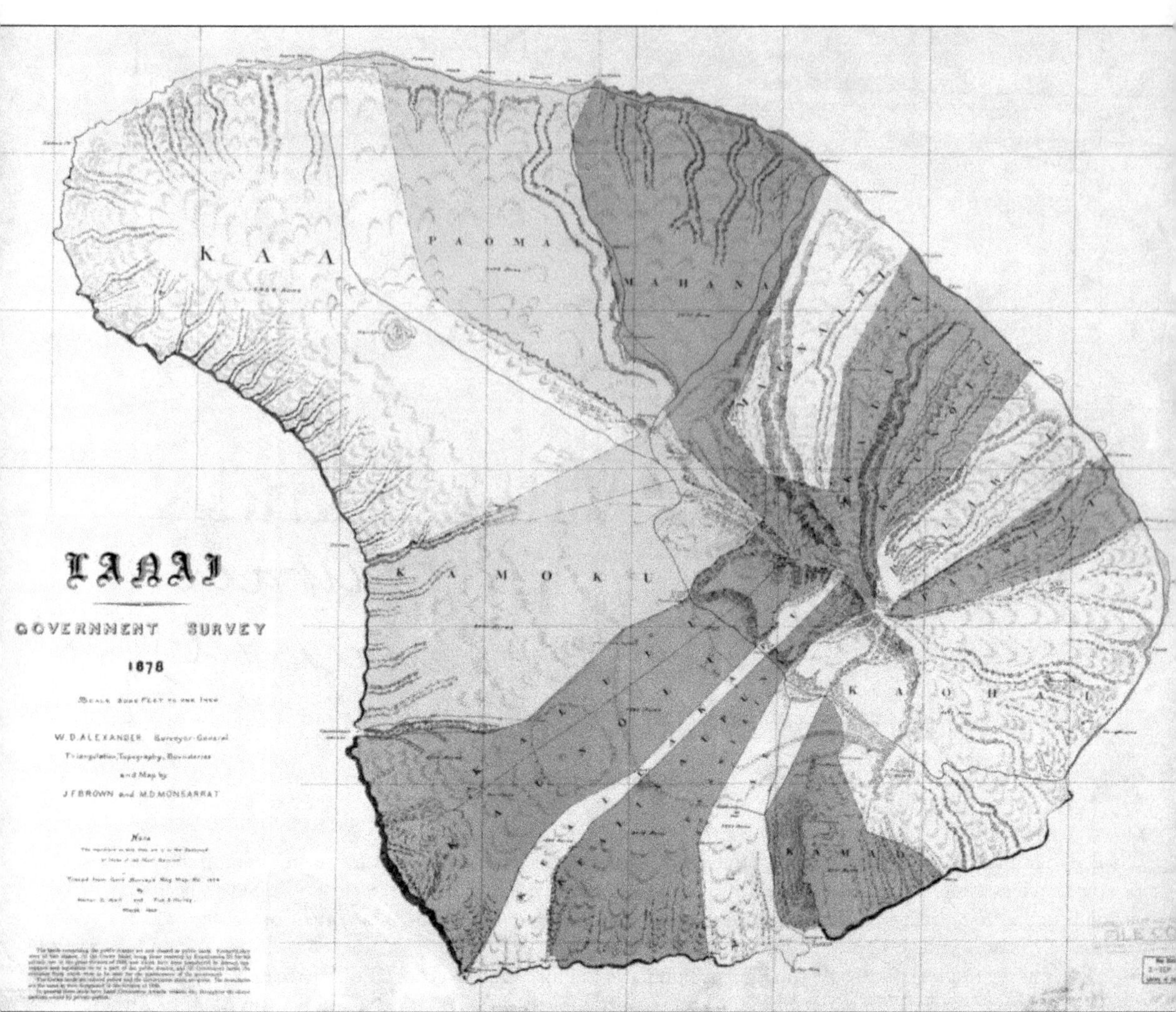

Before Western contact, land was controlled by high-ranking *ali'i* (king or chief), who held it in trust for *maka'ainana* (the people). In 1848, Kamehameha III created the Great Māhele, in which lands were granted to the chiefs, government, and native tenants. *Kuleana* is land assigned to natives to use as a home site and to cultivate crops. They paid labor taxes and annual taxes to a *konohiki* (local overseer), who was responsible for regulating land, water, and the ocean's resources. He supervised communal labor within the ahupua'a and a communal lifestyle following nature's natural rhythms, which also allowed for leisure time for maka'ainana to enjoy their families and lives. (Lāna'i CHC collection.)

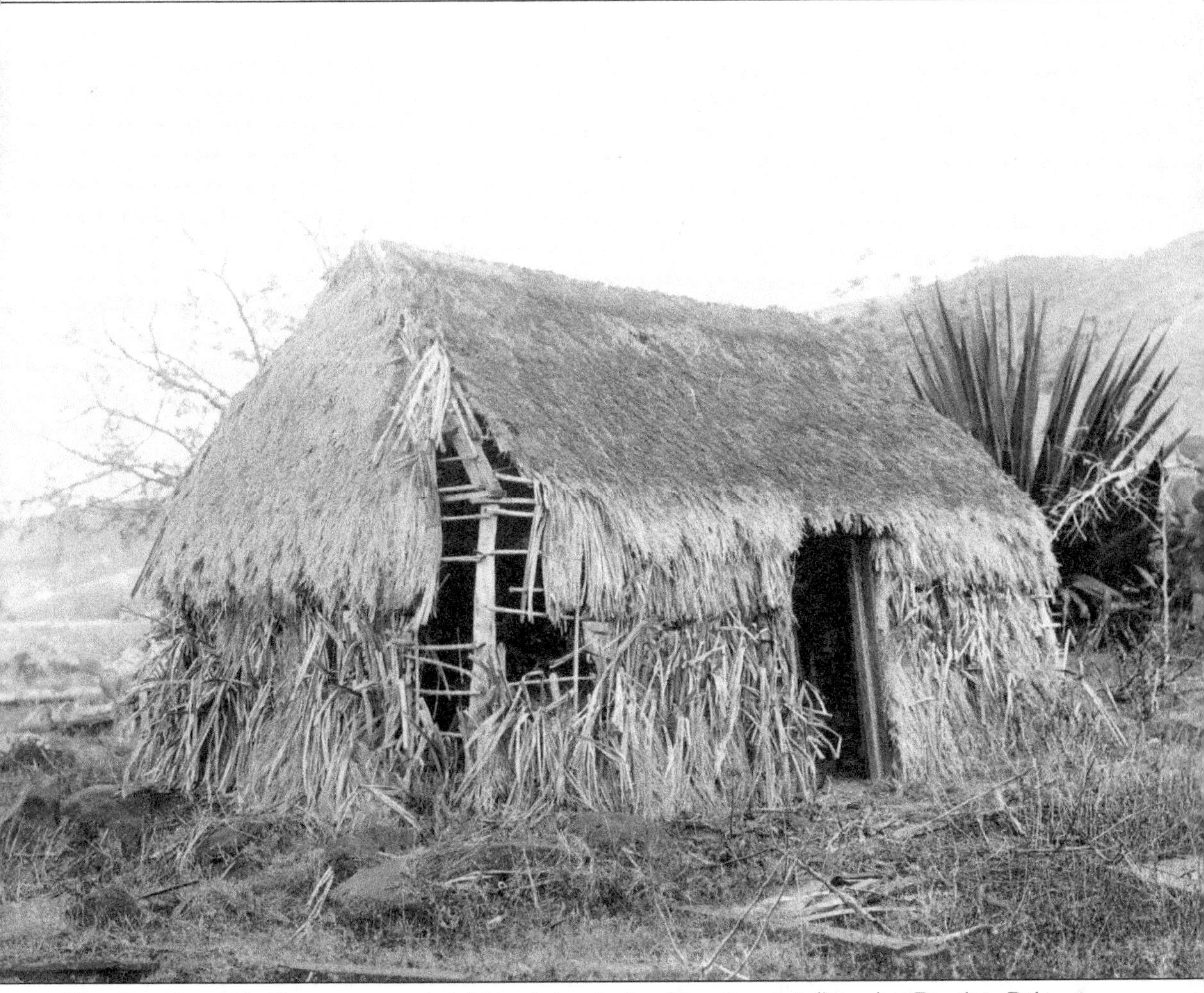

Hawaiian Pineapple Company recorded this as being the last Hawaiian *hale* (house) at Pāwili in Pālāwai in 1912. It was the home of Kahikanaka and his wife, Hakawai. They lived there with their granddaughter Kaupē Kaopuiki and her husband, Joseph Makahanaloa. In 1907, the hale may have been visited by Jonah Kūhiō Kalanianana'ole when he visited Charles and Louisa Gay on Lāna'i. Kūhiō was a royal prince when his uncle David Kalākaua assumed the Hawaiian kingdom's throne in 1884. Kūhiō served in various kingdom offices and was often called Ke Ali'i Maka'āinana, the Prince of People, for his work on the passage of the Hawaiian Homestead Act. This photograph was taken by Ray Jerome Baker. (HAPCo collection.)

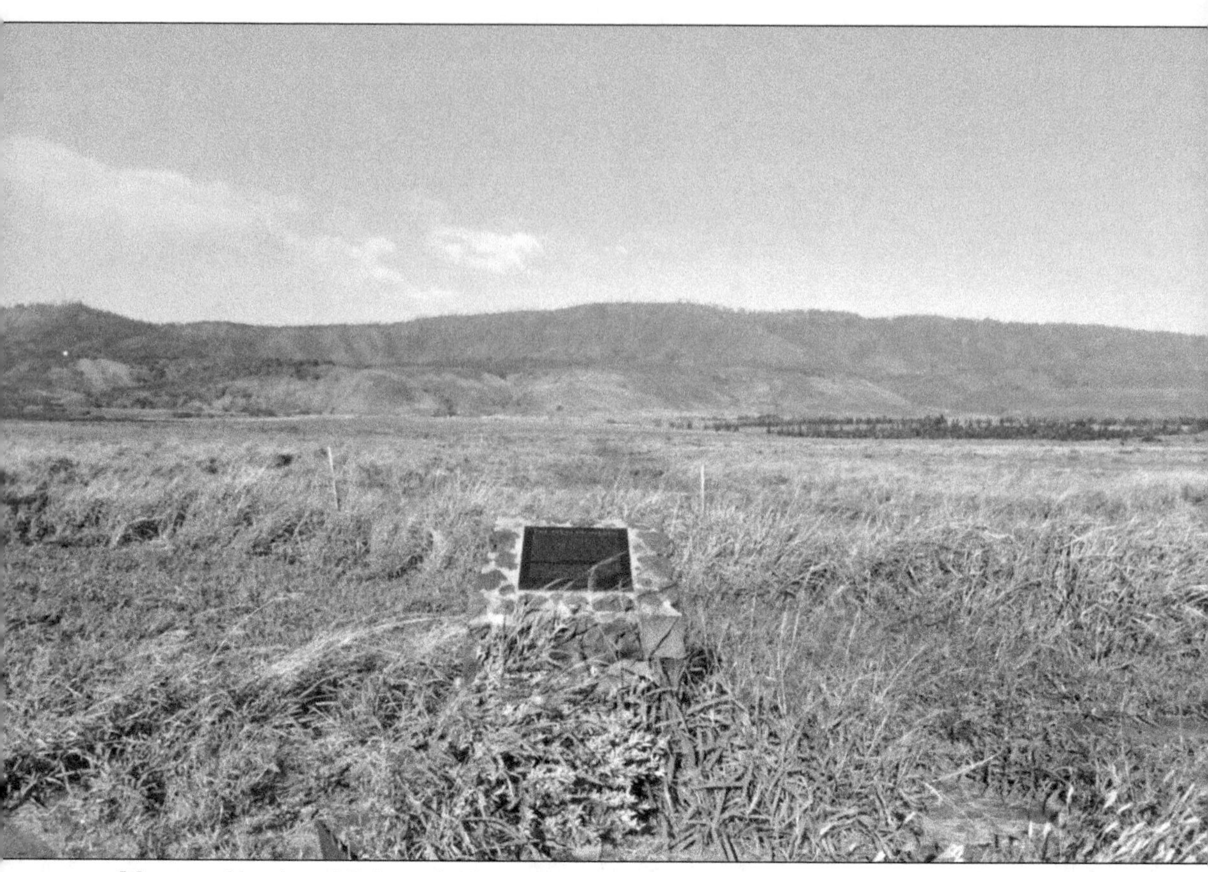

Mormon elders leased Pālāwai land in 1854 to establish Iosepa, the "City of Joseph." They hoped to gather Hawaiian "saints" and Mormons from the United States to it. However, the elders were called back to Utah in 1857 and left the settlers to carry on alone. By 1858, they were struggling; without adequate water, they could not grow crops. They abandoned Pālāwai and moved to Lāʻie on Oʻahu's windward side. In 1862, Walter Murray Gibson arrived to reorganize the settlement. He purchased the ahapuaʻa of Pālāwai for $3,000 from Chief Levi Haʻalelea, recorded it in his own name, and started his ranch. Gibson was excommunicated from the church and purchased more land. He moved his ranch headquarters to Kōʻele and planted its giant Norfolk pine tree in 1875. Alongside Mānele Road, this stone marker with a metal plaque commemorates the Mormon settlement. (Author's collection.)

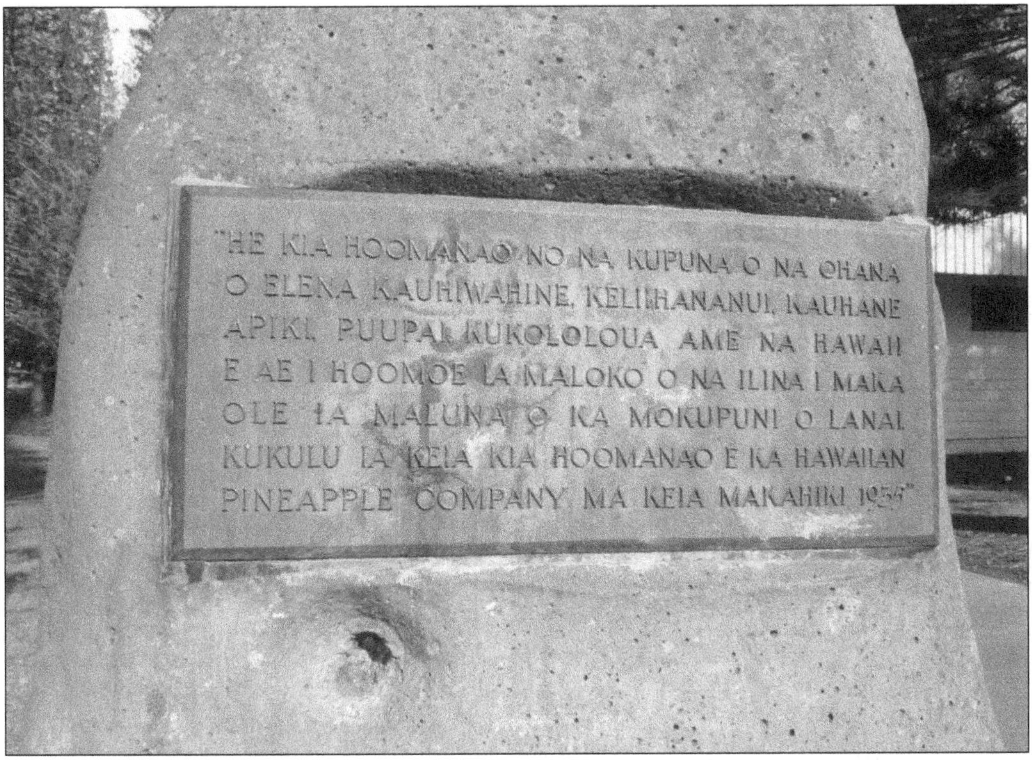

This memorial in Dole Park was installed by Hawaiian Pineapple Company in 1935 in remembrance of *kūpuna* (elders) who are laid to rest in unmarked graves on Lāna'i. Many had native land rights and grant lands from Kamehameha III and Kamehameha IV. When the plantation began, many had already abandoned or sold their land interest to the plantation or to other parties. This memorial acknowledges and honors them as the island's first residents. (Author's collection.)

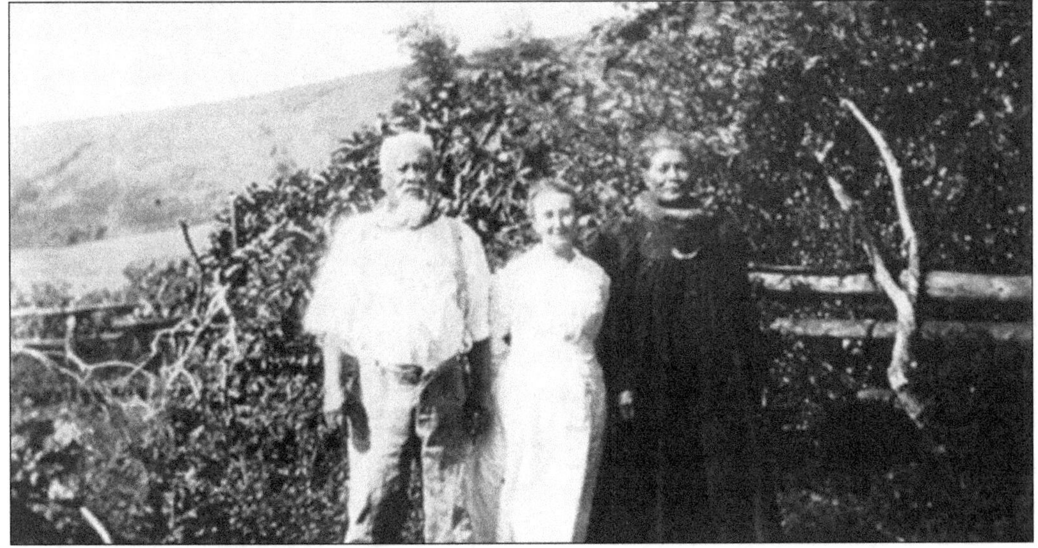

David S. (left) and Makaimoku Keliihananui (right) are pictured here with Jean Munro. Mrs. Keliihananui wears a feather *lei* and a formal black muumuu in contrast to her husband's working clothes and Munro's simple housedress. (George Munro collection.)

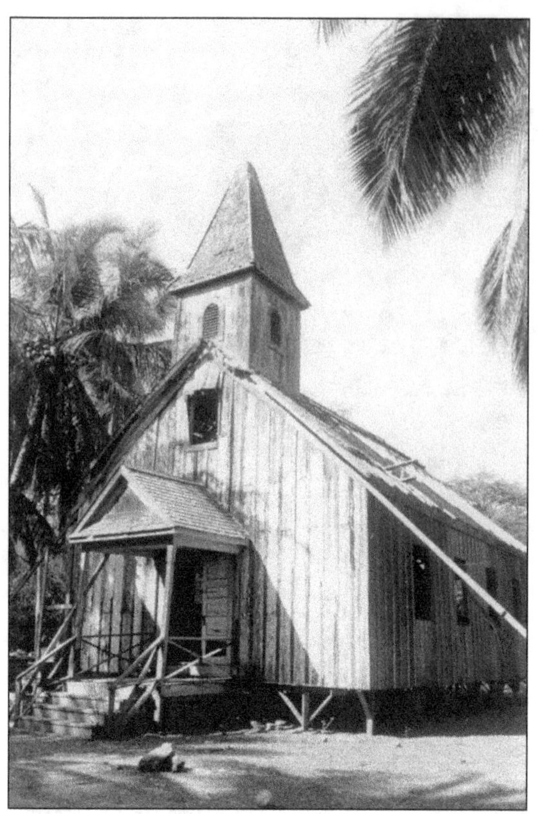

Erosion and weather have taken their toll on the last remaining building at Keōmoku village in this mid-1980s photograph of the church. A diagram of the village as drawn by the late Rev. Daniel Kaopuiki in 1940 shows a thriving village with a hospital, school, and another church in addition to homes for the Maunalei Sugar Company's workers. (Author's collection.)

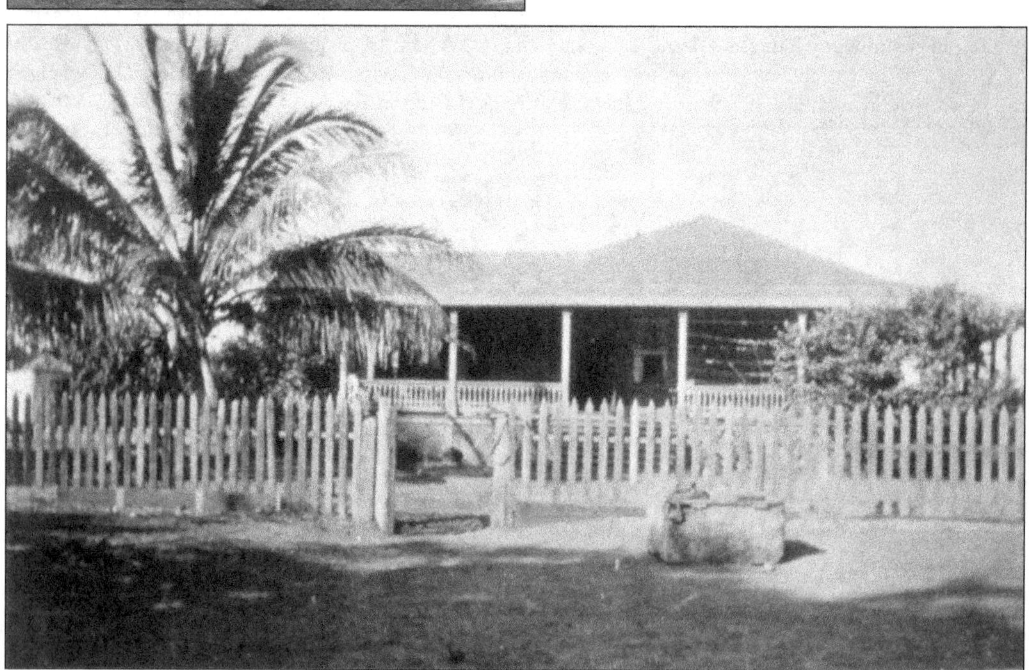

This house, originally built in Keōmoku by the Maunalei Sugar Company as a residence for its manager, later became the home of the Cockett and Kaopuiki families. The Rev. Daniel Kaopuiki and his family left the home in 1951 to move to Lāna'i City. (Chas. Gay collection.)

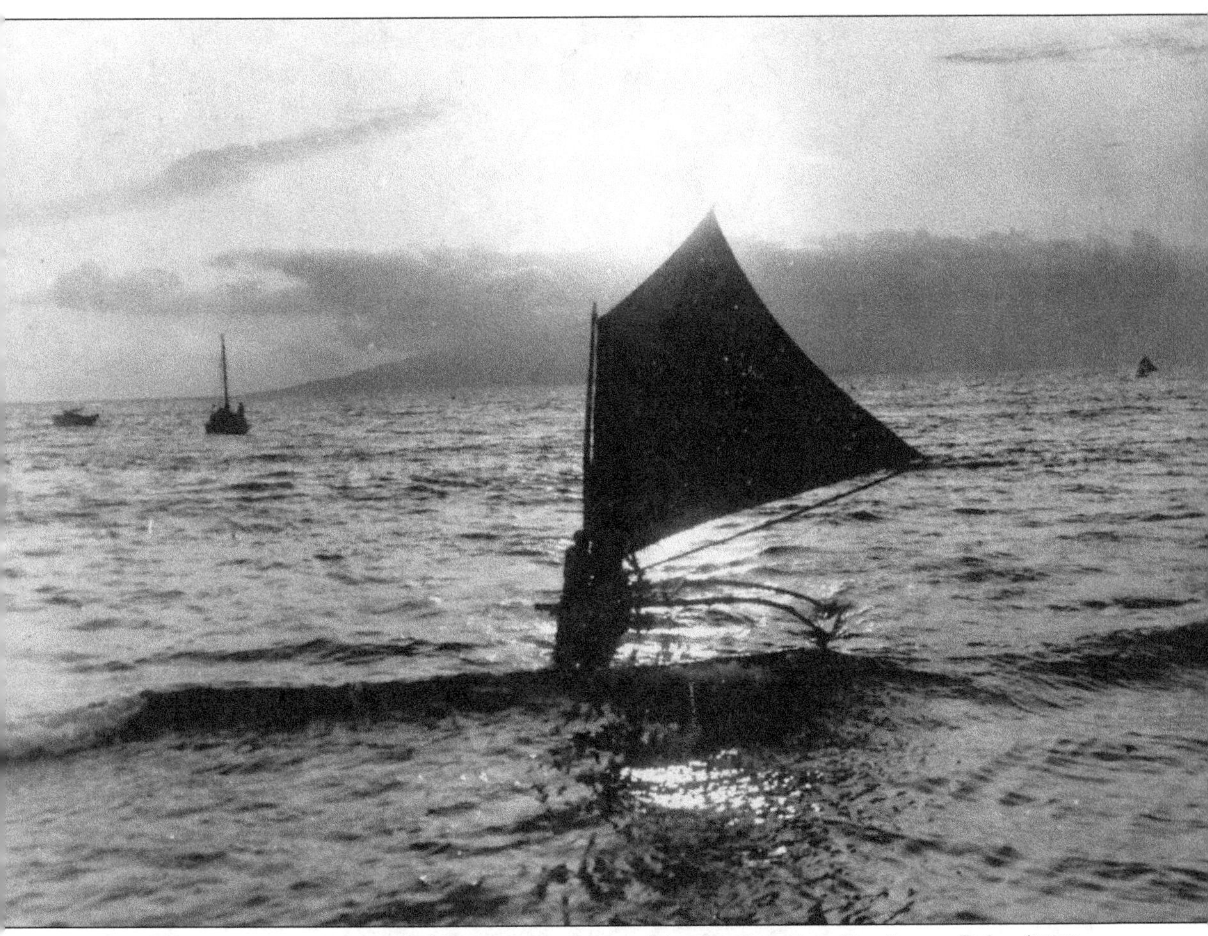

At Keōmoku, as many as 10 sailing canoes went to sea in all kinds of weather. Ray Jerome Baker (1880-1972), an American photographer who moved to Honolulu in 1910 with his wife, Edith Frost, and their son Earl Frost Baker, took this photograph of a Hawaiian canoe under sail captained by Kapena Kaopuiki while visiting Lāna'i. Gay commissioned a San Francisco boat builder to build a Western-style boat to carry letters and passengers between Kalahalepalaoa, Lāna'i, and Lāhainā, Maui. It was named *Nunu Lawe Leka* (pigeon transport letter). Captained by Daniel Kaopuiki Sr., *Nunu Lawe Leka* was famed for its swiftness and agility in navigating the nine miles of 'Au'au Channel between the islands. A highly skilled seaman, Kaopuiki was revered for his knowledge of open-sea sailing and navigating by the stars. Kaopuiki called the North Star Ka Hoku Paa Kea, the fixed star. (Ray Jerome Baker collection.)

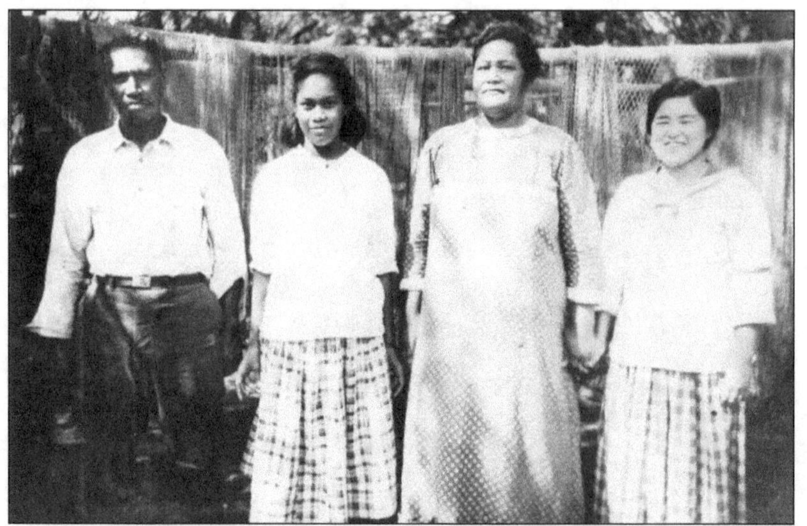

From left to right, Johnny, Makaleka, and Ulia Nakihei with Japanese bride Ayako Tamura from Hiroshima, Japan, pose in front of fishnets set out to dry on a pole at Keōmoku. (Emory collection.)

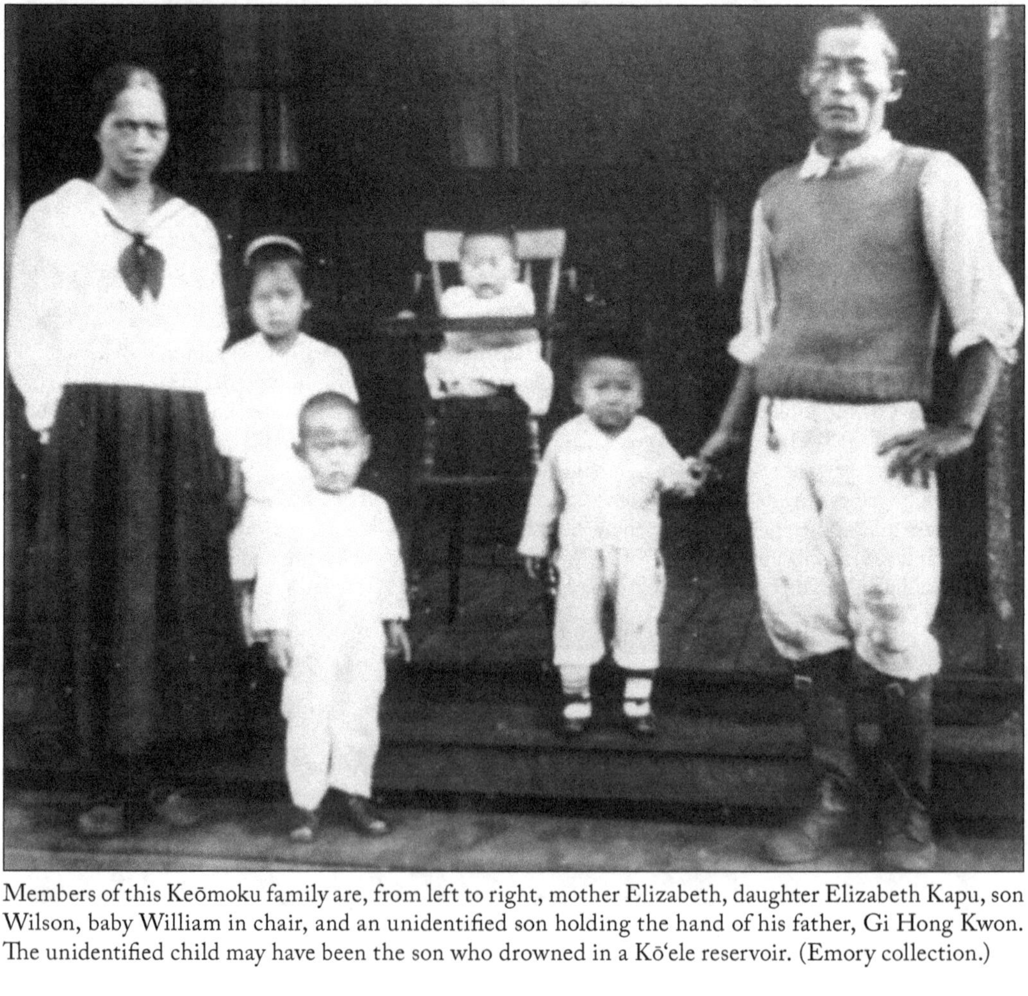

Members of this Keōmoku family are, from left to right, mother Elizabeth, daughter Elizabeth Kapu, son Wilson, baby William in chair, and an unidentified son holding the hand of his father, Gi Hong Kwon. The unidentified child may have been the son who drowned in a Kō'ele reservoir. (Emory collection.)

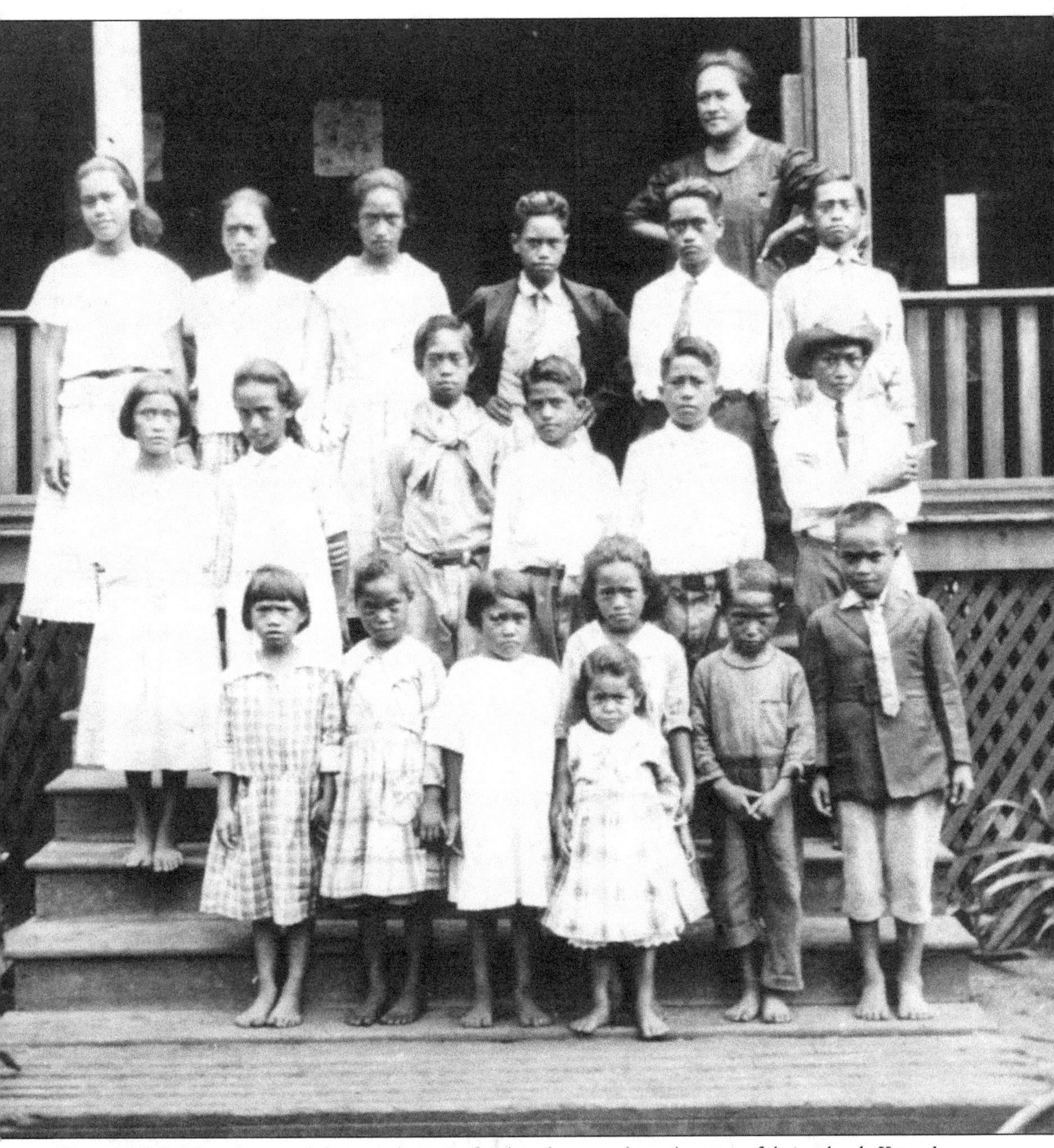

Keōmoku School students and their teacher pose for this photograph on the steps of their school. *Keōmoku* means "the sandy section" in Hawaiian, but as spoken by kūpuna and native speakers, it means "white ship." Ships with huge white sails may have been shipwrecked on this sandy section in the island's early history. During the Maunalei Sugar Company's short existence, Keōmoku became the largest village on the island. It had a post office, more than 100 homes, a school, and a church. Ka Lanakila o ka Malamalama Hoomana Naauao was built in 1903, and in recent years was restored by Lāna'i CHC through community grants. Although it is no longer used on a regular basis, it is open to the public to view. Many of Keōmoku's residents eventually moved to Kō'ele to work at Lāna'i Ranch or to Lāna'i City. By 1955, only a few houses remained, and they collapsed and rotten away. (Emory collection.)

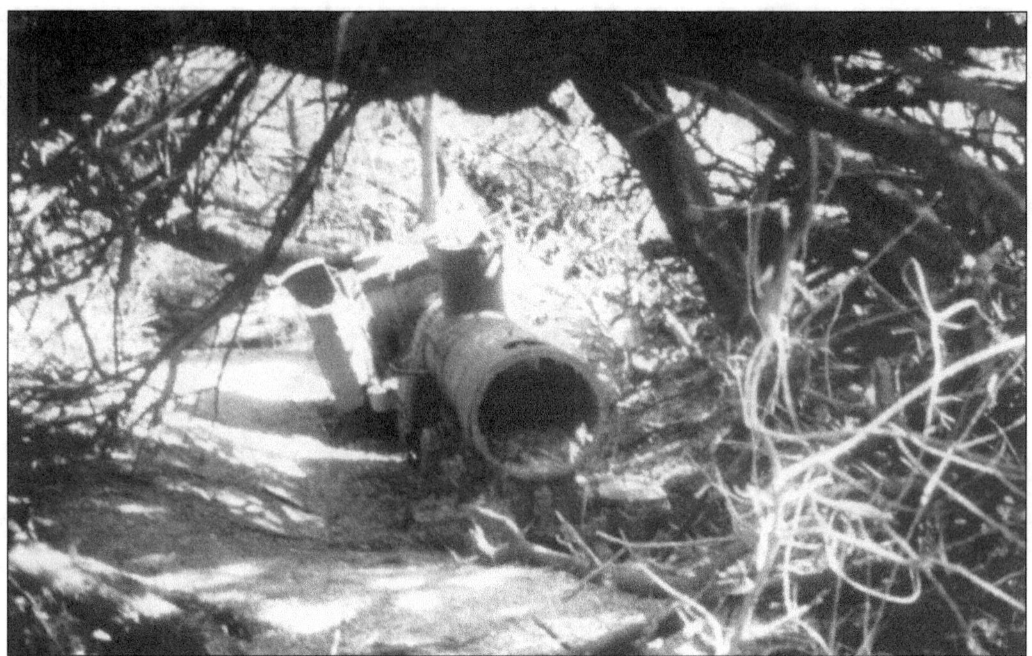

When the Maunalei Sugar Company went bankrupt in 1901, most of its equipment was sold to other sugar plantations. *Kiawe* (mesquite) branches form an alcove around the engine of the Kahalepalaoa locomotive in this photograph from about 1964. Today, the area surrounding it has been cleared and visitors can take a walking tour. (Lāna'i CHC.)

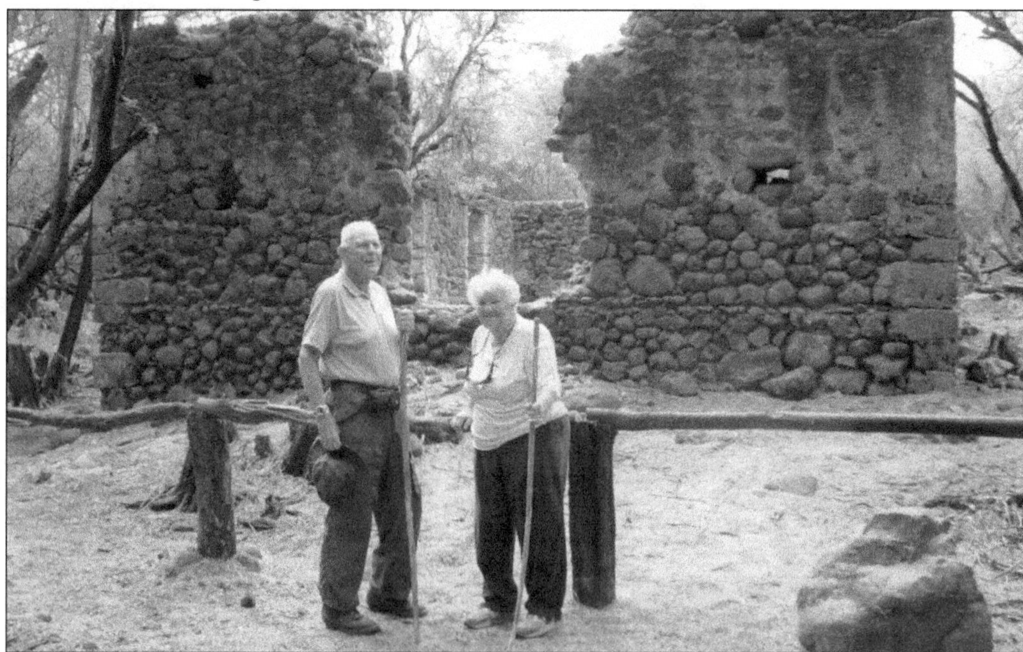

Between 2,000 and 3,000 people lived on Lāna'i when Protestant missionaries from Lāhainā came to the island to build four missionary schools between 1825 and 1840. The first building was near Kahalepalaoa and opened in 1828. William and Jean Munro are pictured here at the Maunalei schoolhouse. At Kihamāniania near Kō'ele, the schoolhouse/church had a thatched roof. (Albert Morita collection.)

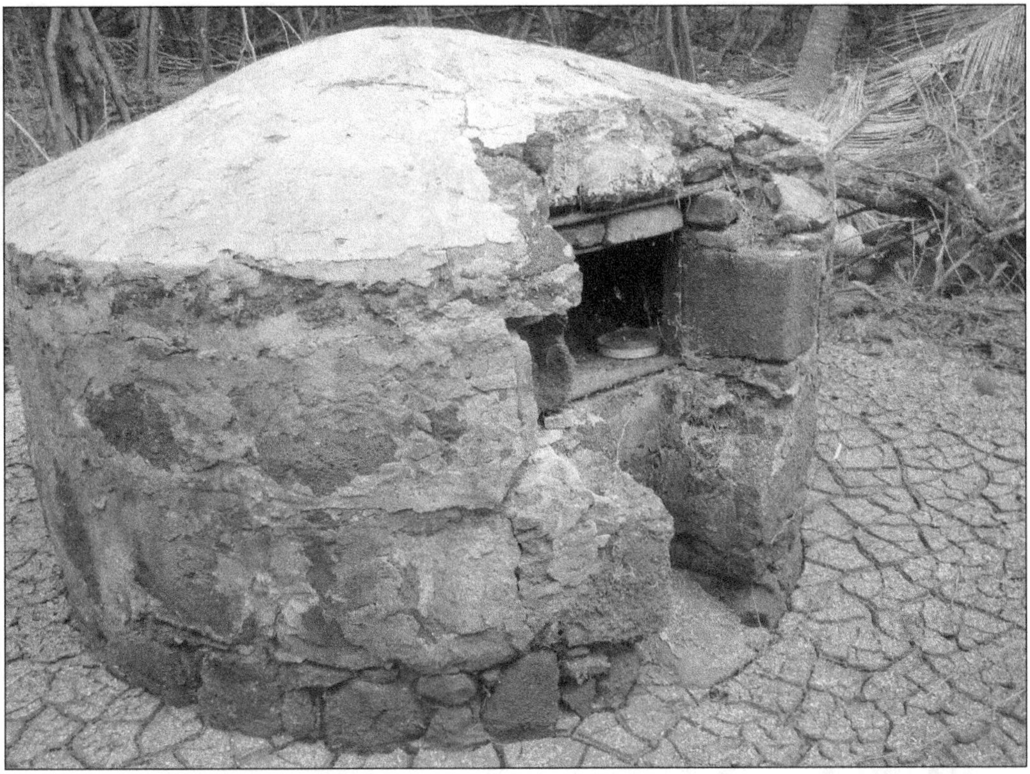

This stone oven used by Japanese workers at Maunalei Sugar Plantation is a stark reminder of the failed venture. The company was incorporated in 1898 with a capital investment of $1 million in 1899. By 1901, the company had closed down. Its water sources turned brackish and could no longer sustain its population of approximately 700 residents. (Lāna'i CHC.)

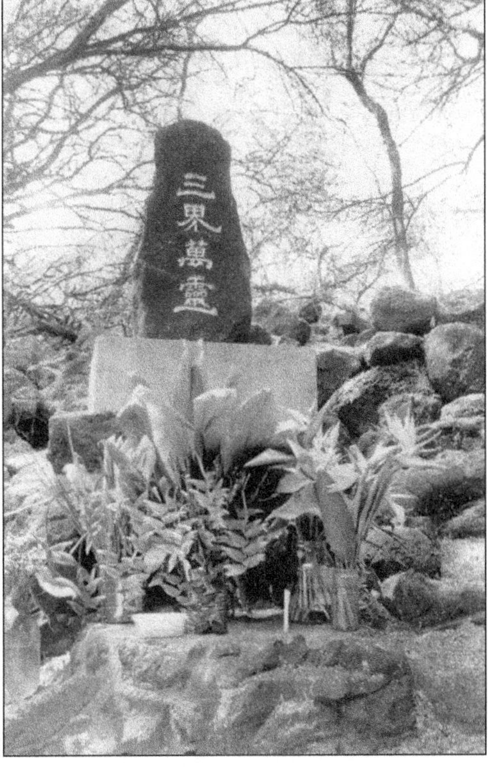

Kiawe branches form a protective arch over a monument at Keōmoku in remembrance of Japanese workers of the Maunalei Sugar Company who lost their lives after an illness swept through the village in 1901. Located near the Kahalepalaoa Landing, the monument's site is cleaned by the Lāna'i Honwanji temple members annually at Obon, a customary time for Japanese to honor the spirits of their ancestors. (Author's collection.)

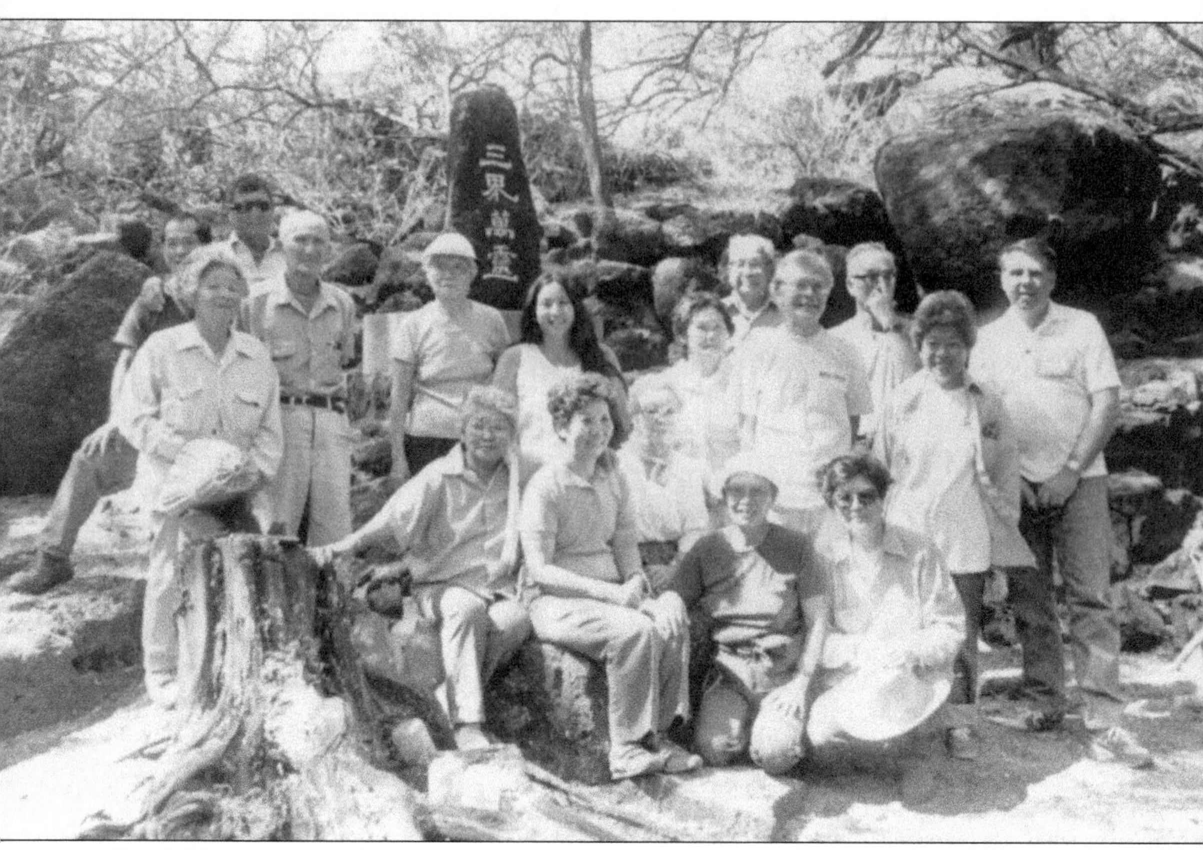

Lāna'i Hongwanji temple members and friends gathered for a group photograph in the 1980s. The group traveled to the monument to clean it for Obon. After their work was completed, they performed traditional ceremonial dances and enjoyed a picnic luncheon before making the long drive back to Lāna'i City. (Author's collection.)

Four

Kō'ele

Ranching Days

Thousands of sheep, goats, and cattle grazed on Lāna'i's wind-swept land. The lack of adequate rain produced little or no grass, and measures had to be taken to reduce herd sizes. In 1902, Charles and Louisa Gay purchased a portion of Walter Murray Gibson's estate from his daughter and son-in-law, Tulula and Fredrick Hayselden, and moved into Gibson's Kō'ele ranch house.

Over a nine-year period, the Gays transitioned their ranch from sheep to cattle, reduced the number of wild goats and sheep, and acquired all of the island's government-owned lands. There was great concern in the Territory of Hawai'i that one family would own two Hawaiian islands, as other Gay family members had purchased the island of Ni'ihau in 1864. The Gays' acquisition extinguished all government interest in ceded lands on the island.

With the purchase, the Gays mortgaged their holdings to meet expenses. In 1910, Honolulu investors William G. Irwin, Robert Singleton, and Cecil Brown foreclosed the mortgaged properties. The Gays retained 600 acres of land about two miles from Kōe'le, moved their family into a new home they named Lālākoa, and planted pineapple to sell to Ha'ikū Pineapple Company on Maui.

The investors formed Lāna'i Company and Lāna'i Ranch and hired New Zealander George Munro as ranch manager. An environmentalist at heart, Munro recognized the importance of watershed management and began the reforestation of Lāna'ihale and planted drought-resistant grasses and windrows to stop wind erosion of the island's topsoil. Many of his ranching methods were unusual at the time, but today, they are considered a holistic approach to raising livestock. In 1917, Lāna'i Company conveyed its holdings to Maui ranchers Frank and Harry Baldwin, who retained Munro as their manager. The Baldwins sold the ranch to James Dole in 1921 for $1.1 million to start his Hawaiian Pineapple Company (HAPCo). Lāna'i Ranch rounded up its last herd of pipi in 1951 and shipped them to market on O'ahu. Kō'ele's ranching days were over.

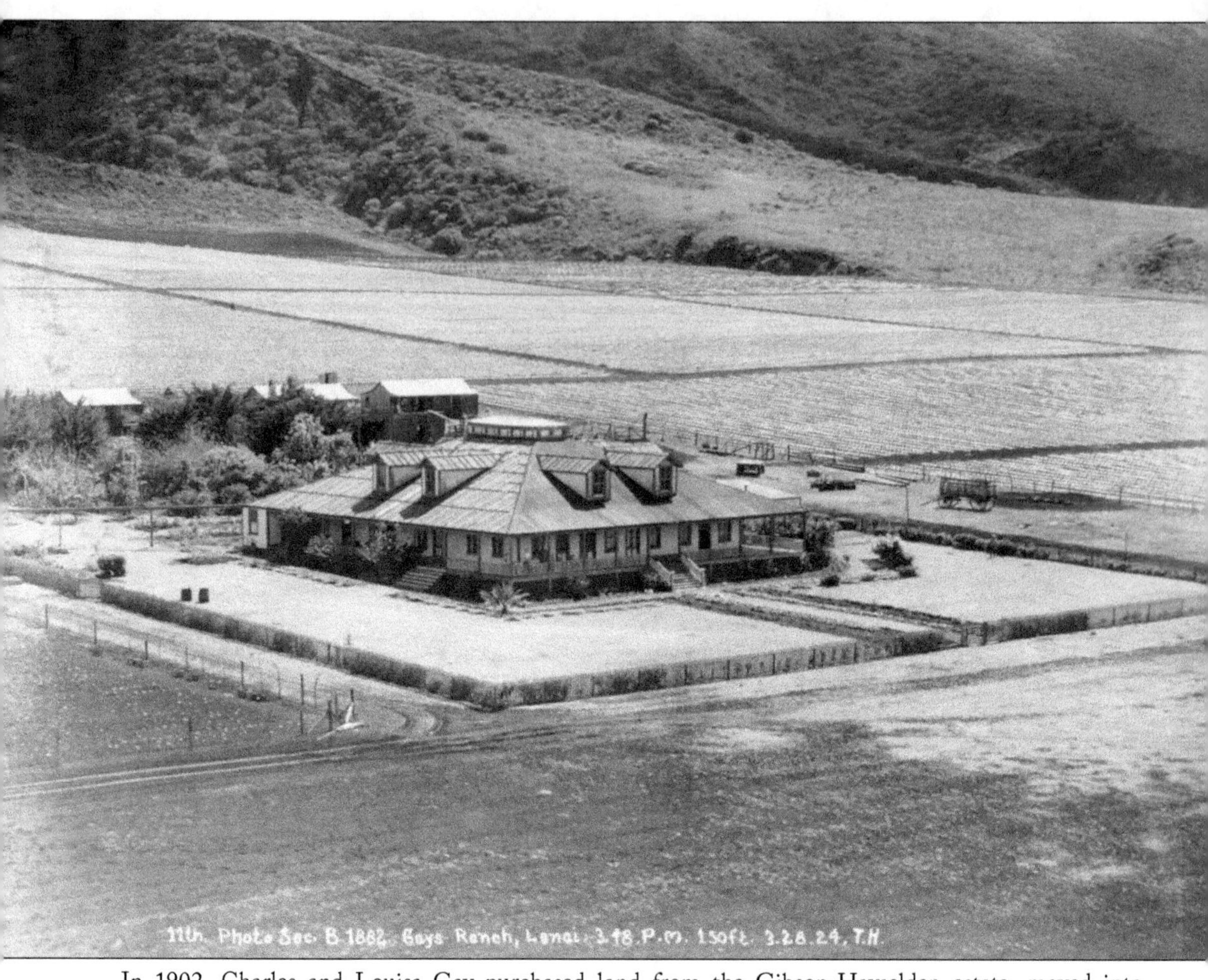

In 1902, Charles and Louisa Gay purchased land from the Gibson-Hayselden estate, moved into Gibson's ranch house at Kō'ele, and began to transition the ranch from raising sheep to cattle. By 1907, the Gays had purchased all eight government ahupua'a on Lāna'i and acquired all previously ceded land rights granted to the island's natives, thus becoming the first single owner of the majority of the island. However, in 1910, after selling some land to O'ahu investors to support their business ventures, they retained only 600 acres and moved to Lālākoa, a new home they built less than two miles from Kō'ele. It had eight large bedrooms, a living room, parlor, and dining room, and numerous outbuildings. Lālākoa's most stunning feature was a central courtyard enclosed by a glass sunroof. Pots of hanging ferns draped over the rails of balconies surrounded the courtyard. In 1919, the Gays planted the first pineapple fields on the island. In this photograph taken on March 26, 1924, their estate is surrounded by cultivated fields. (Army Air Corps.)

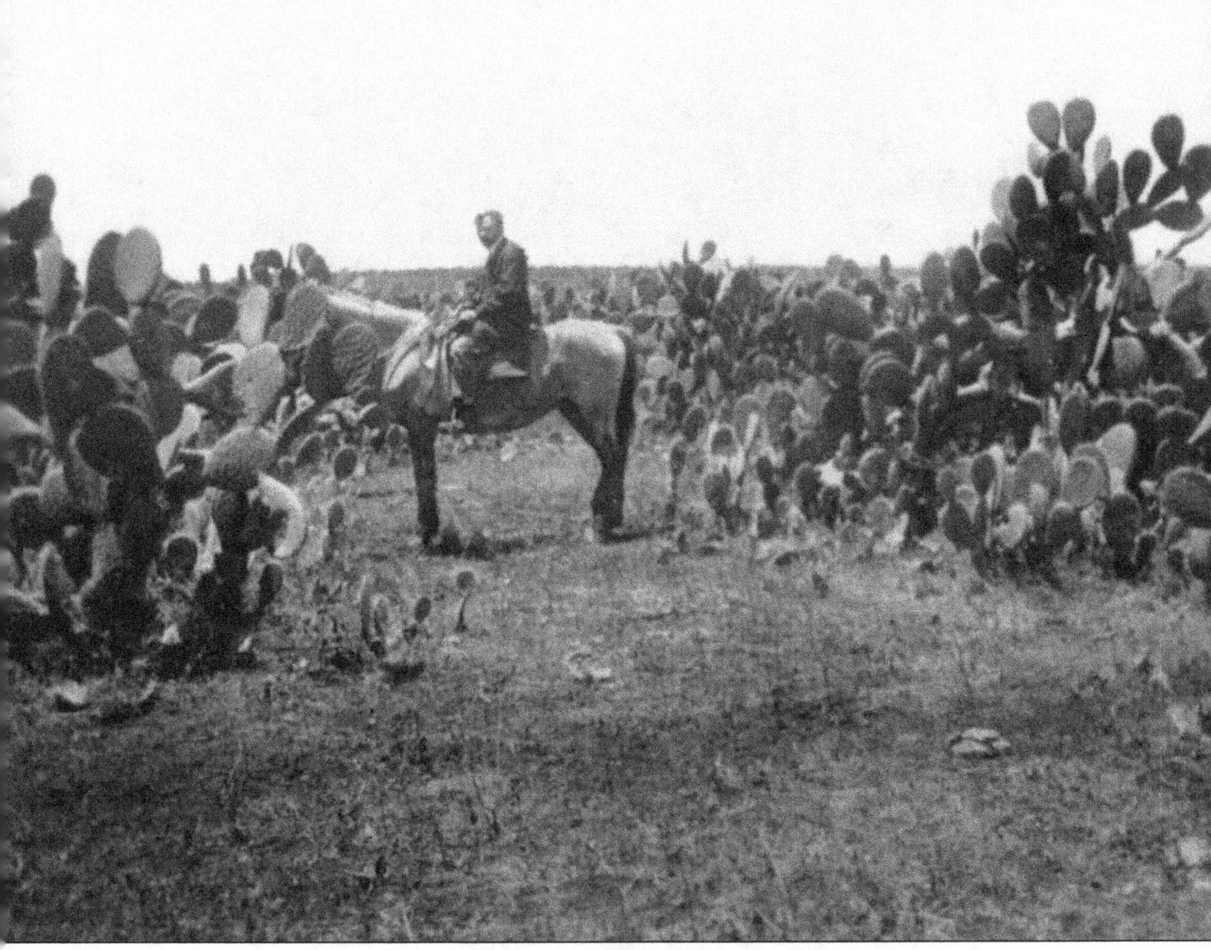

Newspaperman Alexander Hume Ford pauses in the *pānini* (cactus plants) that were burned to remove thorns and fed to pipi in times of drought. After O'ahu investors formed Lāna'i Company and Lāna'i Ranch in 1911, they hired New Zealander George Munro. The investors sold their holdings in 1917 to Maui ranchers Frank and Harry Baldwin, who retained Munro as their Lāna'i manager. Munro was tasked with creating a watershed on Lāna'ihale. (Ray Jerome Baker collection.)

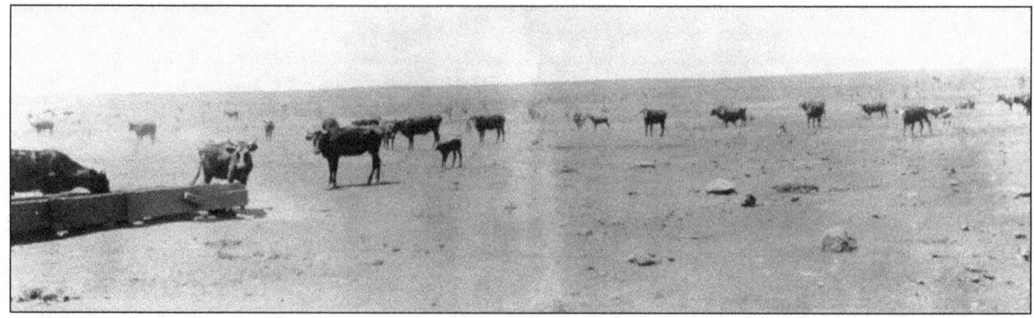

Goats and sheep were introduced onto the island during the 1830s. By the 1900s, wild herds of goats were nibbling the island's vegetation down to its roots, and wind was carrying the island's topsoil away. Walter Murray Gibson was nicknamed the "Shepherd of Lāna'i," by his O'ahu detractors. Records from 1887 show he had 400 head of sheep, 300 head of cattle, and 200 head of horses. (HAPCo collection.)

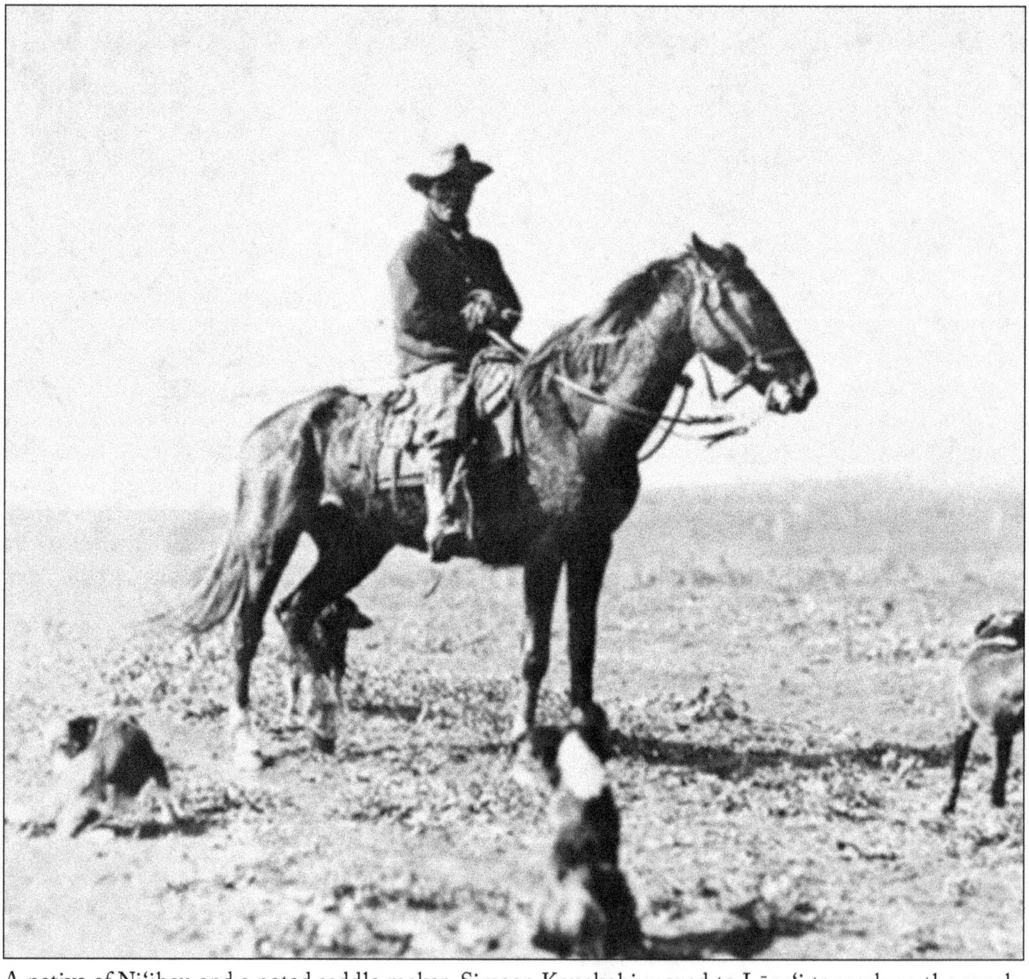

A native of Ni'ihau and a noted saddle maker, Simeon Kauakahi moved to Lāna'i to work on the ranch. His home island of Ni'ihau was purchased by Elizabeth Sinclair from Kamehameha V in 1864 for $10,000 in gold. Her grandson Charles Gay acquired the majority of Lāna'i's land in 1907. (Emory collection.)

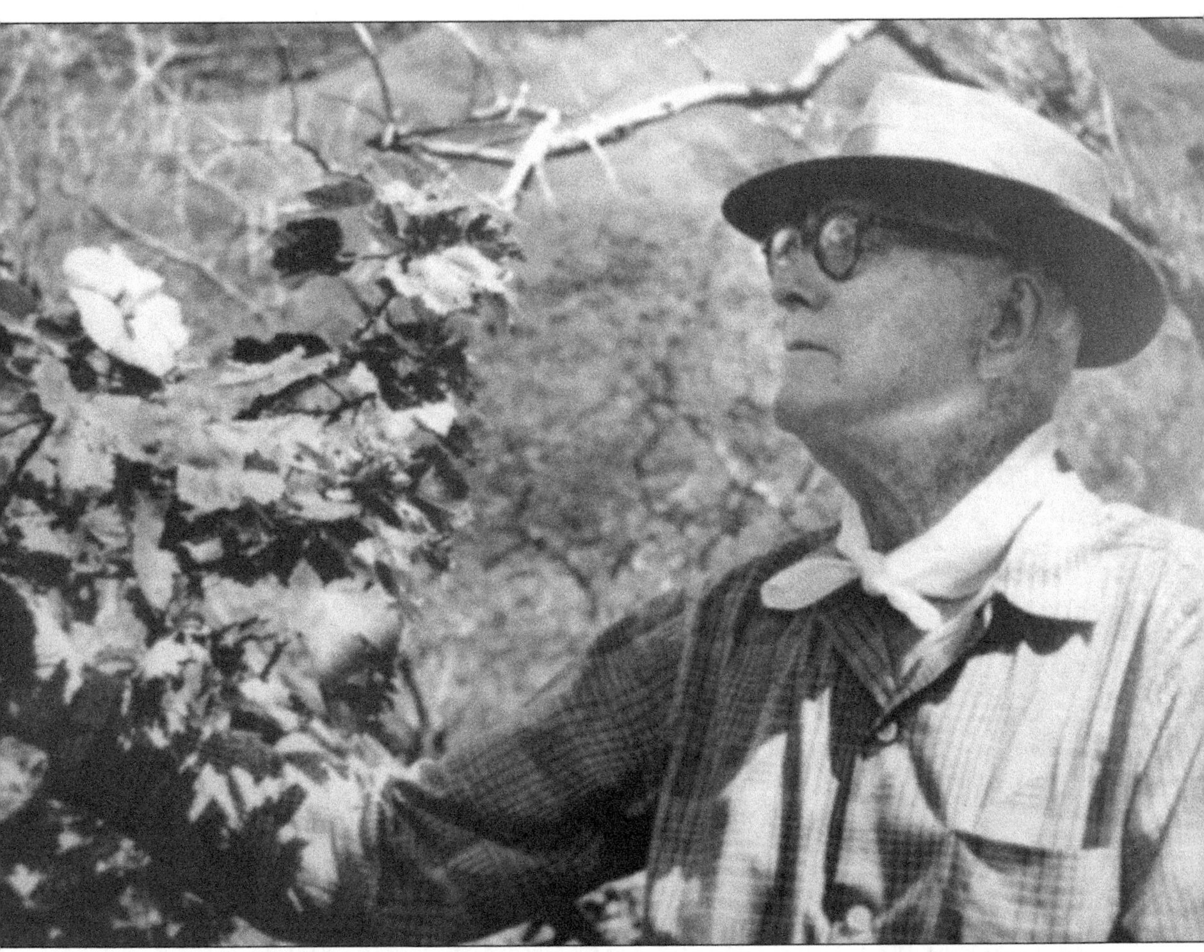

Not unknown in Hawai'i's ranching circles, George C. Munro worked as an overseer for the Gay and Robinson families at Makaweli from 1892 to 1899. He moved to Kualapu'u on Moloka'i in July 1899 to manage a ranch owned by American Sugar Company. The ranch showed significant improvements under his management; however, in October 1906, his employment was abruptly terminated. The Munro family, with five Hawai'i-born children, returned to New Zealand to start a farm at Ruatangata on New Zealand's North Island. When he was offered Lāna'i's ranch manager position in 1911, Munro left his family at home and set sail for Hawai'i in April to see the ranch. A few months later he sent for Jack, his cattle dog. On February 27, 1912, his wife, Jean, and their children, James, Jeanie, Alexandrina, Georgina, and Ruby, arrived on O'ahu. They lived at Kō'ele until his retirement in 1935. (George Munro collection.)

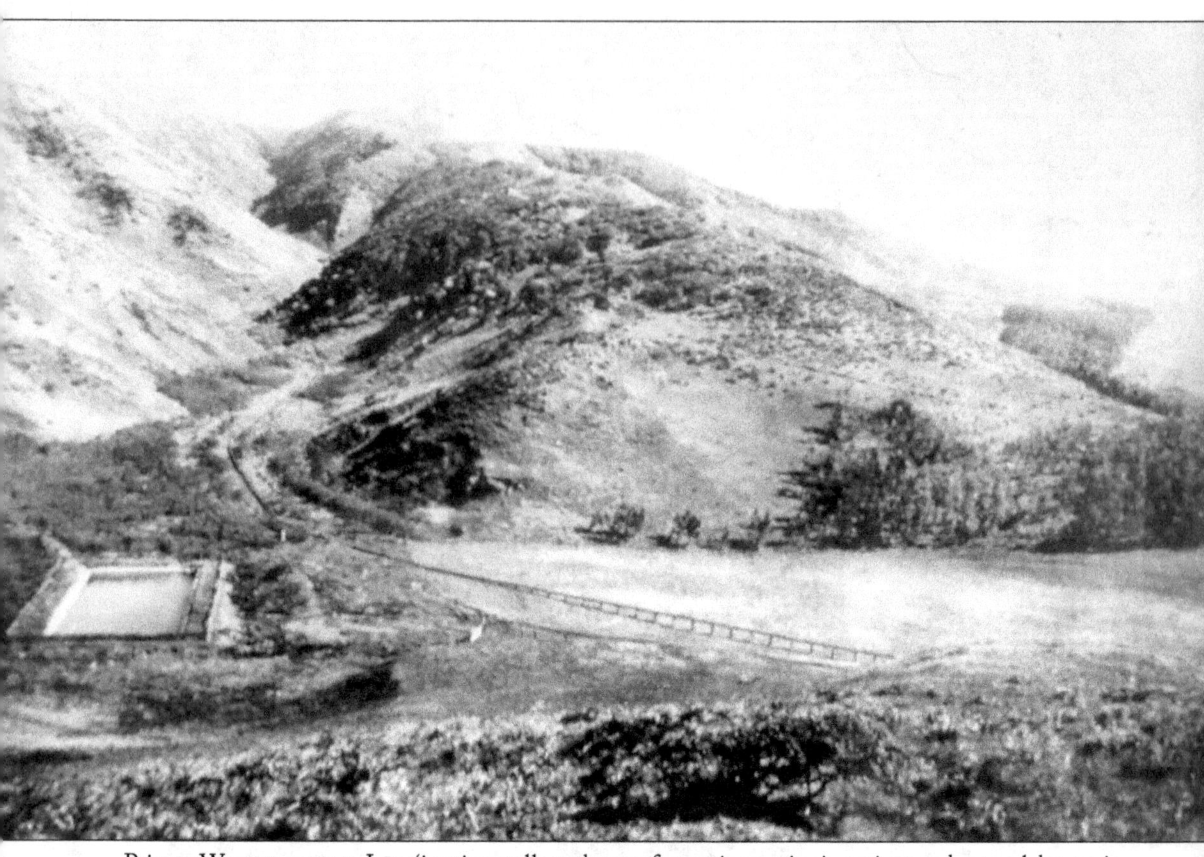

Prior to Western contact, Lāna'i natives collected water from winter rains in ravines and natural depressions or from shallow wells for their domestic use and to water cultivated crops such as sweet potatoes and yams. Some ravines show signs of having been dug deeper so more rainwater could be stored for the dry season. At Kō'ele, Frederick Hayselden, Walter Murray Gibson's son-in-law, built a large reservoir (now the Lodge at Kō'ele reflecting lake) behind the ranch manager's house. At the lower end of Kaiholena Gulch, he built the reservoir pictured here. Lined with stones, it held 400,000 gallons of water and was fed by winter rains. In later years, Charles Gay and Lāna'i Company continued to use it. George Munro noted that if water was always on its bottom, the island's fine silt sealed the leaks effectively. Water from Maunalei was also piped through three tunnels to this reservoir. (Tokumatsu Murayama collection.)

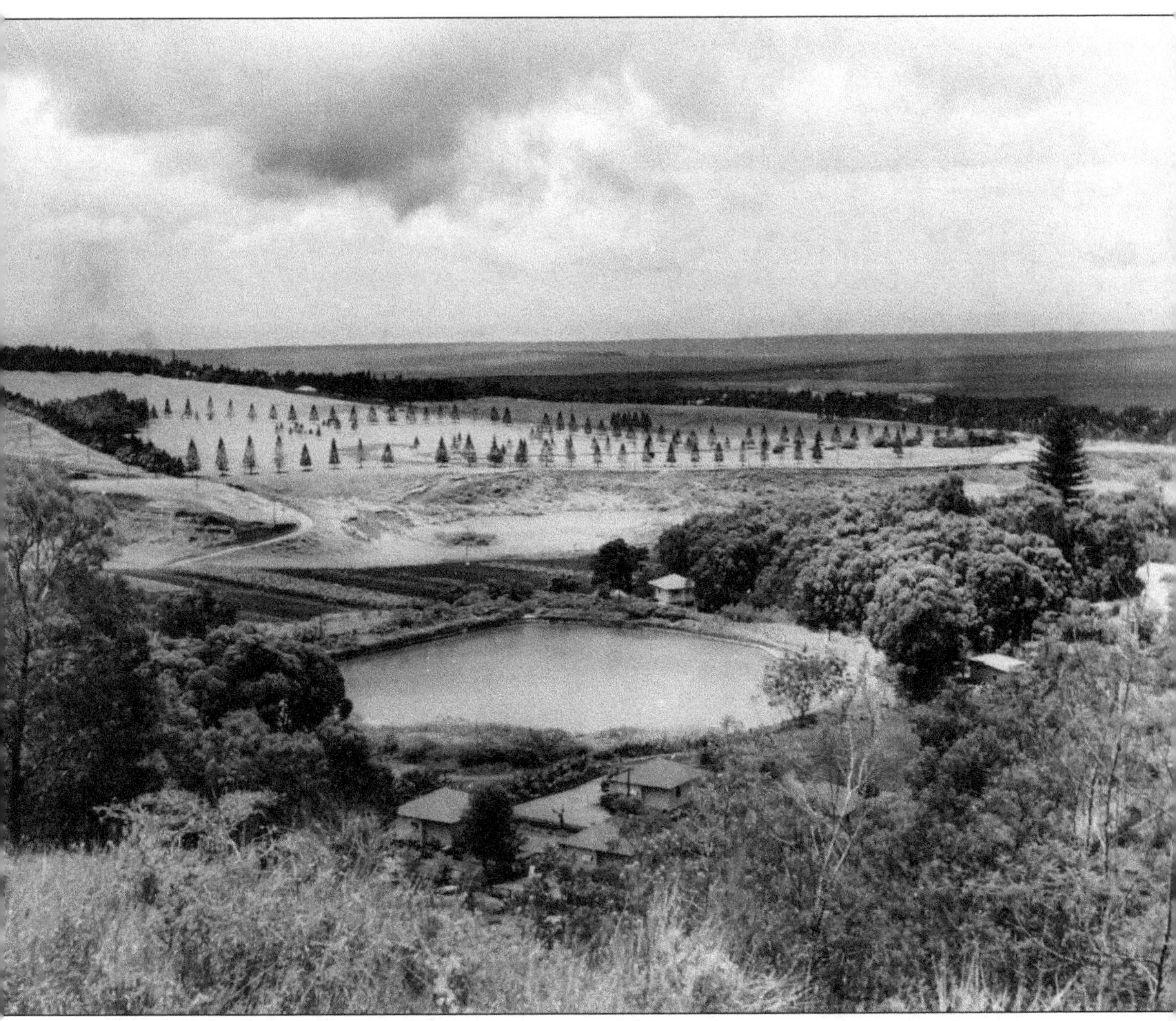

Located in the ahupuaʻa of Kamoku, Kōʻele was headquarters for the ranches of Walter Murray Gibson, Charles Gay, and Frank and Harry Baldwin. In 1875, Gibson planted the giant Norfolk pine tree next to it. The reservoir behind the ranch house was built by Frederick Hayselden, Gibson's son-in-law. When it became Lānaʻi Ranch, George Munro and his family occupied the main ranch house. After Munro's retirement in 1935, his son James, an engineer at Hawaiian Pineapple Company, resided in it. Kōʻele was an oasis of greenery in windswept plains stretching westward toward the ahupuaʻa of Paomaʻi and Kaʻa. After the ranch closed in 1951, several families continued to live at Kōʻele. (Richard Fuller.)

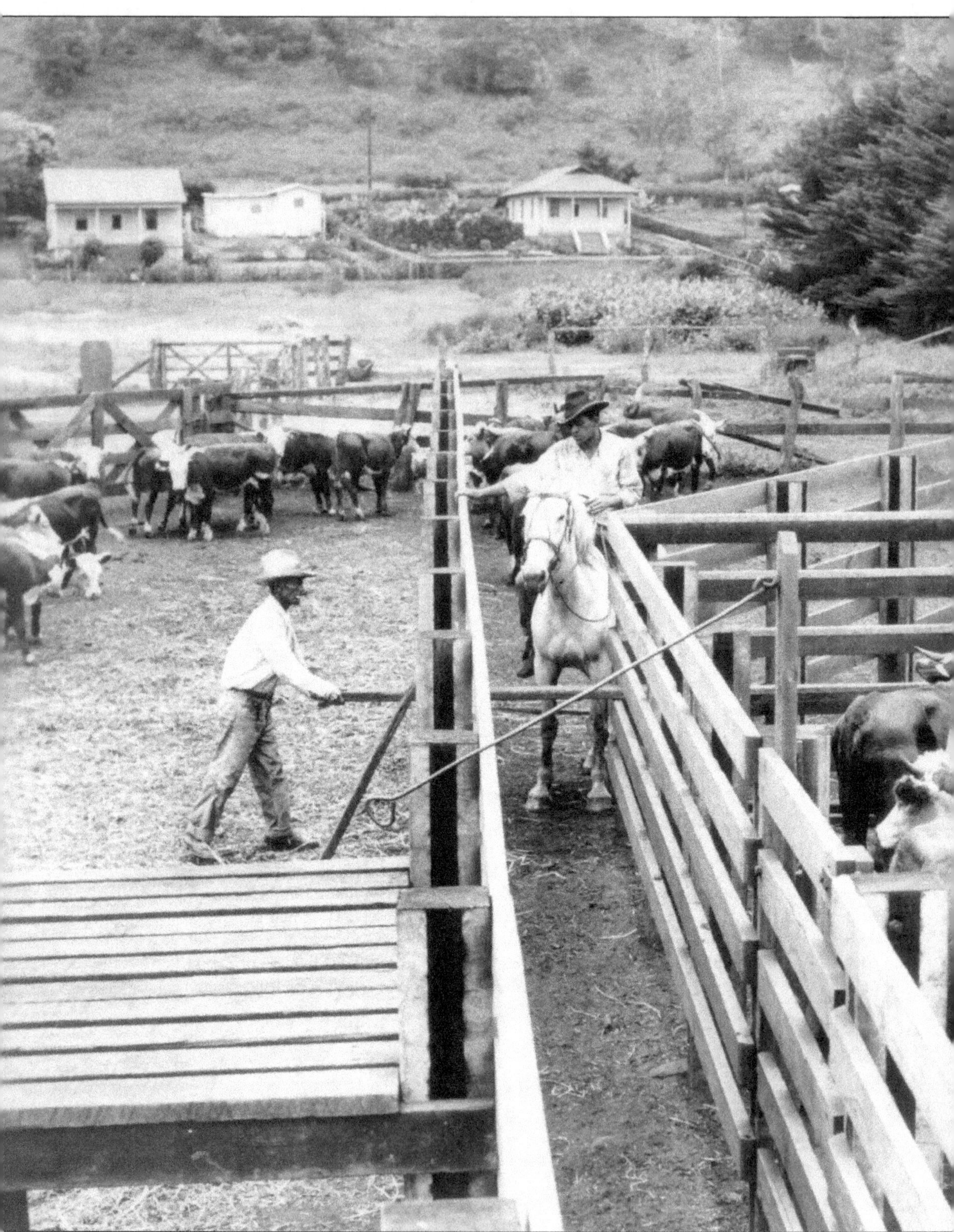

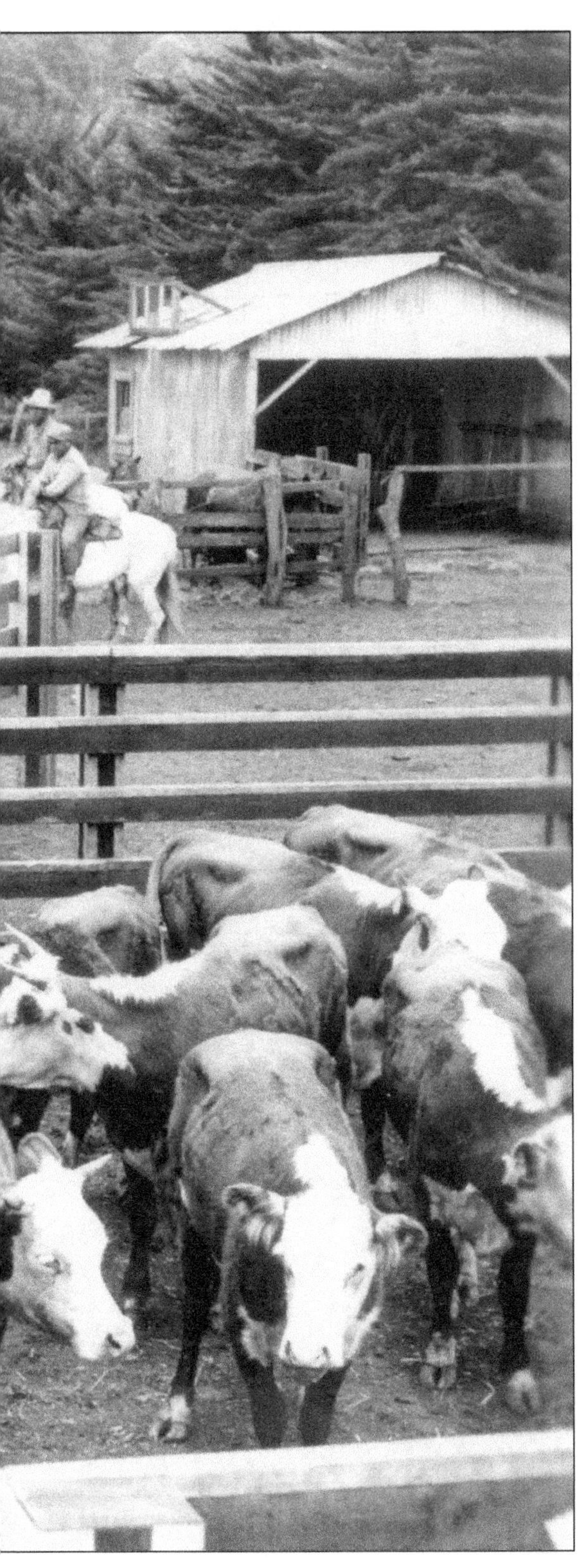

Paniolo move pipi through chutes at Kōʻele to separate the stock that will be shipped to market on Oʻahu. Kōʻele was the headquarters of Lānaʻi Ranch, where Herefords were the preferred breed. In the background, two of the ranch houses are clearly seen. When the ranch closed in 1951, all of its stock pens and other buildings, such as the blacksmith's shop, remained. (HAPCo collection.)

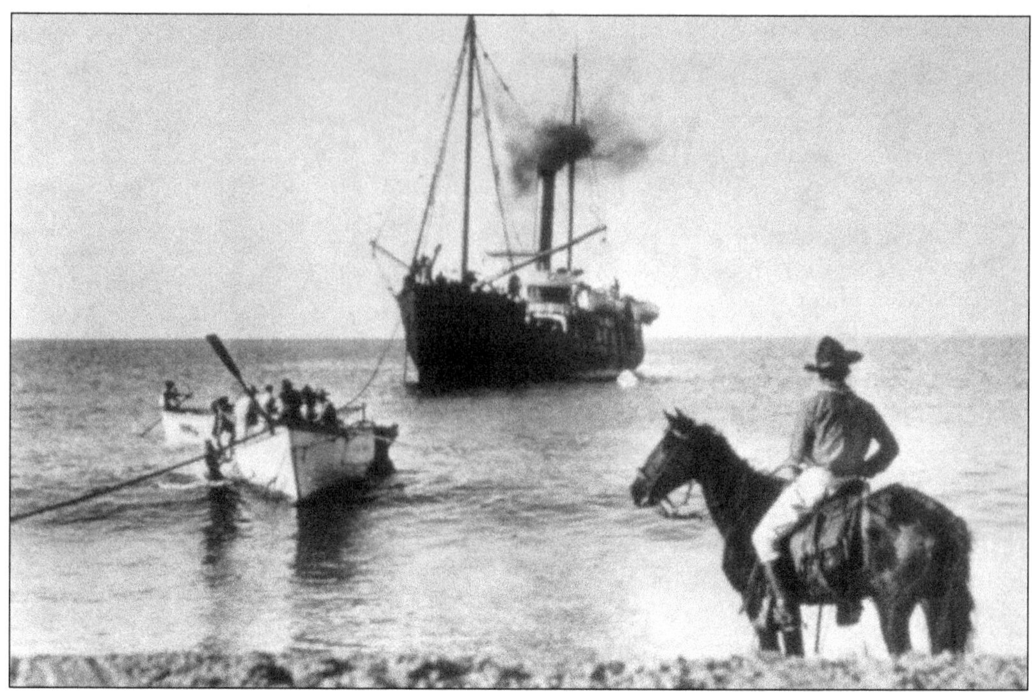

Paniolo on horseback drove the pipi approximately seven miles from Kō'ele to Hulopo'e Beach at Mānele. On the beach, each pipi was forced into the ocean by a paniolo who rode his horse into the sea. Only specially trained horses were used for this task. The men in the waiting rowboat secured each animal to it, and using a long line anchored between the shore and the ship, went out to the waiting steamer. (George Munro collection.)

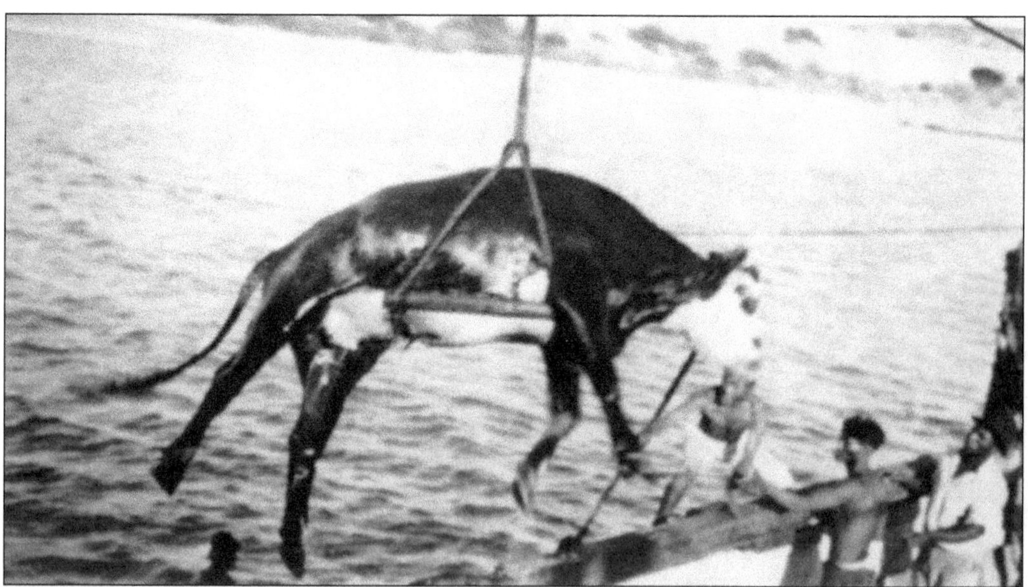

Each pipi was placed into a sling when the rowboat reached the ship and hoisted up onto its deck into a secured corral for the trip to O'ahu. (George Munro collection.)

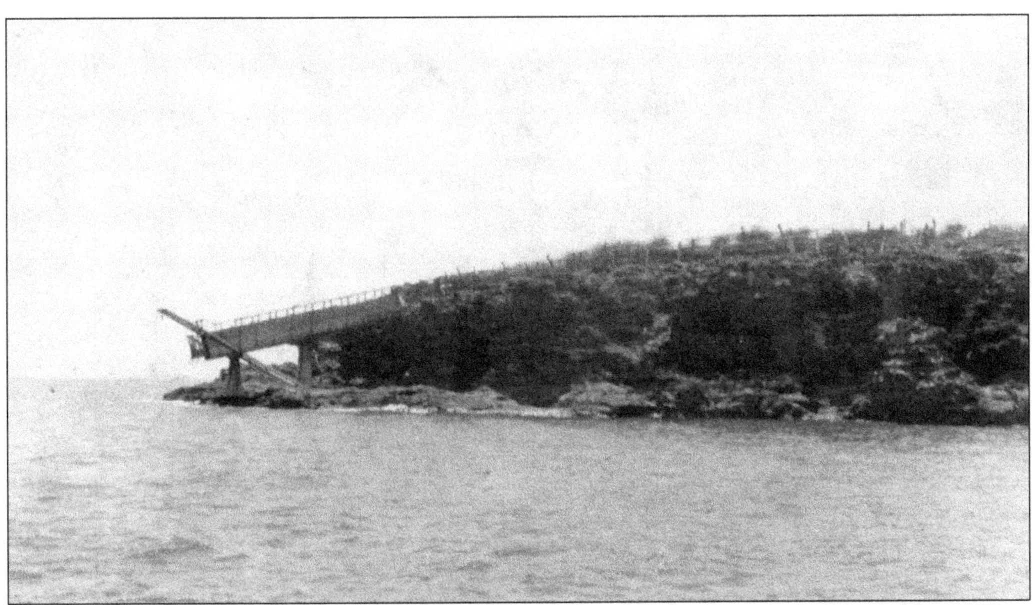

The ranch built a cattle chute at Mānele to make it easier to load pipi onto the waiting steamer. The concrete pillars to support it are still visible today. Shallow concrete salt beds are also located nearby. Residents filled the beds with clean ocean water and returned after it evaporated, leaving salt crystals for them to gather. (A. Duane Black collection.)

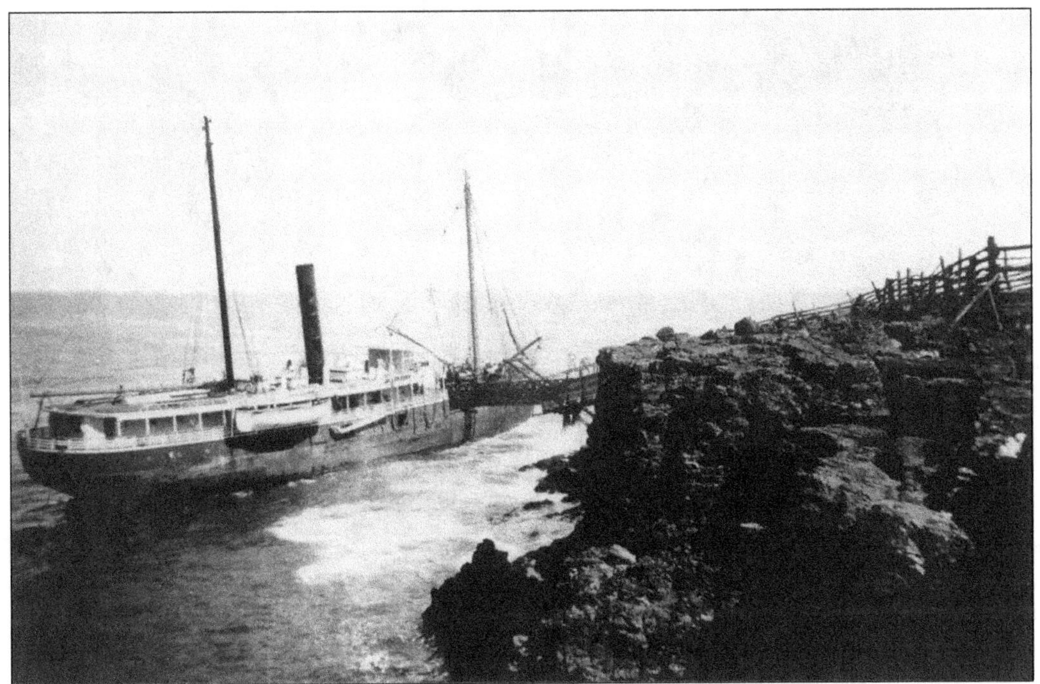

A steamer is anchored at the Mānele cattle chute waiting for livestock to be loaded. This area of Mānele is a favorite resting site of spinner dolphins, which delight in following the arriving boats entering Mānele Small Boat Harbor. (George Munro collection.)

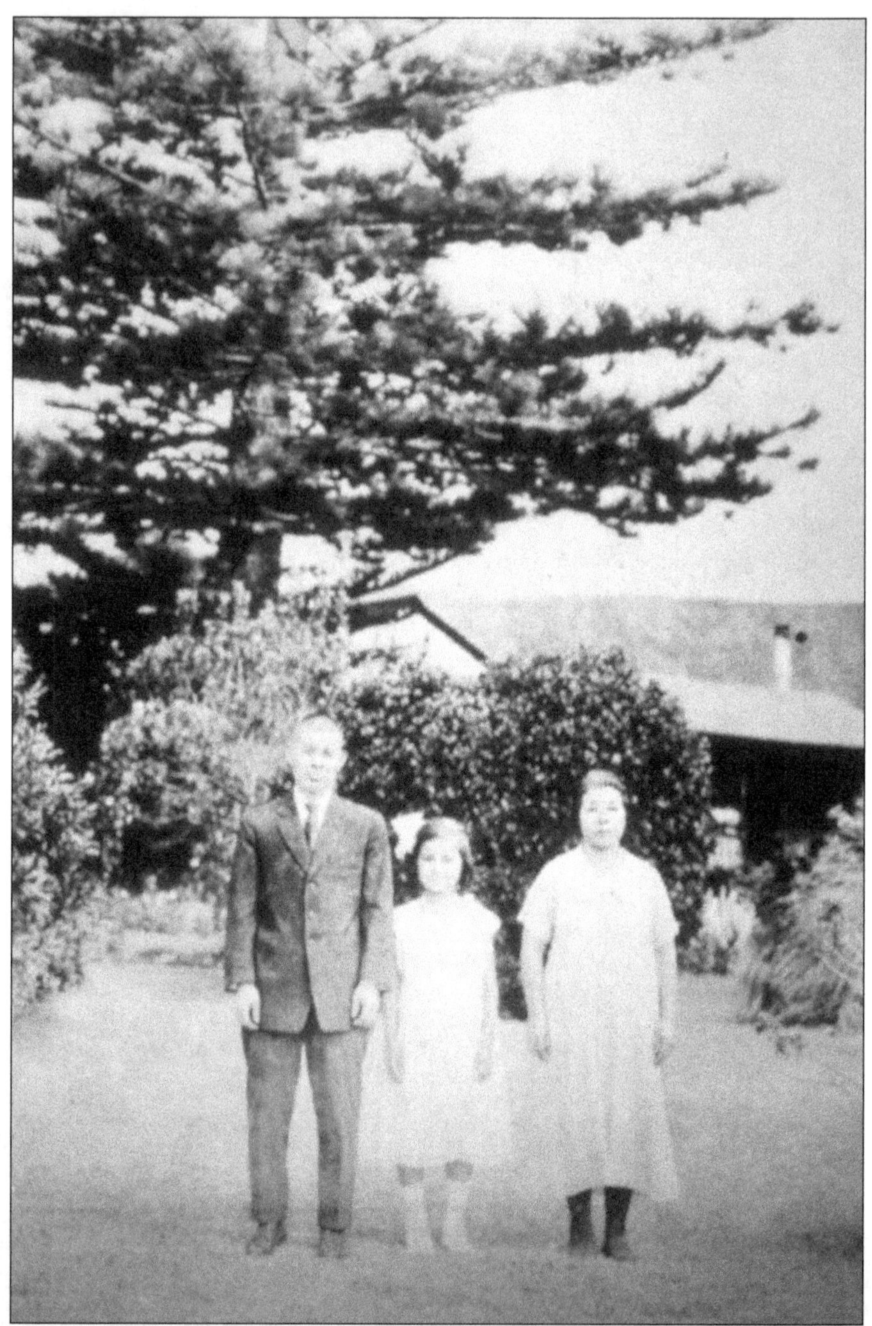

The Abe family pose in front of the Kō'ele ranch manager's house. Although most of the residents of Kō'ele were native Hawaiian, Japanese immigrants were easily assimilated into village life. In the background is one of the two Norfolk Island pine trees given to Walter Murray Gibson by King David Kalākaua in 1875. During a storm in January 1903, the tree was hit by lightning. In an account of the incident, Lawrence Gay, one of Charles and Luisa Gay's 11 children, said the bolt hit the tree, traveled to the house's iron roof, burned a groove down a metal gun-cleaning rod, and hit the floor before it killed the family cat, which was hiding under the house. The ranch children attended their own school at Kō'ele, located on what is now the eighth fairway of the Cavendish Golf Course. (Emory collection.)

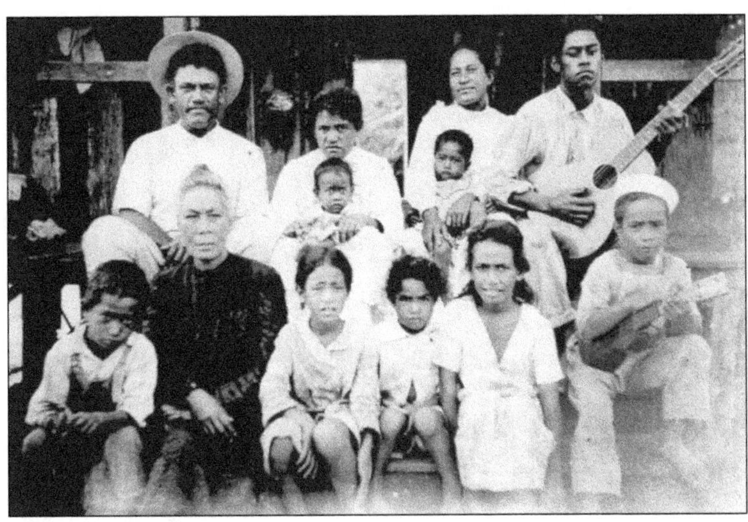

The Kaopuiki family pose on the front steps of their home at Ka'a. Pictured are, from left to right, (first row) Harry Kapena Kaopuiki; Malia Mano; Rebecca, Lei, and Martha Kaopuiki; and Namauu Makaiwi; (second row) Noa and Sarah Kaopuiki, holding baby Abraham; Hattie Kaopuiki, holding baby Alexander; and Roert Kauhane. (Emory collection.)

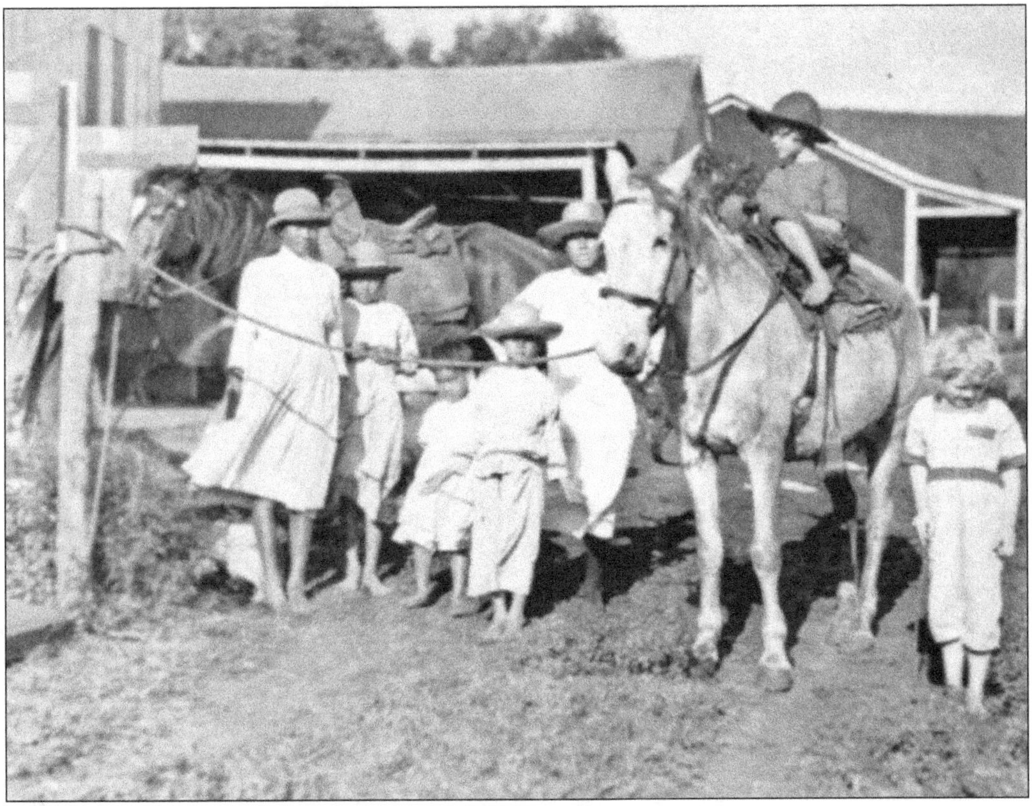

Hawaiian children from Ka'a loaned their horses to the Forbes children in this photograph taken by Dr. Emory. Their father, Charles Forbes, was a botanist at Bernice P. Museum and became George Munro's mentor and close personal friend. After his untimely death at age 37, his widow, Helen "Nell," and three children, Mary, Jean, and Douglas, moved to Lāna'i, where they became a part of the Munro family. Nell was the ranch's bookkeeper and postmistress and also kept records of Kō'ele's rainfall. (Emory collection.)

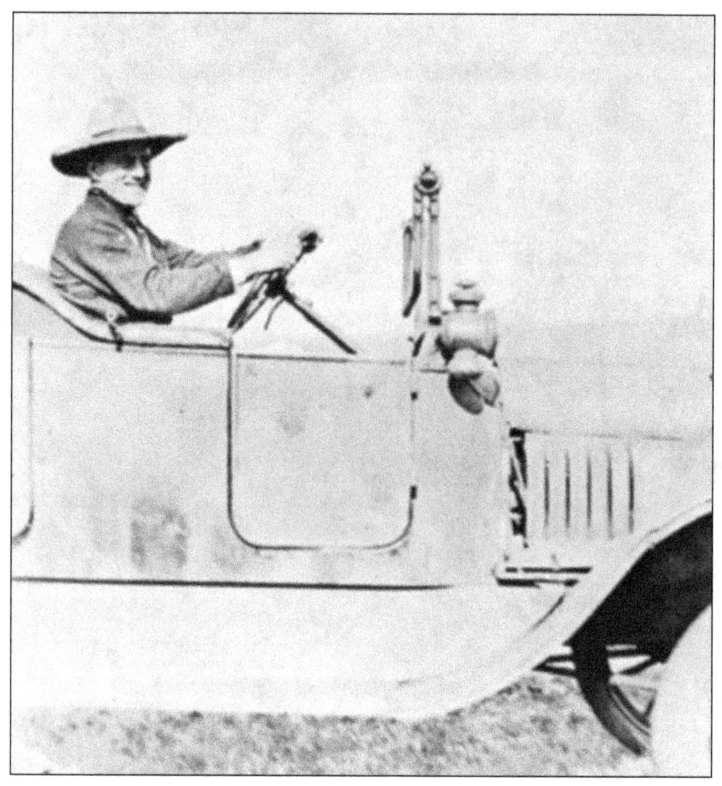

Hector Munro, the nephew of Lāna'i Ranch manager George Munro, enjoyed driving the ranch's vehicles. He frequently accompanied Dr. Kenneth Emory on his field studies of Lāna'i. (Emory collection.)

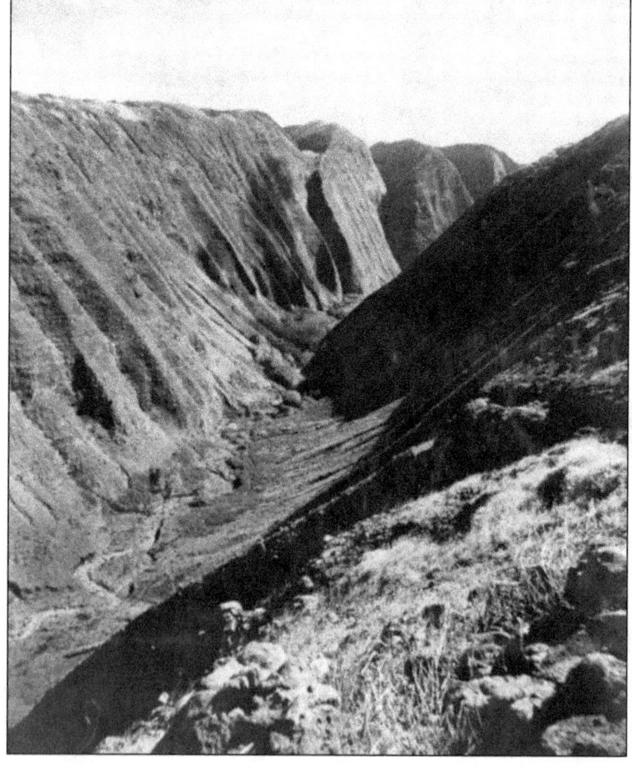

Approaching Lāna'i from the sea reveals a wreath of clouds draped on Lāna'ihale. Maunalei means "lei mountain," and its gulch slices deep into the heart of the island. Within its steep walls, underground springs flow to the surface of the land during the rainy season. Natives cultivated taro and other crops along the banks of a perennial stream that flowed to the sea. In 1917, Harry and Frank Baldwin bought lands previously owned by Charles Gay for $600,000. The Baldwins searched for reliable water sources for their cattle and found it in Maunalei. Drilling a well 600 feet deep, they hit water and pumped it through three tunnels to a three-million-gallon reservoir at Kō'ele. In later years, Hawaiian Pineapple Company built a two-million-gallon storage tank on Nininiwai Hill behind Lāna'i City. The Maunalei well was closed when it became too expensive to operate. (George Munro collection.)

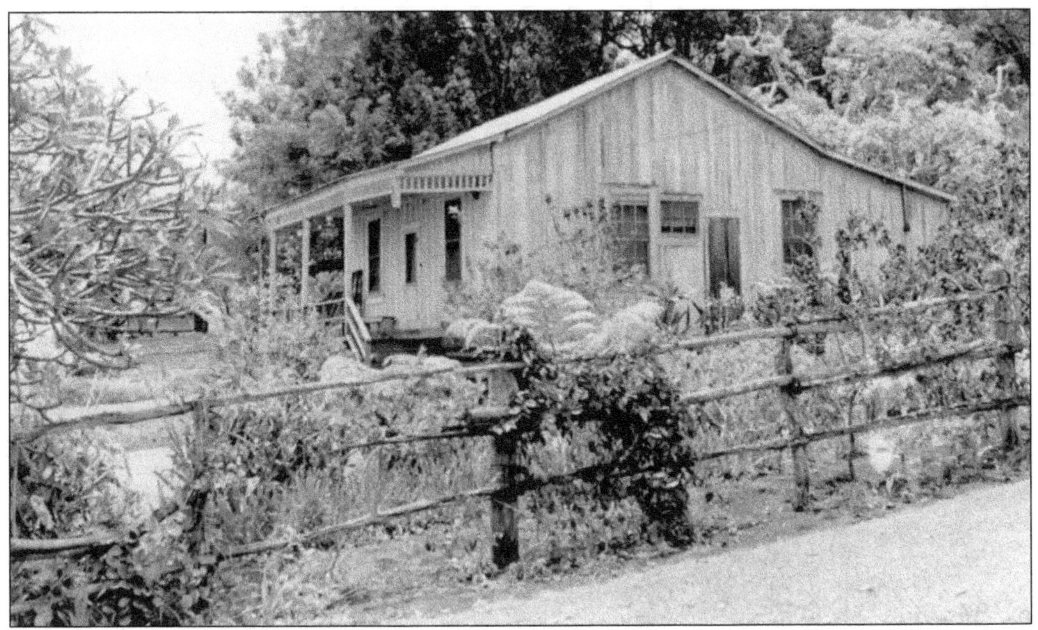

Just before it was scheduled to be demolished, this Kō'ele ranch house previously occupied by John and Hannah Richardson was picked up and moved to another location in the hopes that it could be restored by a nonprofit historical group in the future. Unfortunately, the project did not gain much support, and the building, which was placed on metal drums near the company's old power plant, rotted away. (Author's collection.)

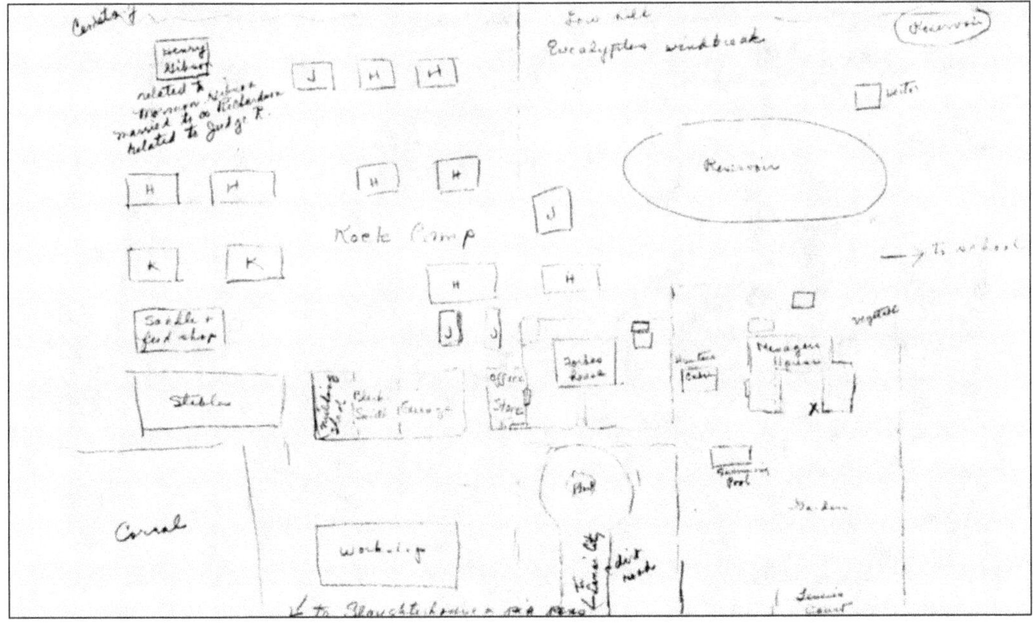

Helen "Nell" Forbes, the bookkeeper for Lāna'i Ranch, sketched this map of the Kō'ele houses and main buildings. Her family lived in the house where the Lodge at Kō'ele is located today. After the ranch closed in 1950, it was occupied by the Richard Morita family for 17 years and was moved when the lodge was being constructed in the late 1980s. It was then occupied by former ranch paniolo Ernest Richardson and his wife, Rebecca, until their passing. (Charlotte Bacock, Lāna'i CHC.)

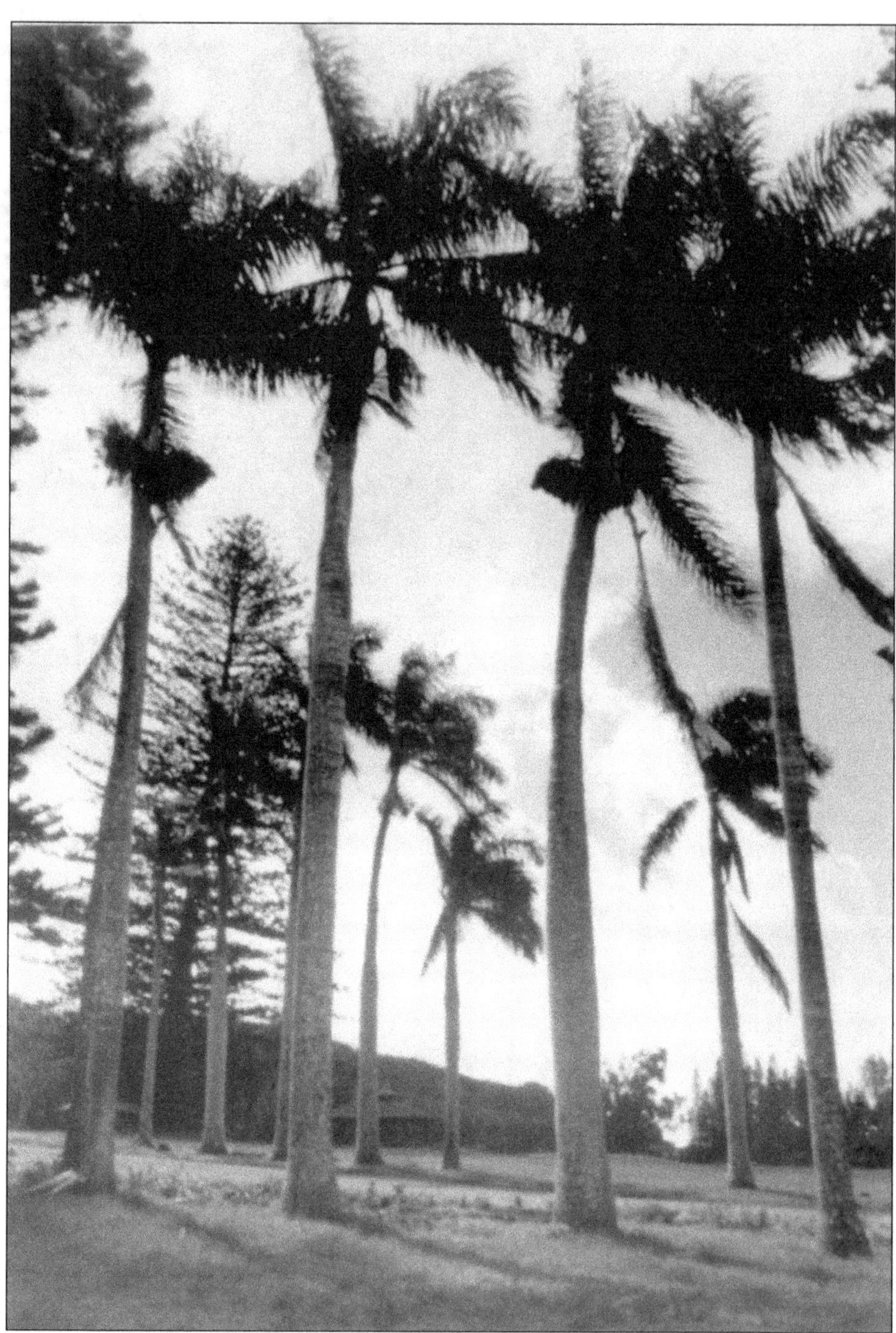

In years past, royal palms were frequently planted along the main entryway leading to the manager's or owner's homes of large companies. These palms may have been planted when Walter Murray Gibson moved his residence from Pālāwai to Kōʻele. When the lodge was built, the palms were dug up and relocated to their present location on the hillside behind the Lodge at Kōʻele. It was the first time royal palms of this size had ever been relocated in Hawaiʻi. The move was accomplished with the help of a skilled helicopter pilot. Only one palm did not survive the move. (Author's collection.)

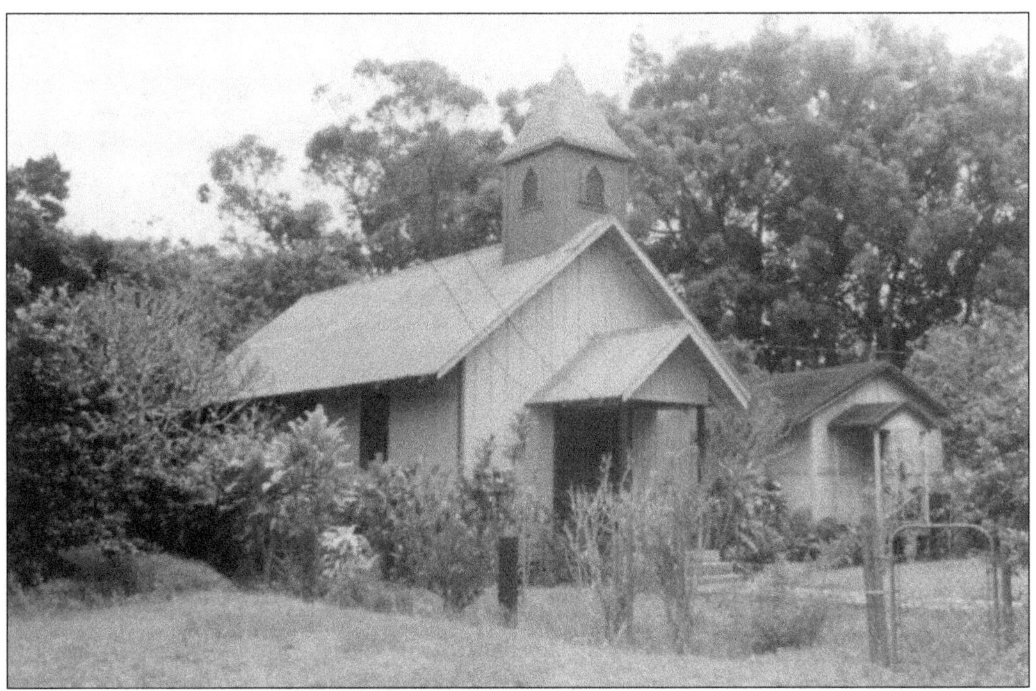

The church at Kō'ele was moved from the rear of the ranch headquarters to its present location on Keōmoku Road. The eucalyptus trees pictured behind the church and its adjacent hall are still growing today. (Roberta Kauffman collection.)

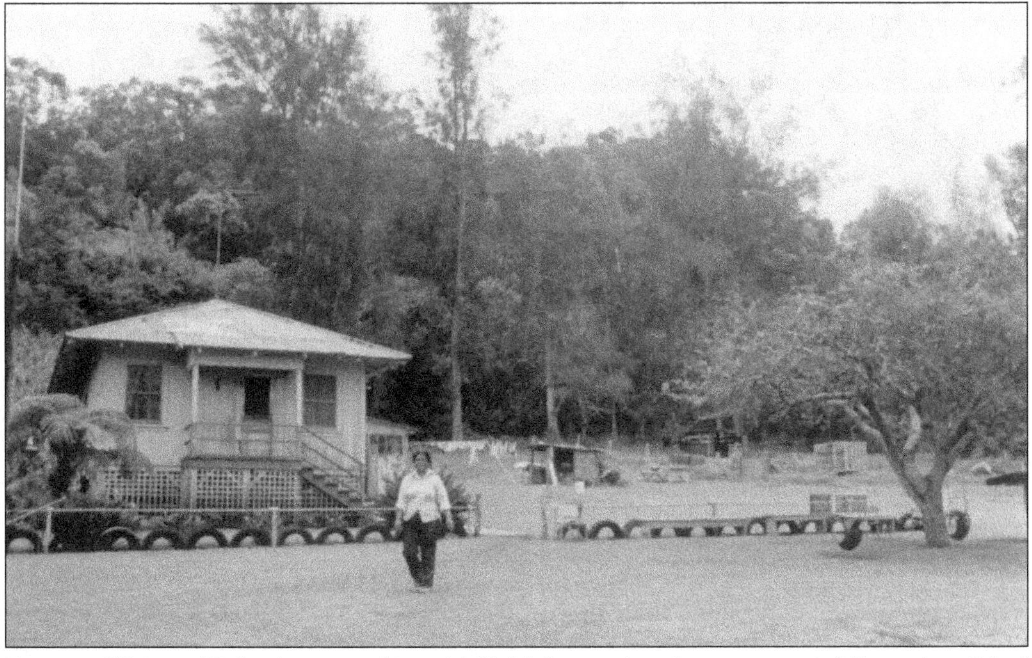

Ernest and Rebecca Richardson moved into this Kō'ele house when they were married. It was demolished when the Lodge at Kō'ele was under construction. Another house was moved and renovated for them so they could live out their remaining years at Kō'ele. In the foreground is their daughter Mary Ellen "Suki" Nakoa. (Roberta Kauffman collection.)

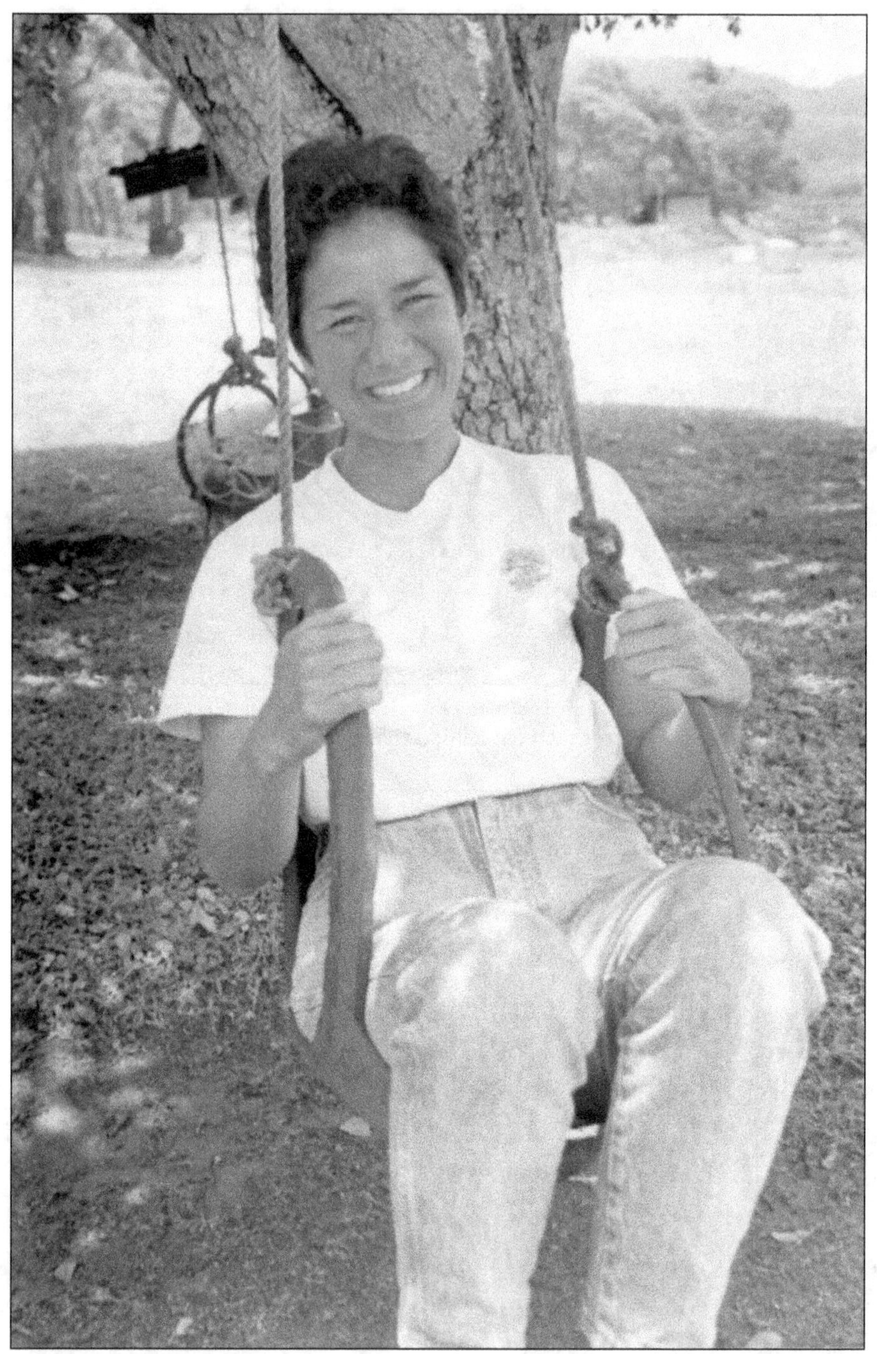

When Hermina "Mina" Morita was a toddler, she became the hānai, adopted Hawaiian-style, daughter of Ernest and Rebecca Richardson. Uncle Ernest built her a special swing in a tree in their front yard along with a sandbox made from an old bathtub. The swing and sandbox were enjoyed by other children as well. When the Lodge at Kō'ele was under construction, the University of Hawai'i's oral history division contracted her to help with interviews of previous residents of Kō'ele and Keōmoku Village. Two volumes of the interviews were published and are available for researchers at the Lāna'i Culture and Heritage Center and at the Lāna'i Public/School Library. (Author's collection.)

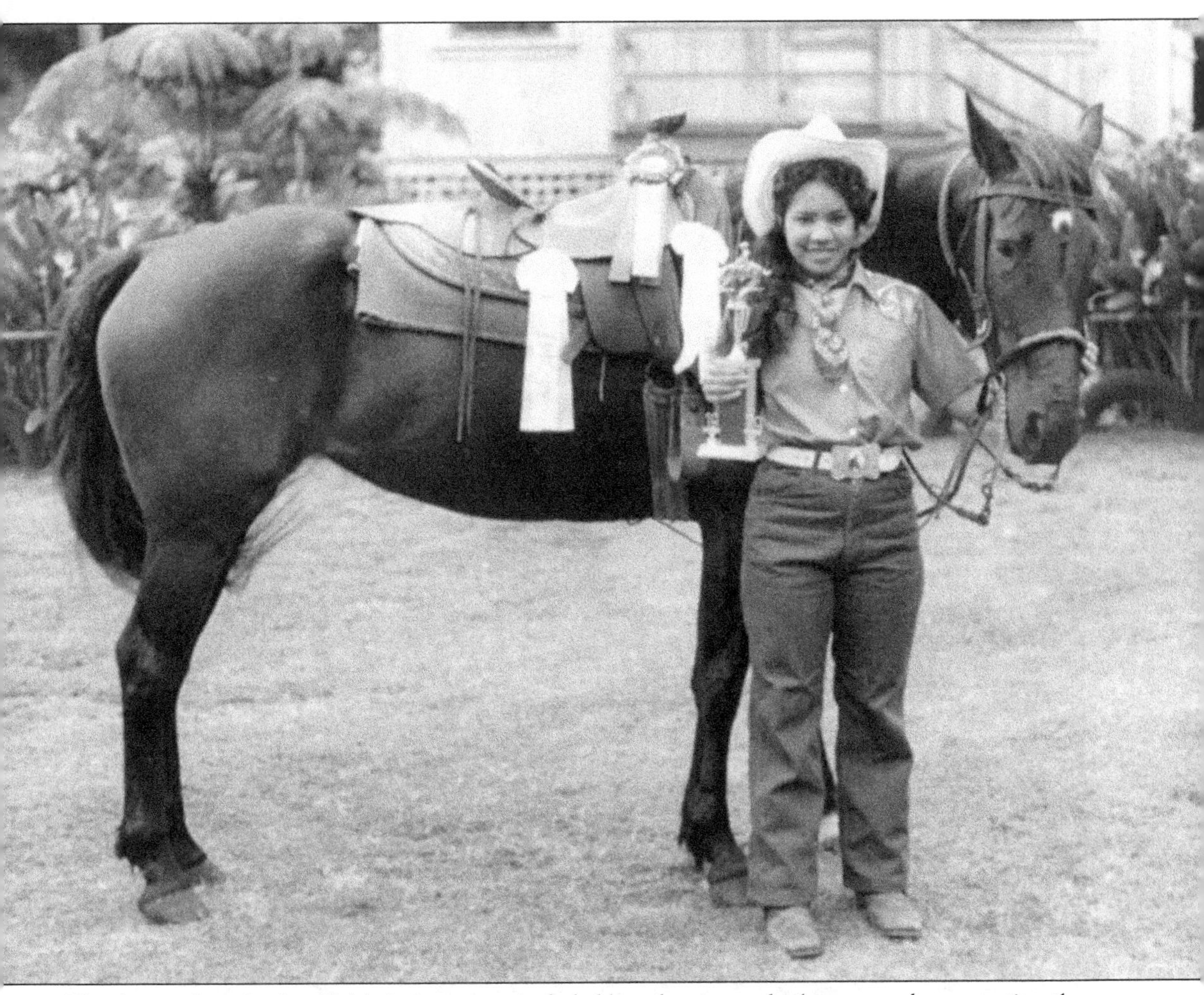

Play days on horseback at Kōʻele in later years included barrel racing and other games demonstrating the horseback riding skills of participants of all ages. Hoss Richardson's daughter Karen proudly displays the ribbons and trophy she won with her horse. (Clarence "Hoss" Richardson collection.)

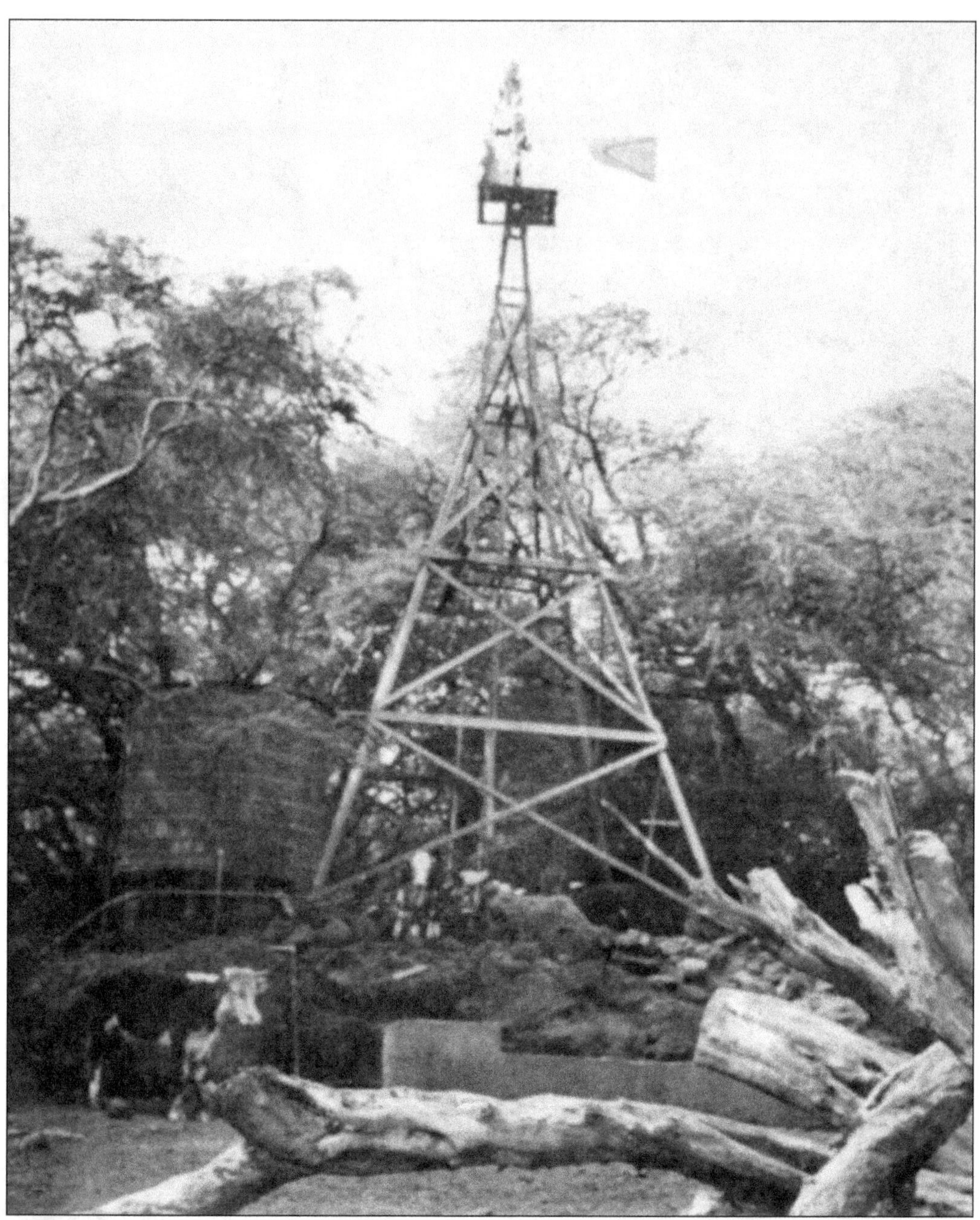

Hawaiian Pineapple Company's Dole field supervisor Adolph Desha's collection of photographs at the Lāna'i Cultural Center yielded this photograph of a windmill used to draw water from a well at Keōmoku. During Charles Gay's ownership of the island, he dug wells and installed windmills to draw water from them. Under George Munro's management of Lāna'i Ranch, his sons were tasked with checking all of the watering stations within five miles of Kō'ele daily. If a windmill broke down, a contingency plan was in place to repair it by taking parts off a windmill from another area not being grazed by pipi. If there was no wind, paniolo had to turn the windmill by hand. An engine-driven portable pump later relieved them of this chore, as it could be hauled to each well as needed when winds were *malia* (calm). (Adolph H. Desha collection.)

Five

Pineapple Builds a New City

A Torch to Hawai'i's Youth

In 1922, when James D. Dole purchased Frank and Harry Baldwin's Lāna Keōmoku island holdings for $1.1 million, he was not just purchasing land, he was purchasing a future for thousands of families. In addition to creating a pineapple plantation, James D. Dole set out to create a community of people who worked and played together and who would send their sons and daughters out of the pineapple fields into every sector of business and professions in the United States.

"In the isle of golden pines, torch to Hawai'i's youth," is a line in Lāna'i High School's alma mater. During the summer months, in addition to teenagers from the community, the plantation hired hundreds of teenagers from Hawai'i and the mainland to work in its fields. The money they earned helped to pay for college tuitions; the calluses on their hands and aching muscles helped them understand the value of hard work and the sacrifices made by their parents to provide them with a better life.

During the 1950s, more than 3,000 people lived in Lāna'i City and enjoyed a variety of activities outside of work. The company supported clubs such as boxing, baseball, and basketball. They had tennis courts and the nine-hole Cavendish Golf Course, where residents could golf for free. Residents went bowling, dancing, hunting, fishing, and camping. HAPCo flourished, and by the 1970s, expanded its Lāna'i plantation to over 18,000 acres. However, the island's population was declining as more young people were moving away. By 1980, competition from growers in other countries and rising expenses in Hawai'i were becoming a concern. In 1986, multimillionaire California land developer David H. Murdock purchased shares of Dole Company and became its largest stockholder.

Lāna'i's population was aging, Hawai'i's pineapple industry was phasing out of canned fruit and entering the fresh-fruit market, and a new industry had to be found to support the island's economy. In 1992, the last field of pineapple was harvested and sent to the Dole cannery on O'ahu. Lāna'i's fields were left fallow, its 70 years of growing pineapple were *pau*, finished.

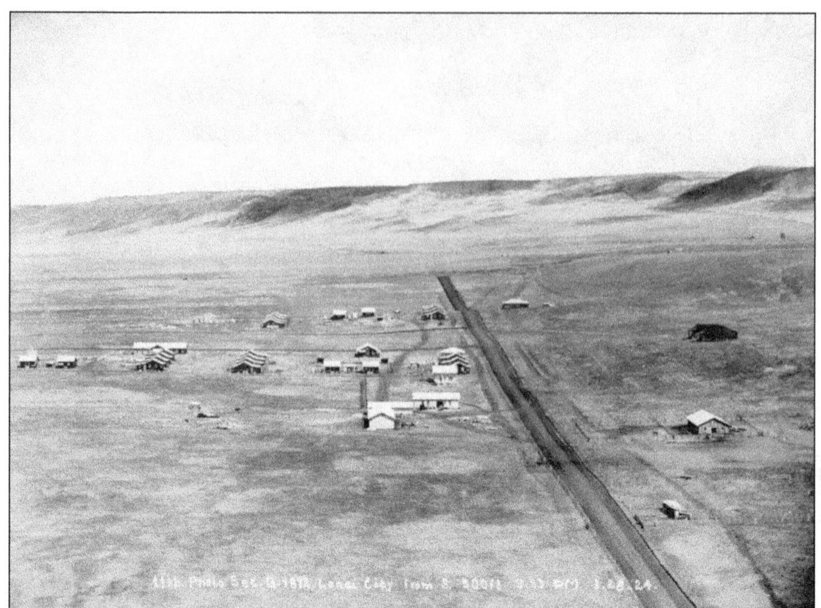

Lāna'i Avenue is the only clearly defined street in this 1924 photograph. The first planned city in the Hawaiian Islands, its dirt roads, tents, and the desolate terrain must have been a challenge to its new residents. (Air Army Corps.)

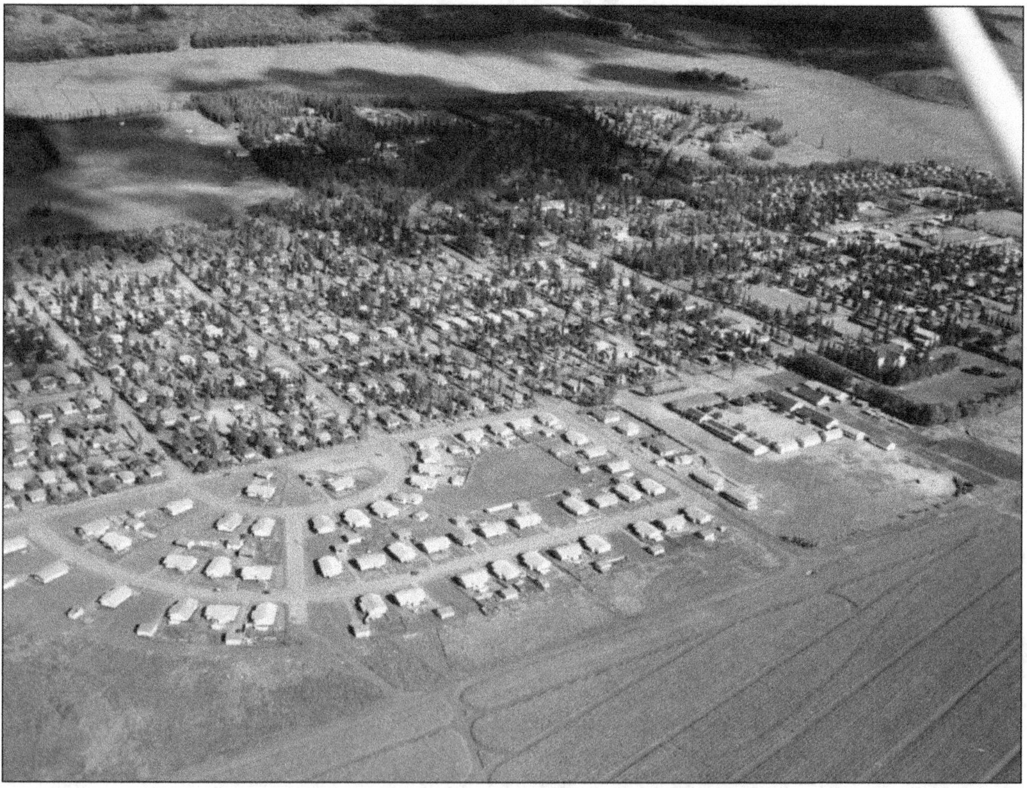

The progress made in building Lāna'i City is clearly shown in this photograph from 1953. Streets going from north to south converged on Dole Park in the town's center and were named for people, places, or plants. Streets going mauka, toward the mountains, and makai, toward the sea, were numbered. Cook Isle pine trees were planted in Dole Park and where the Dole building, hospital, and Hotel Lāna'i are today. (Richard Fuller collection.)

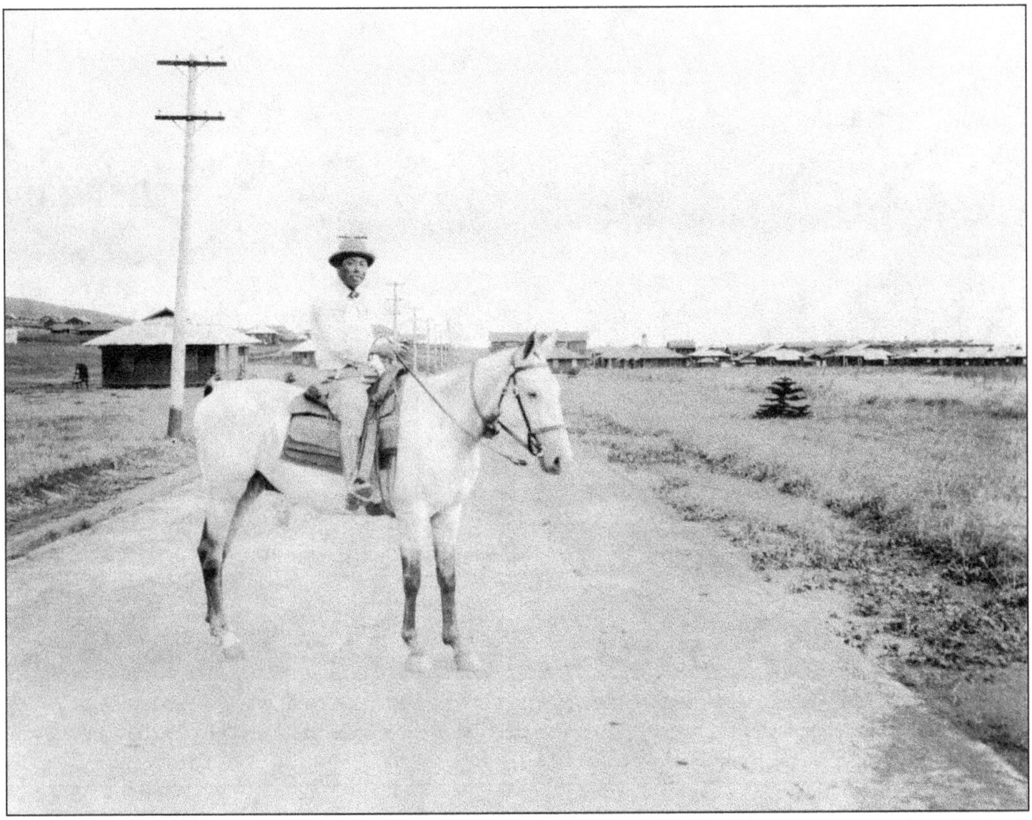

The unofficial mayor of the new city was a Japanese man named Fuji. He was in charge of all of the city's dwellings and regularly made his rounds on horseback to see if everything was kept in an orderly fashion. (HAPCo collection.)

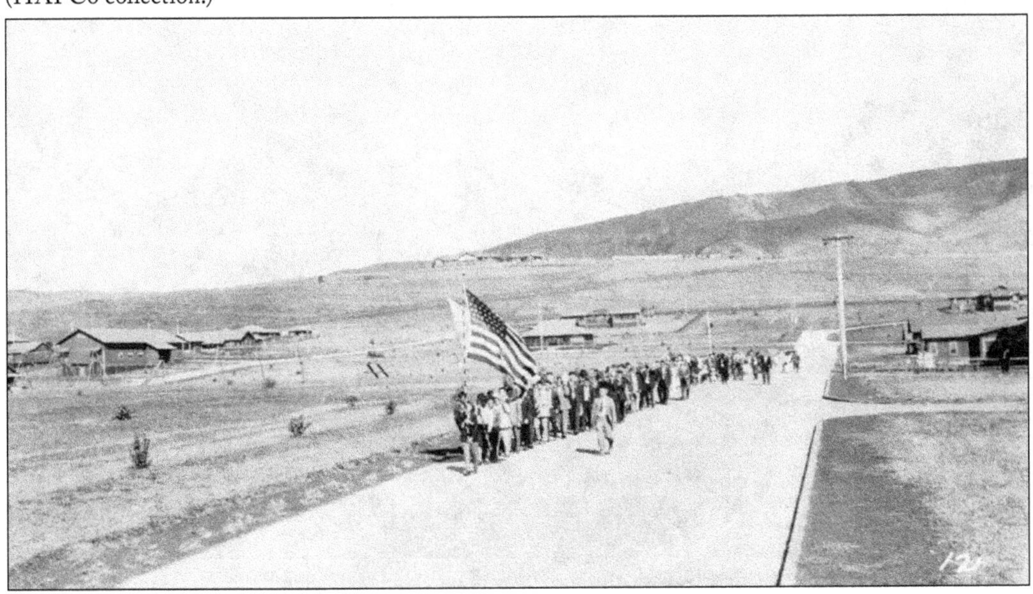

Formally dressed in their Sunday best, residents of the new city parade along Lāna'i Avenue with the American flag fluttering in the breeze above them in this 1921 photograph. (HAPCo collection.)

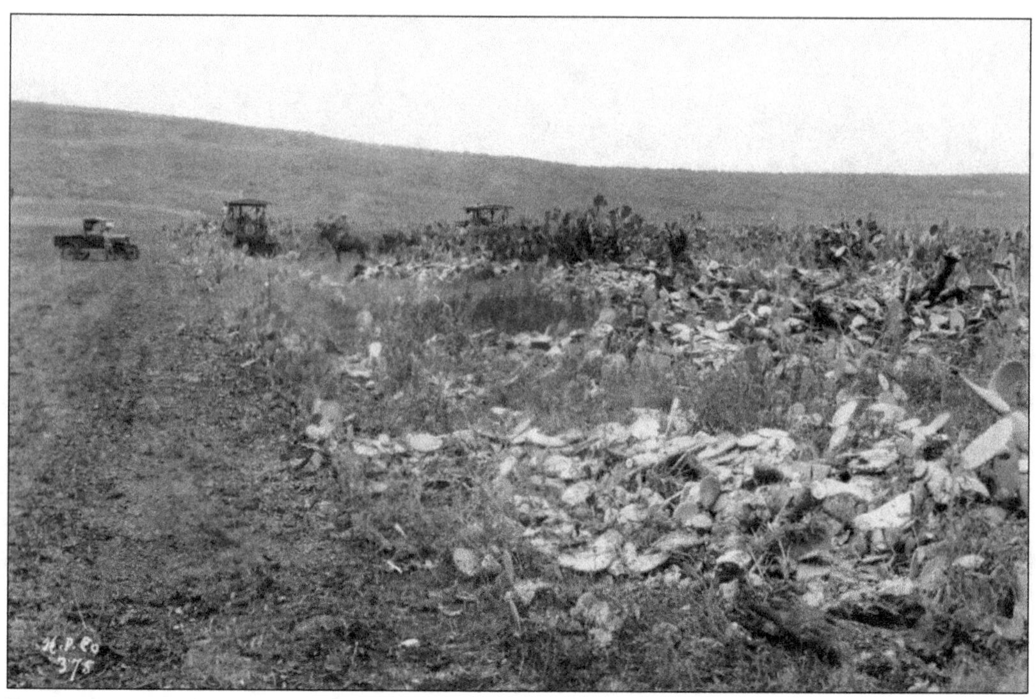

Pānini are removed with a tractor before they can be plowed under to make way for pineapple fields. A rider on horseback supervises the work. After axis deer were introduced to Lāna'i in 1920, they moved into the pānini patches. (Donald Rietow collection.)

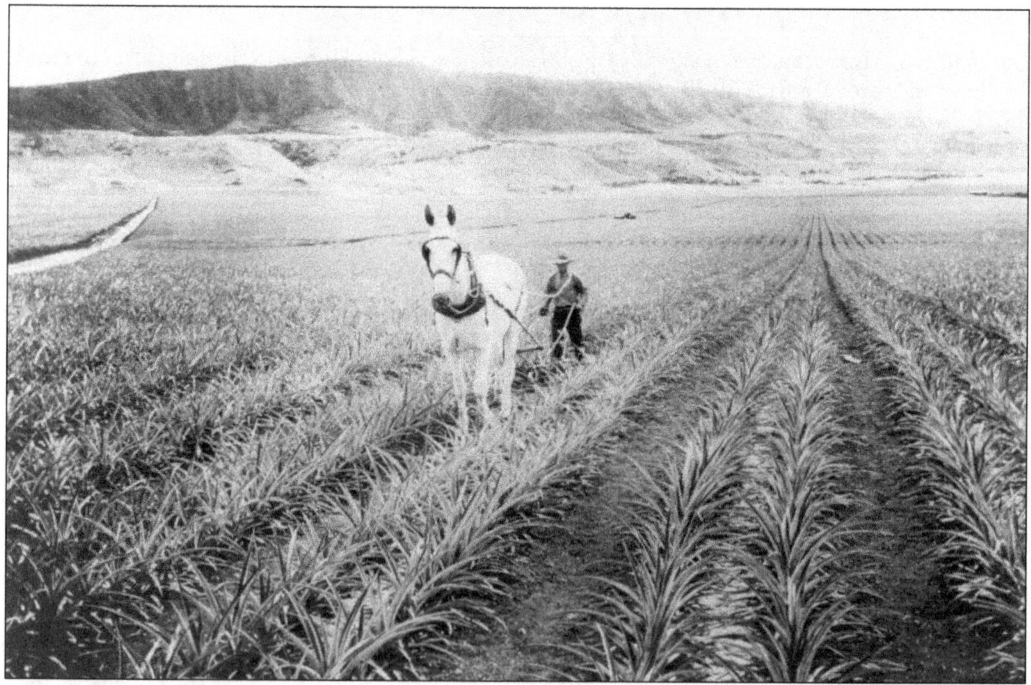

Pulling a cultivator, a mule patiently plods through rows of pineapple plants in Pālāwai. As more fieldwork became mechanized, the mules were retired. The mules were stabled in Miki Basin and just outside of the south end of Lāna'i City. (HAPCo collection.)

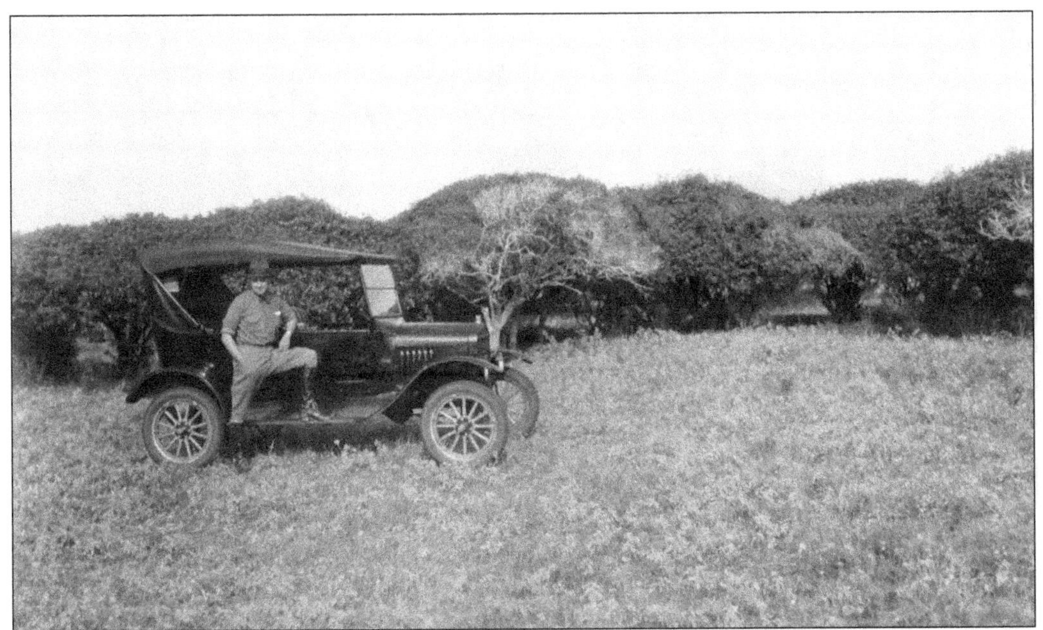

Hawaiian Pineapple Company's first Lāna'i plantation manager, Bloomfield Brown, stands in front of the Olopua section of the Kānepu'u Dryland Forest. It is the largest remaining dryland forest in Hawai'i today. Visitors may take a self-guided tour along a pathway with descriptive signage about the native and endemic plants. The forest is enclosed with fencing to protect it from axis deer. (HAPCo collection.)

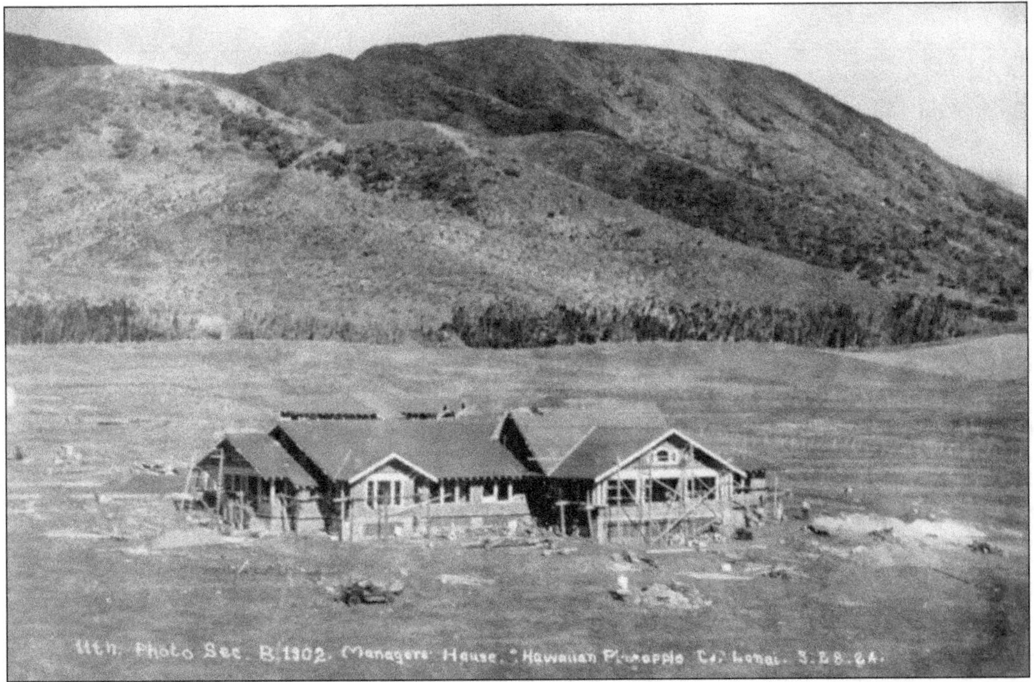

From the glass-enclosed front porch of his house, located on the hillside above Lāna'i City, plantation manager Bloomfield Brown could look down onto the plantation and see everything occurring in it. A very strict man, he was known to personally reprimand anyone he saw littering. Brown was the only manager to ever live in this building; it later became a social hall for the residents. (HAPCo collection.)

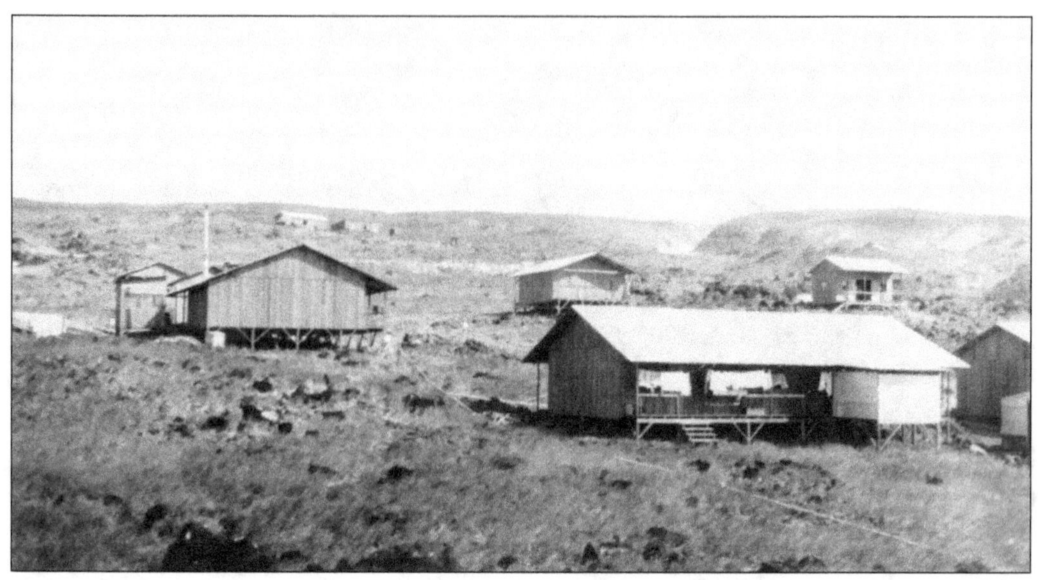

Housing for the harbor's workers was constructed on the hillside overlooking the harbor. In later years, neat yards filled with mango trees and flowering bougainvillea plants helped to soften the appearance of its rocky location. Kaumālapaʻu Village was also called "harbor camp," and its children were transported to and from school by bus. Today, although three houses remain perched above the harbor's cliffs, only one dwelling is still occupied. (HAPCo collection.)

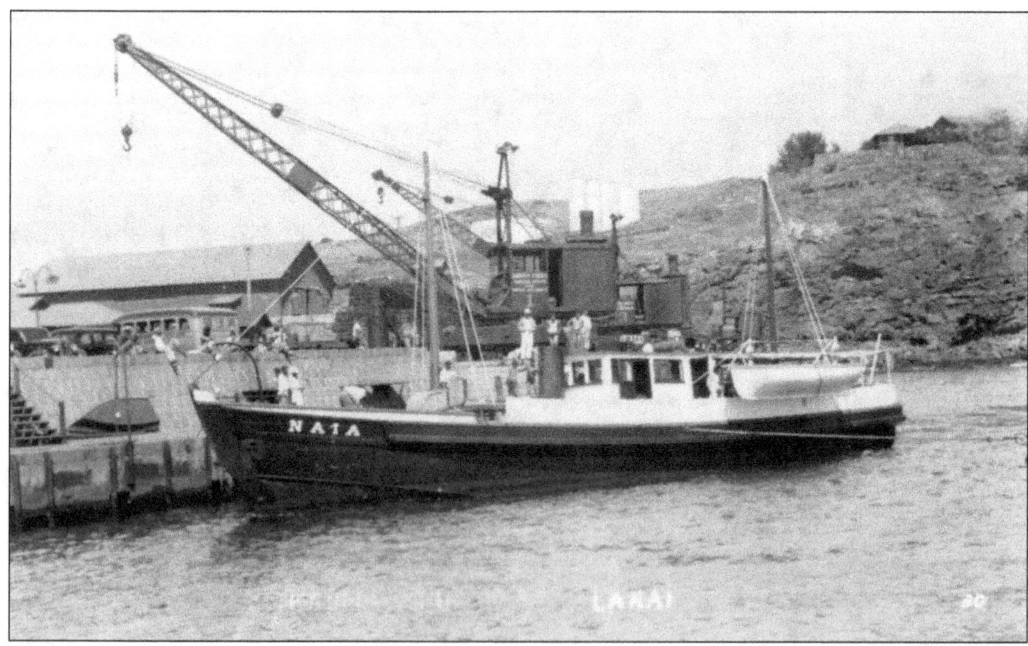

Naia, an inter-island boat that carried passengers between the islands, is docked at Kaumālapaʻu Harbor. James Dole developed the infrastructure needed to transport pineapple to the cannery on Oʻahu. On the dock behind the boat is one of the two steam engine cranes used to load the bins of fruit. (HAPCo collection.)

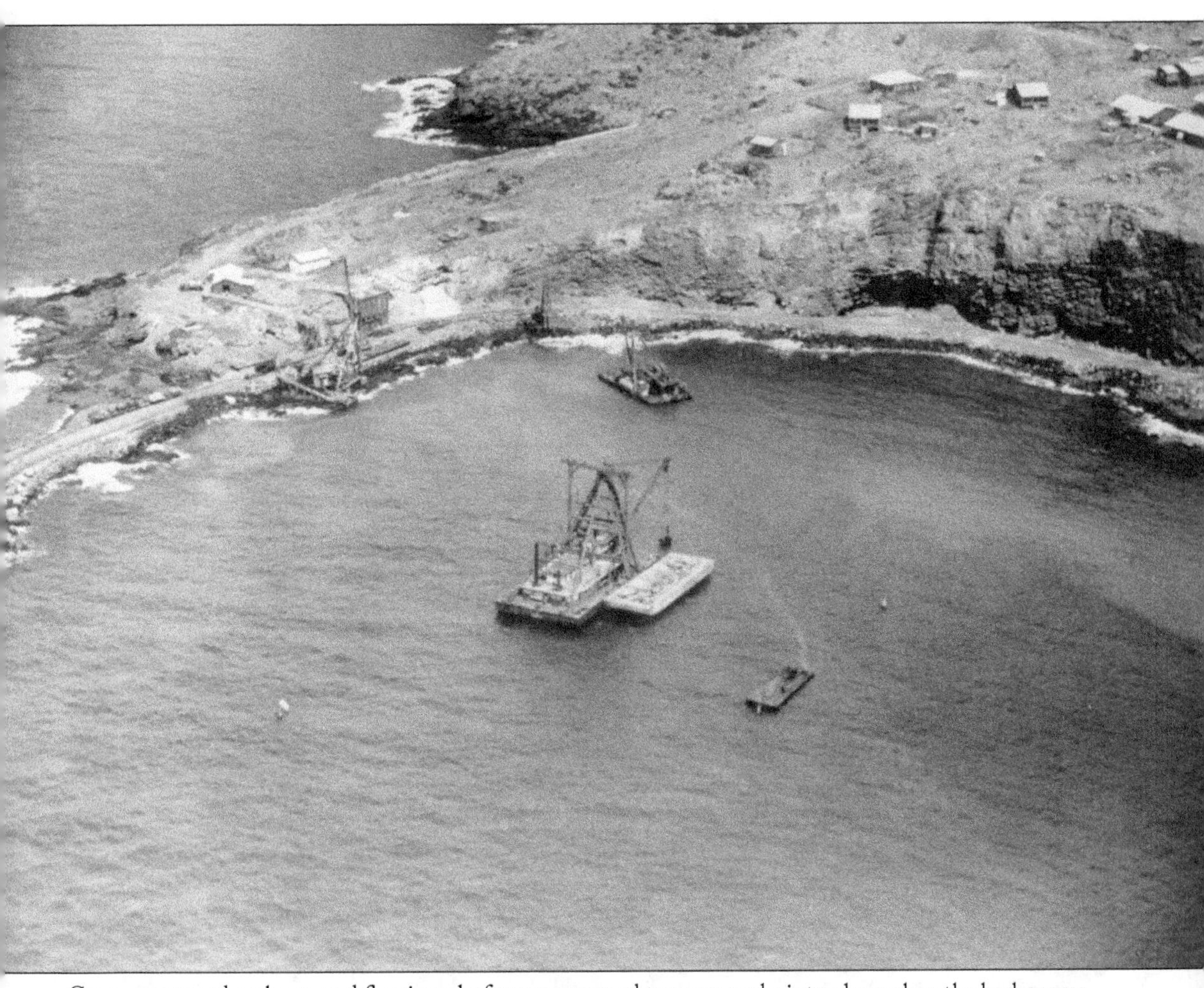

Cranes mounted on boats and floating platforms were used to move rocks into place when the harbor was built. Cliffs line the coastline of the harbor's southwest side, and storms coming from the south create swells that crash into its dock. (HAPCo collection.)

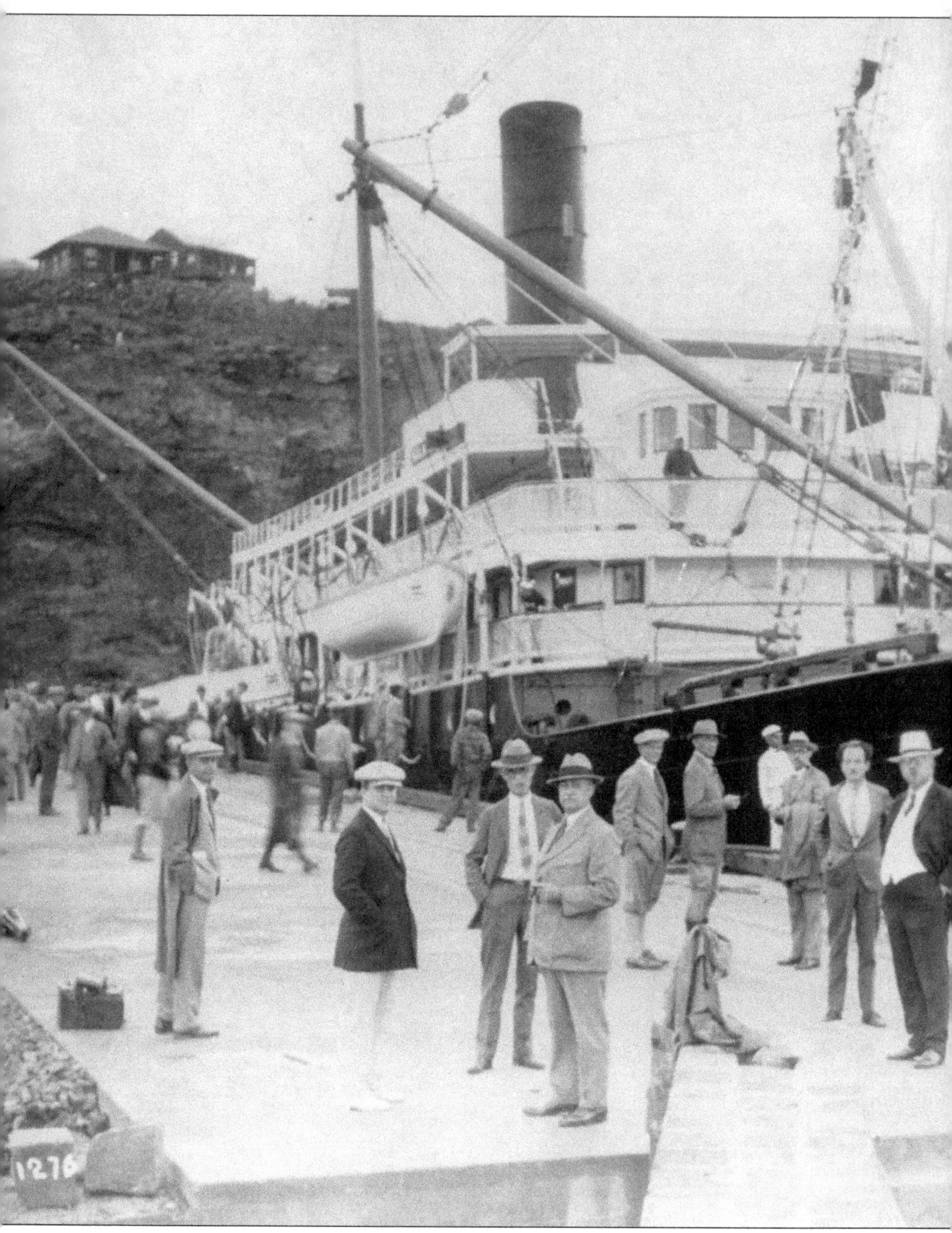
1276

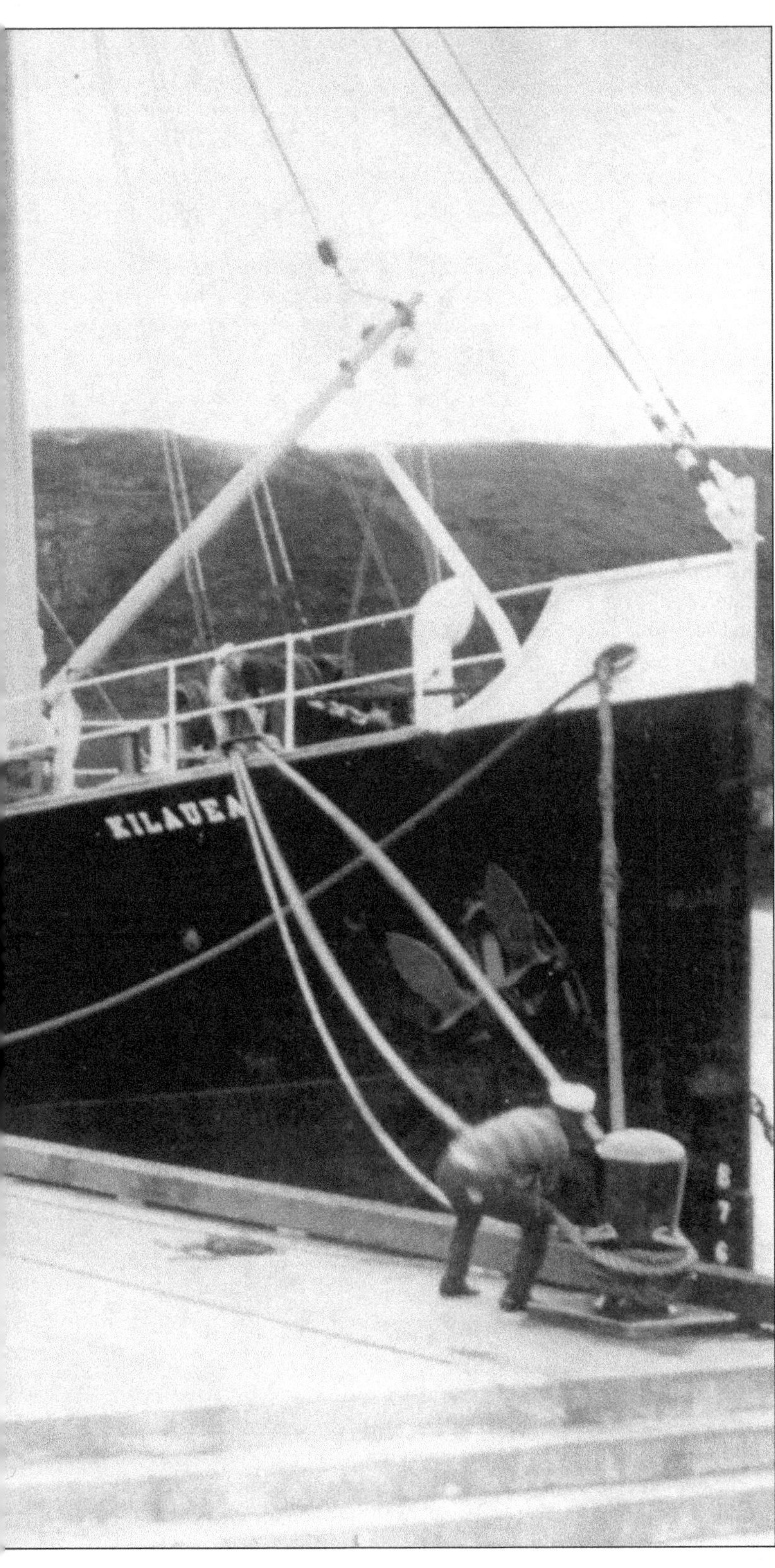

In 1901, James Dole incorporated the Hawaiian Pineapple Company on 60 acres of land on the island of O'ahu. In 1922, Dole bought out the Lāna'i land holdings of Frank and Harry Baldwin of Maui for $1.1 million and set about creating what would become the world's largest pineapple plantation. He hired David Root, James Munro, Tokumatsui Murayama, and others to help him create a town for his field workers. By 1923, the first buildings were being constructed. On January 31, 1926, James D. Dole invited 150 Hawai'i dignitaries to the "unveiling" of his Lāna'i plantation. Lāna'i City was the first planned community developed in the Hawaiian Islands. (HAPCo collection.)

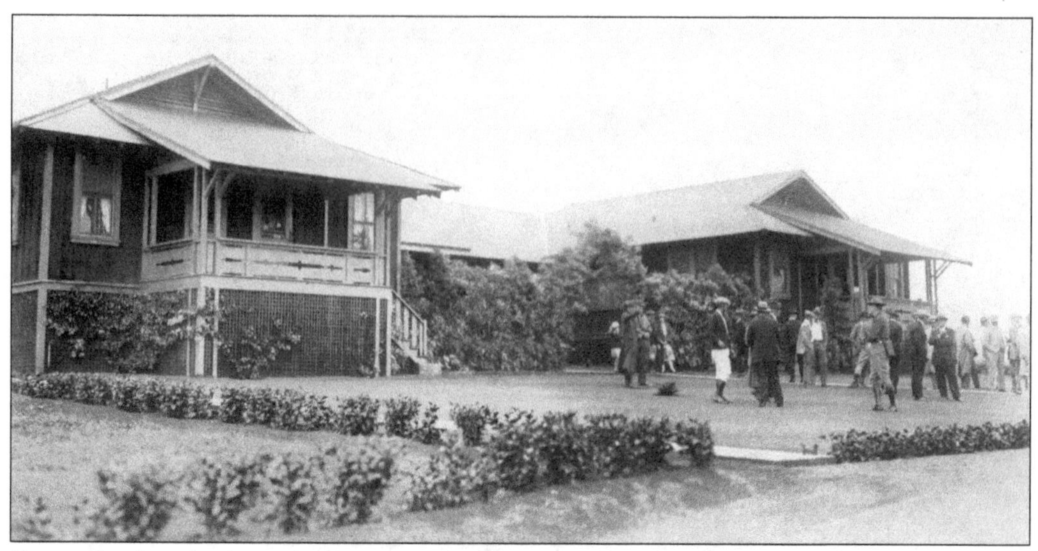

Originally a boardinghouse for the plantation's single supervisory staff, this building later became the Lāna'i Inn, then the Lāna'i Lodge; today, it is the Hotel Lāna'i. The 11-room hotel was a social gathering place for residents and the only hotel accommodations for business travelers and tourists until the Lodge at Kō'ele opened in 1990. (HAPCo collection.)

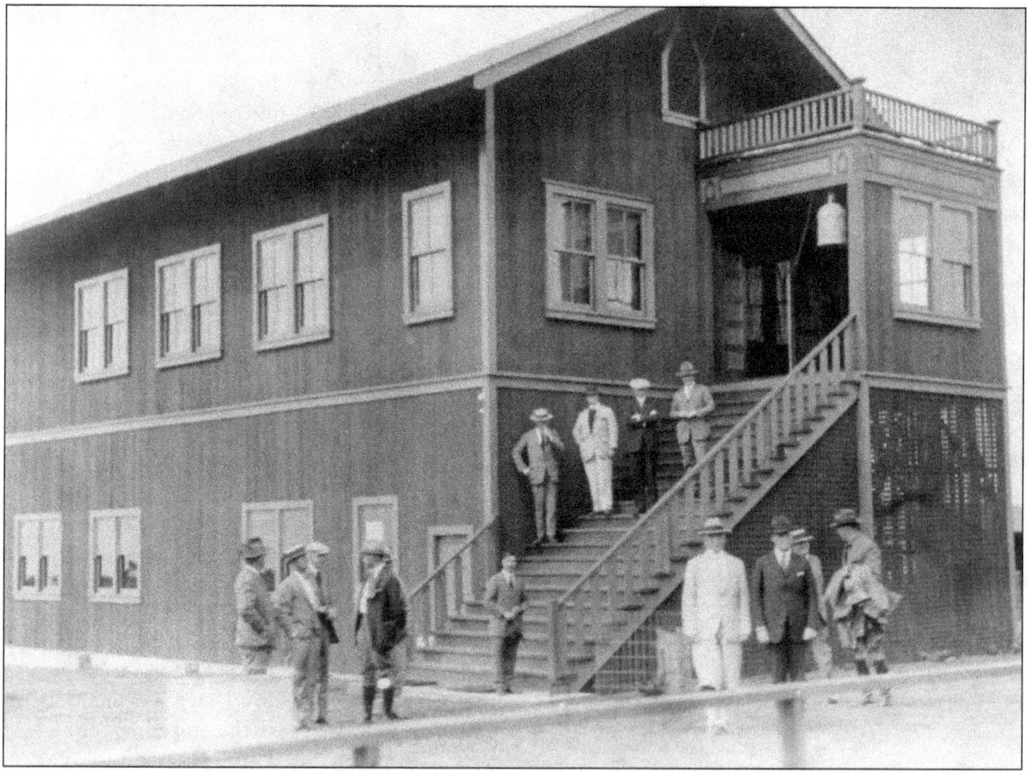

Residents of Lāna'i's Japanese community used this building as their temple. When World War II began, the building was confiscated and turned over to United Church of Christ and renamed Lāna'i Union Church. After the war was over, another building on Fraser Avenue was built for the Lāna'i Hongwanji Temple and continues to be used today. (HAPCo collection.)

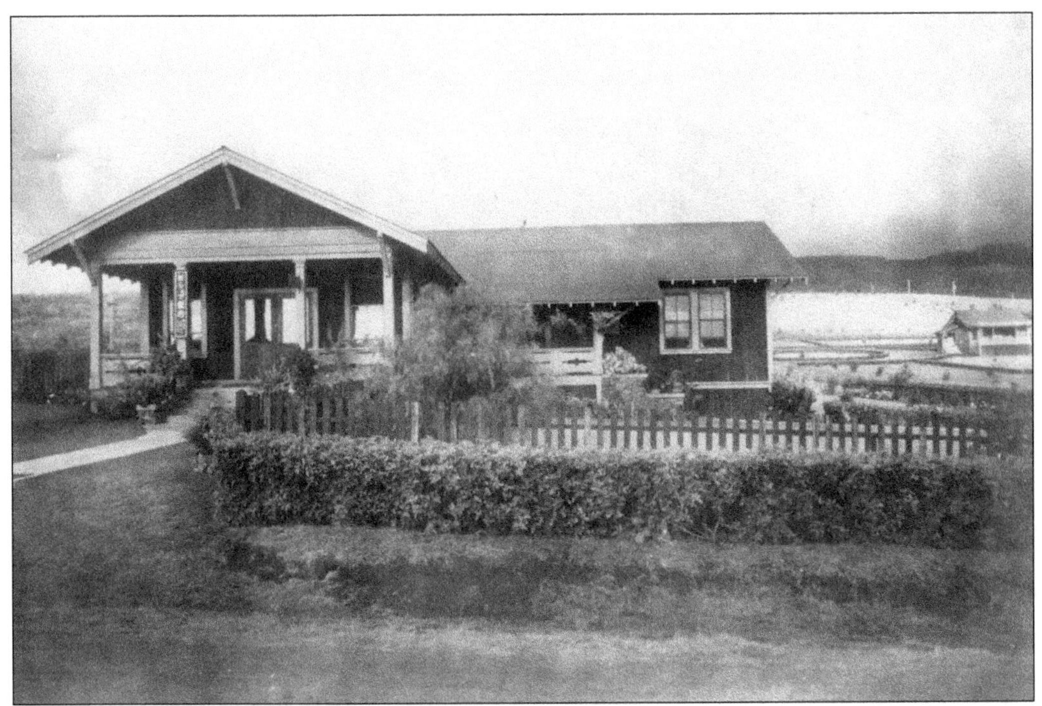

This building on the corner of Lānaʻi Avenue and Seventh Street housed Bishop Bank in 1926. Built by the Hawaiian Pineapple Company's skilled Japanese carpenters, it reflected their influence. Modernized to comply with ADA requirements, the present-day building retains its original charm and is occupied by First Hawaiian Bank. (HAPCo collection.)

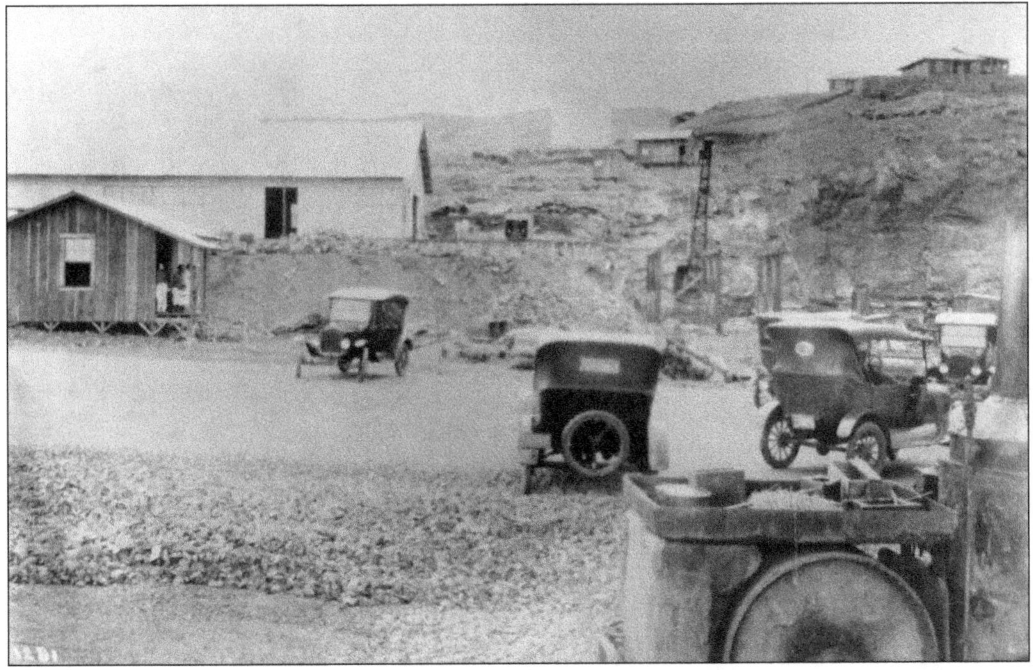

Vehicles accompanied the visiting dignitaries on board the *Kilauea* to take them on a tour of Lānaʻi City and the Hawaiian Pineapple Company's plantation. (HAPCo collection.)

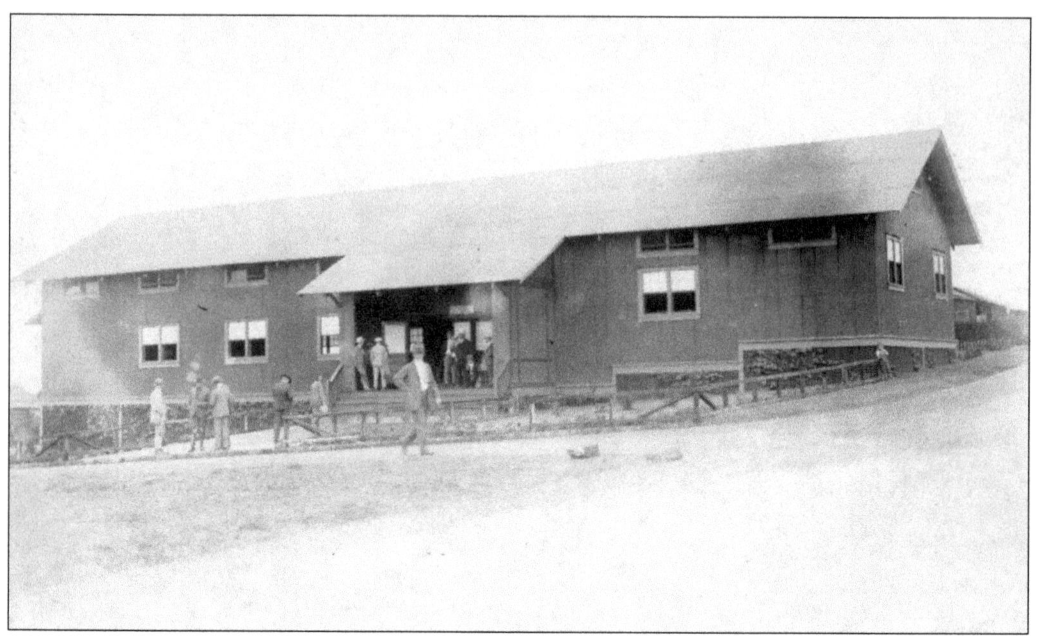

Lānaʻi was not only a place to work. James Dole wanted to create a community for families, a place where his workers could enjoy activities together. Hale Keaka (house of theater) opened on January 31, 1926. Today, the building retains it original appearance on the outside, but its interior was rebuilt to house two 90-seat theaters with state-of-the-art technology. It reopened in time for Christmas 2014. (HAPCo collection.)

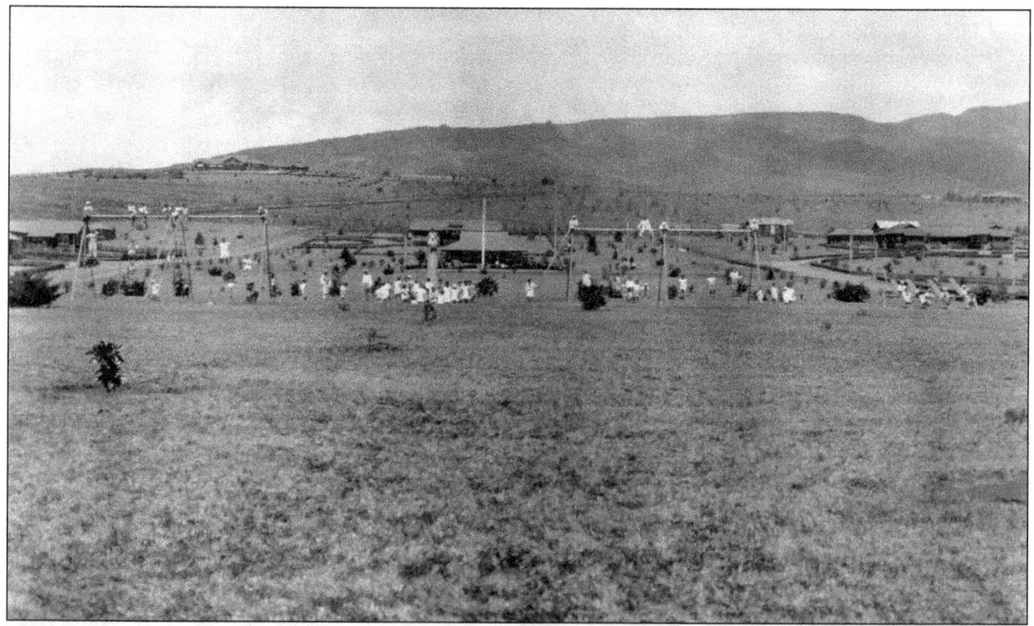

Lānaʻihale is barren in this Hawaiian Pineapple Company photograph taken in 1926. Dole Park's majestic Cook Island pine trees are less than three feet tall, but several buildings can be seen: the original plantation manager's house, the boardinghouse for supervisors, and part of the company's administrative building. Children fill the playground, but as many of them are formally dressed in white, they may have gathered there for a special occasion. (Cookie Hashimoto collection.)

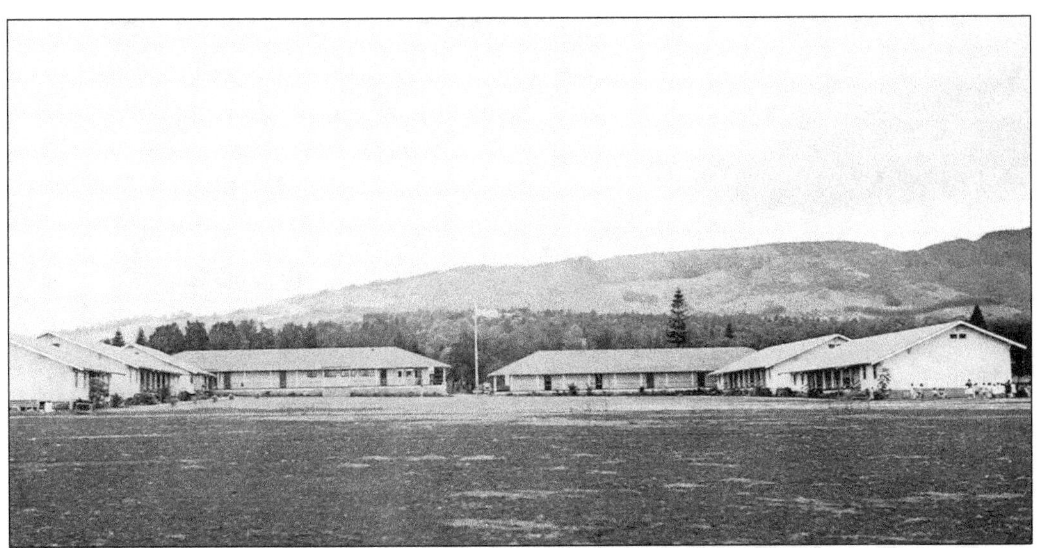

The ranch's Kō'ele School was located on what is now the eighth fairway of the Cavendish Golf Course. Founded in 1938, Lāna'i High and Elementary School was built at its present location on Fraser Avenue. The school's original wooden buildings surrounded a quadrangle lined with fig banyan trees. Over the years all of the buildings have been replaced, with the exception of two buildings by the cafeteria, which are now used for storage. Through the years, the school's flagpole has remained in its original location. (Cookie Hashimoto collection.)

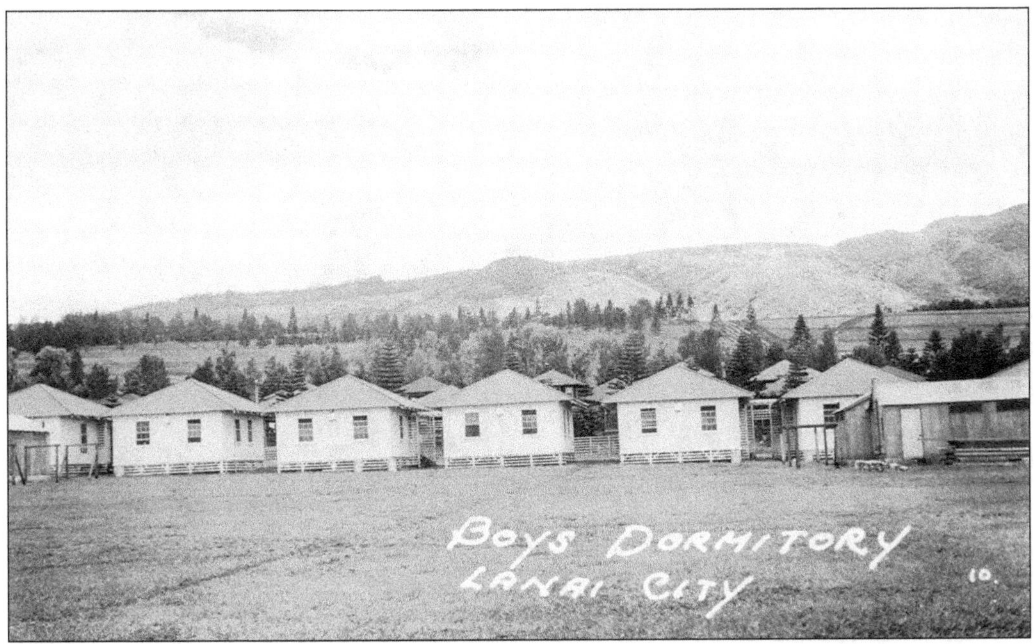

The plantation relied heavily on seasonal workers to get the ripening pineapples harvested. Each summer, students from Hawai'i and other states came to Lāna'i to work. They were housed in dormitories like the buildings pictured here. The students were accompanied by an adult chaperone or counselor who became their *luna* (field supervisor). (Cookie Hashimoto collection.)

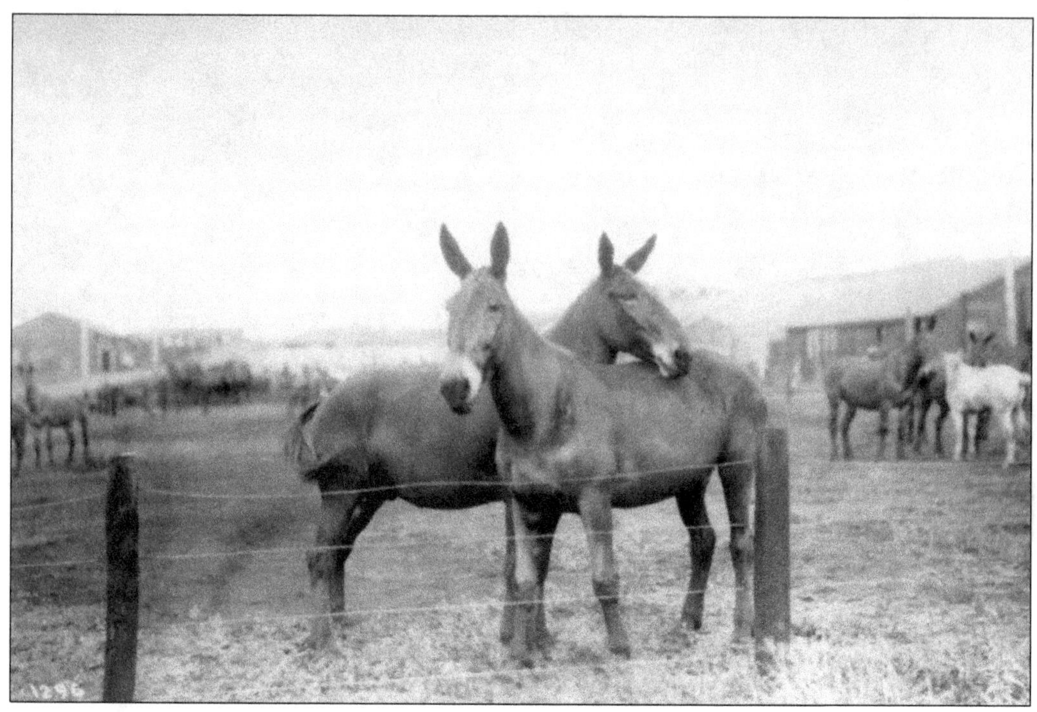

"Workhorses" of the plantation, mules, were valued and carefully tended to at stables located in different areas, making it convenient for their handlers to tack them up for their workday. These handsome mules were stabled near the present-day Lāna'i City Service. (HAPCo collection.)

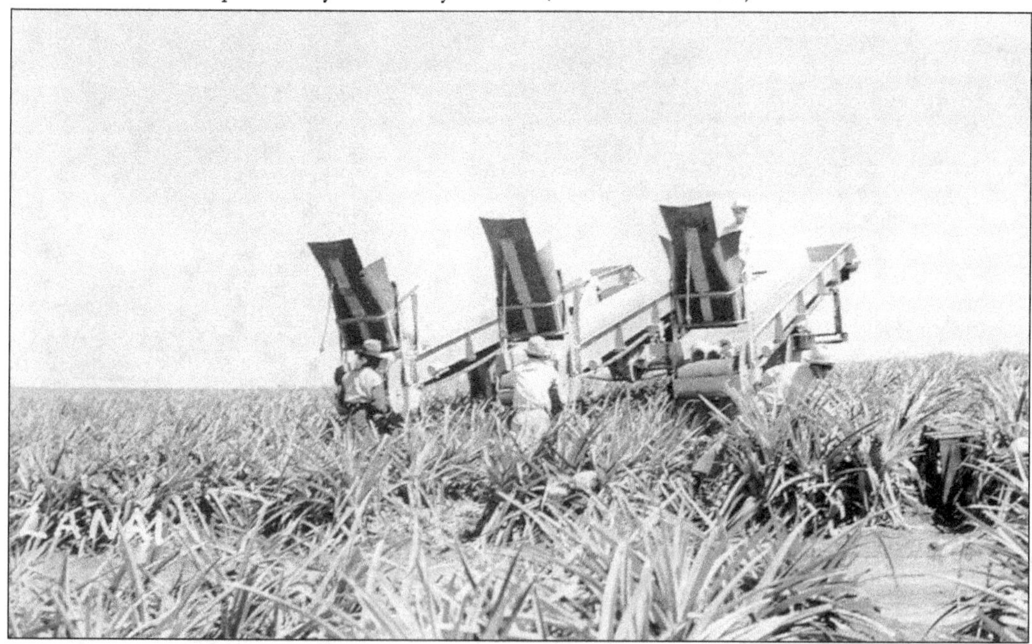

Pineapple is harvested by hand. When Hawaiian Pineapple Company's plantation started, workers carried ripening fruit out of the fields in sacks slung around their shoulders and waists. The bags were emptied by the roadside, and the pineapples were repacked into crates and loaded onto a truck. This early prototype harvester shows a machine for three workers. (Cookie Hashimoto collection.)

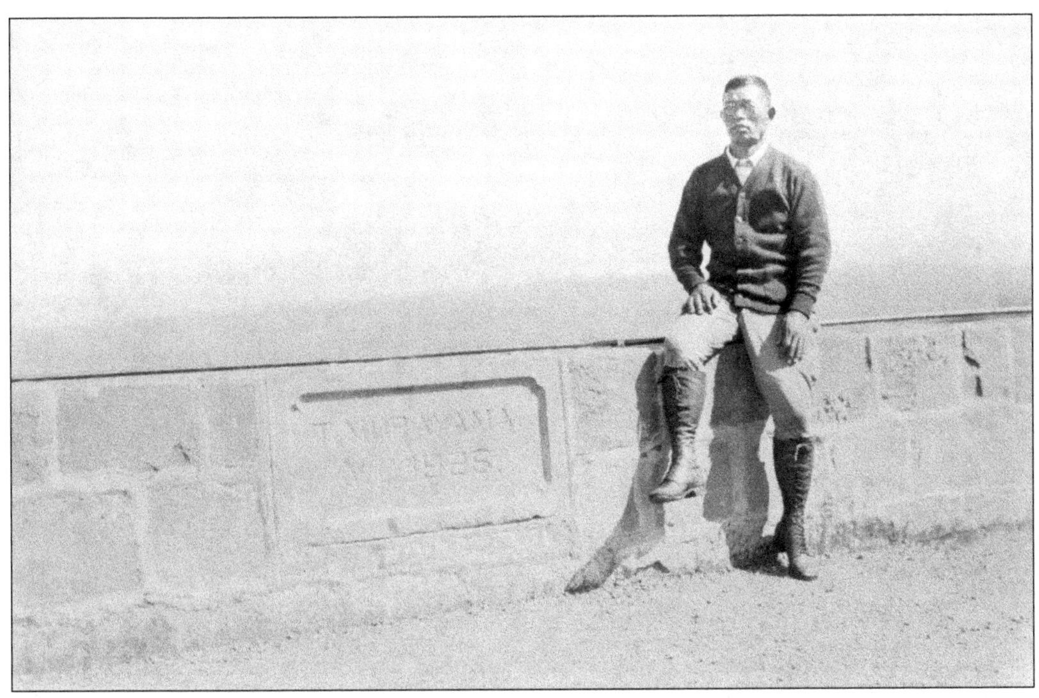

Tokumatsu Murayama sits on the rock wall he designed at Kaumālapaʻu Harbor. To his left on the wall is a plaque with his name and the date the project was completed. In a letter dated February 28, 1926, Hawaiian Pineapple Company's resident engineer David E. Root expressed his appreciation of Murayama's work. It included the construction of a three-and-a-half-million-gallon reservoir and over 4,400 linear feet of tunnels, among other projects. (HAPCo collection.)

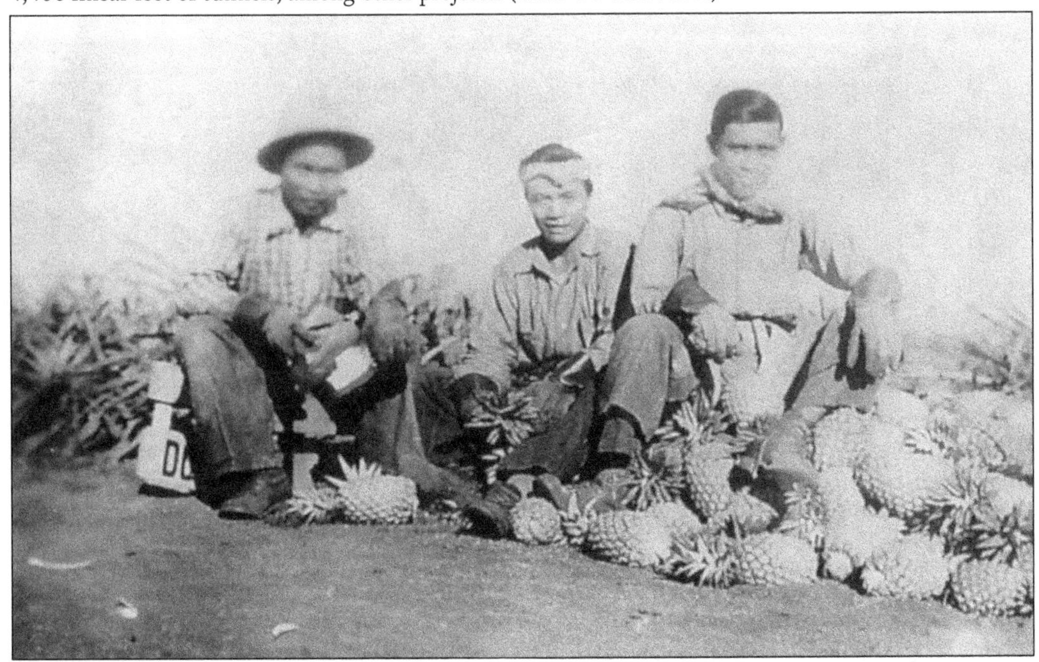

Picking pineapples was heavy work. From left to right, Fractoso Agapay, Ernesto Mercado, and Jaime Saturninio pose with some of the pineapples they have just harvested. (Rosita Camero collection.)

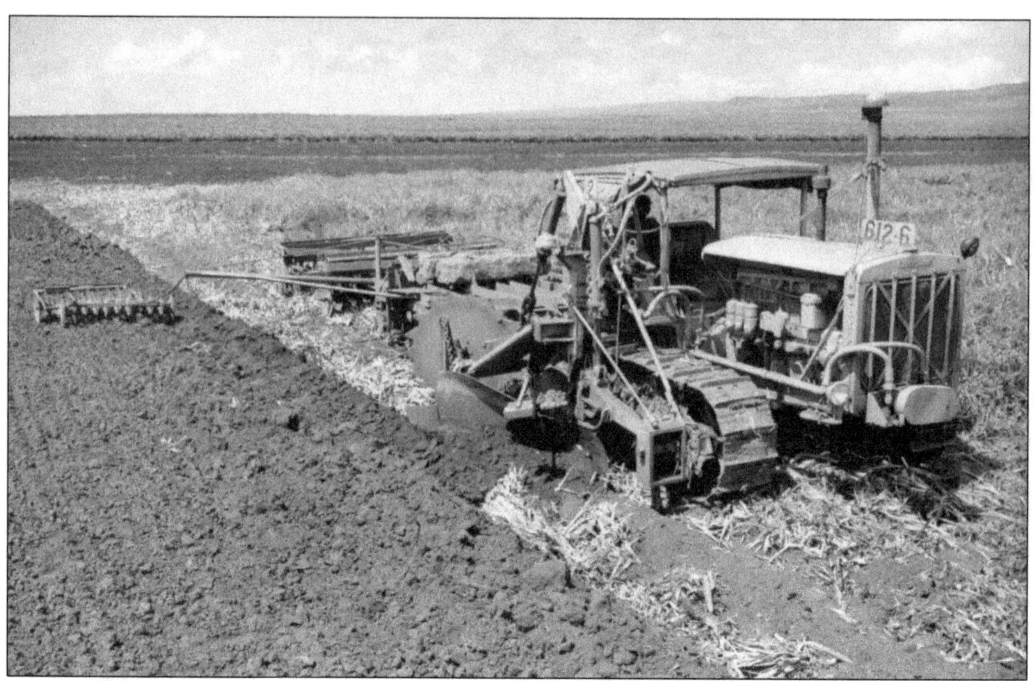
A tractor, pulling a specially designed side plow, turns the crushed pineapple plants back into the soil and makes a furrow for new planting at the same time. However, they were never able to design a machine to plant the pineapple tops or harvest the fruit. (HAPCo collection.)

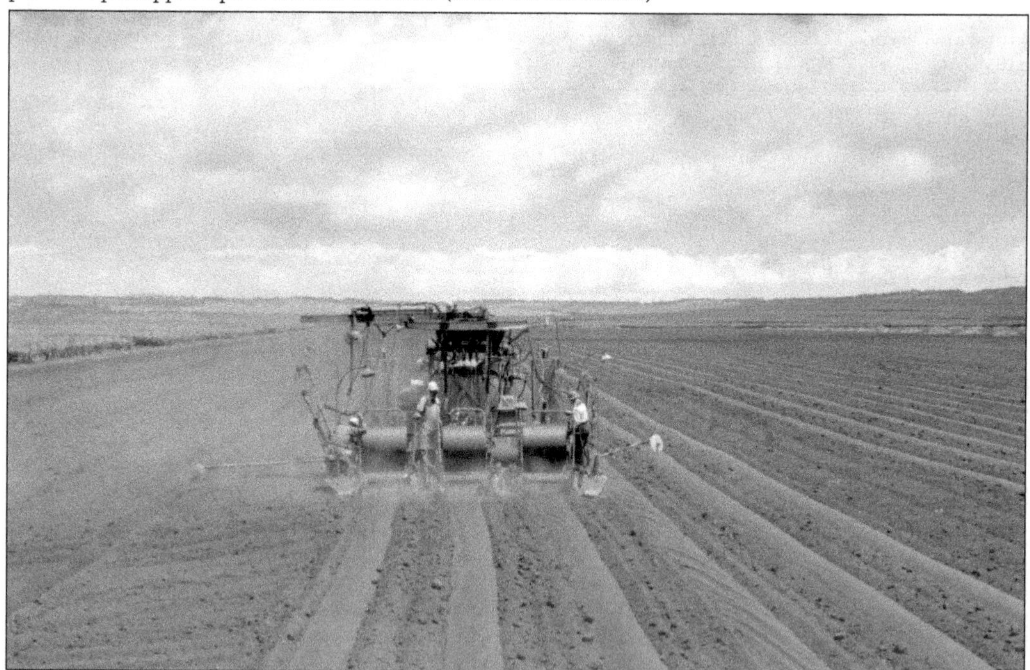
A paper-laying machine designed by James T. Munro, George Munro's son, furrowed three rows of heavy black paper at a time, laid fertilizer under it, and covered its edges with earth. As the plantation's engineer, Munro worked with other employees to make improvements and perfected furrowing, spraying, and harvesting methods as well as the loading of the barge. (Aurelio Del Rosario collection.)

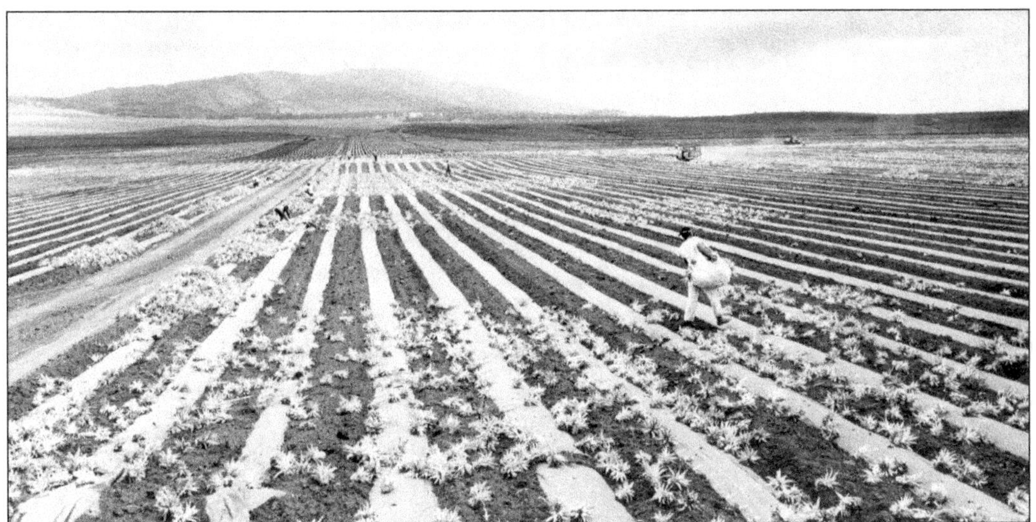

Pineapple tops are piled high on the roadside. Each planter fills his bag with the tops and scatters them across the rows of plastic. Bent over, he or she will move through the field, slit open each marked line on the plastic, and plant a pineapple top. Planters received bonus pay based on the amount of pineapple tops they planted each day. (HAPCo collection.)

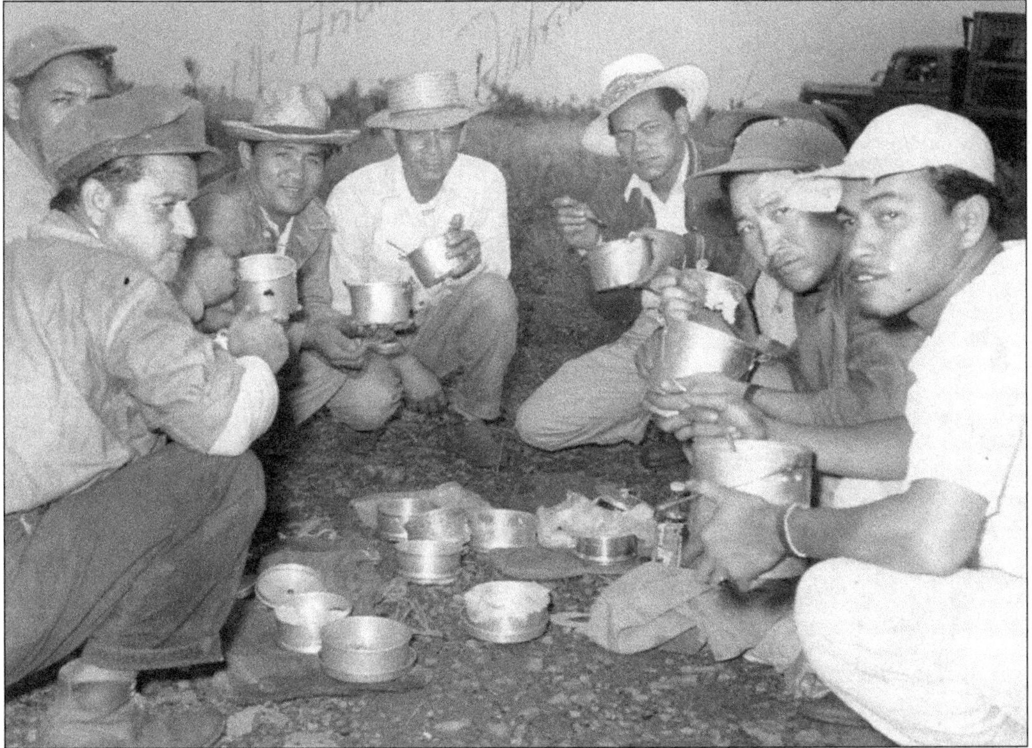

Field workers carried their *kaukau* (food) in a two-compartment tin pail they carried to work with them each day. The bottom section of the container was usually filled with rice; the smaller upper compartment contained their meat, fish, or vegetables. Many plantation wives earned extra money for their families by cooking and preparing kaukau for single men in the neighborhood camps. (Cookie Hashimoto collection.)

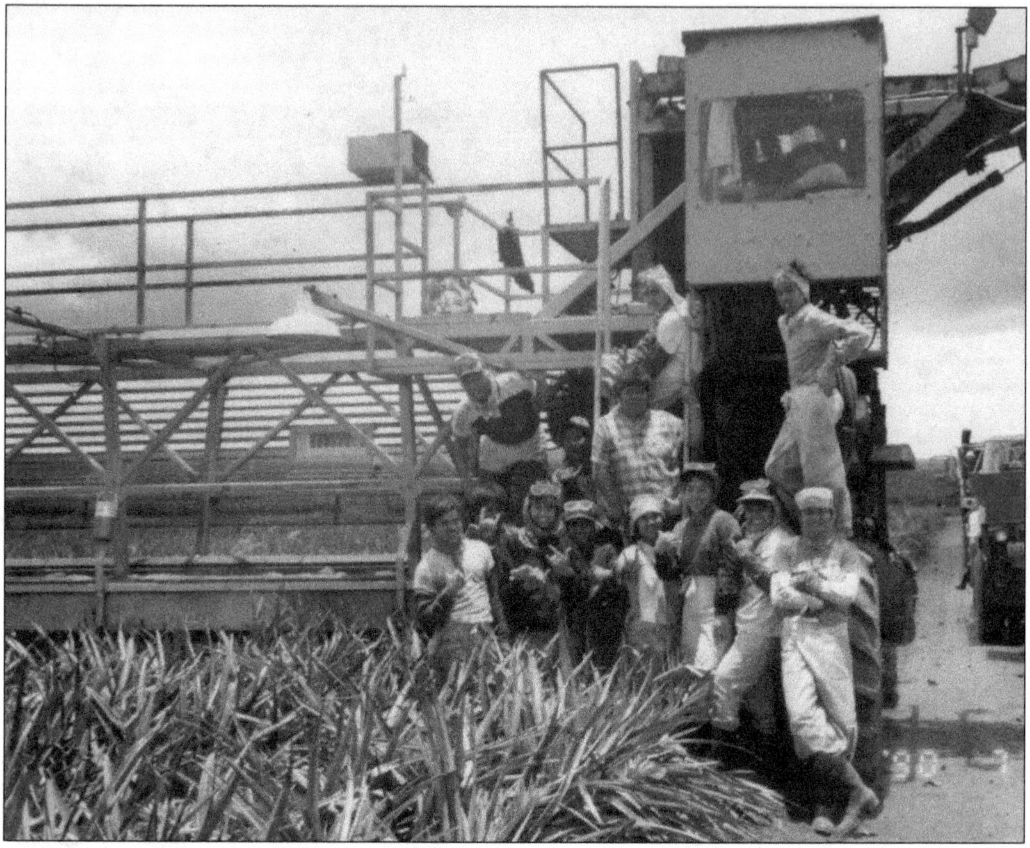

Teenaged seasonal workers were placed together into a gang. Each gang was assigned to the same field luna for the entire summer. When following the harvesting machine, everyone was responsible for harvesting the fruit in their own rows, but they quickly learned to help each other when one person's row was swamped with fruit. The gangs developed a close-knit bond many retained for life. (Frances Pagay collection.)

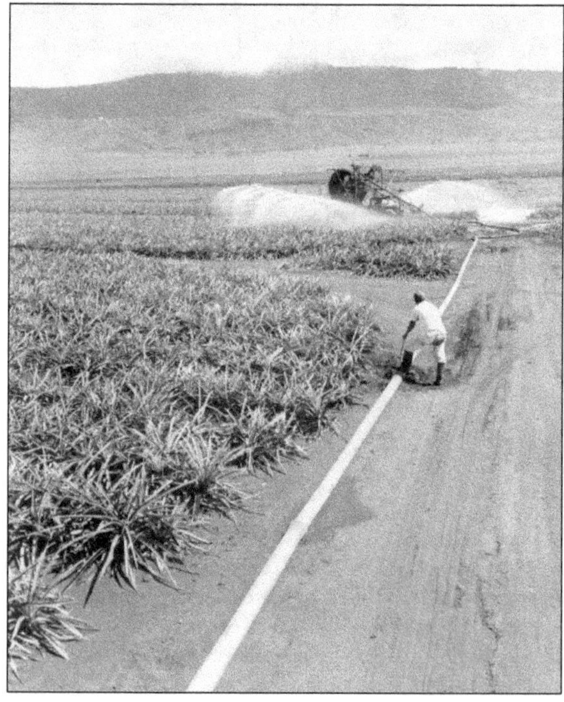

Mormon settlers experienced difficulties raising their crops due to a lack of rain in the Pālāwai Basin. Hawaiian Pineapple Company developed water resources and designed large sprinklers capable of watering rows of pineapple at one time. (HAPCo collection.)

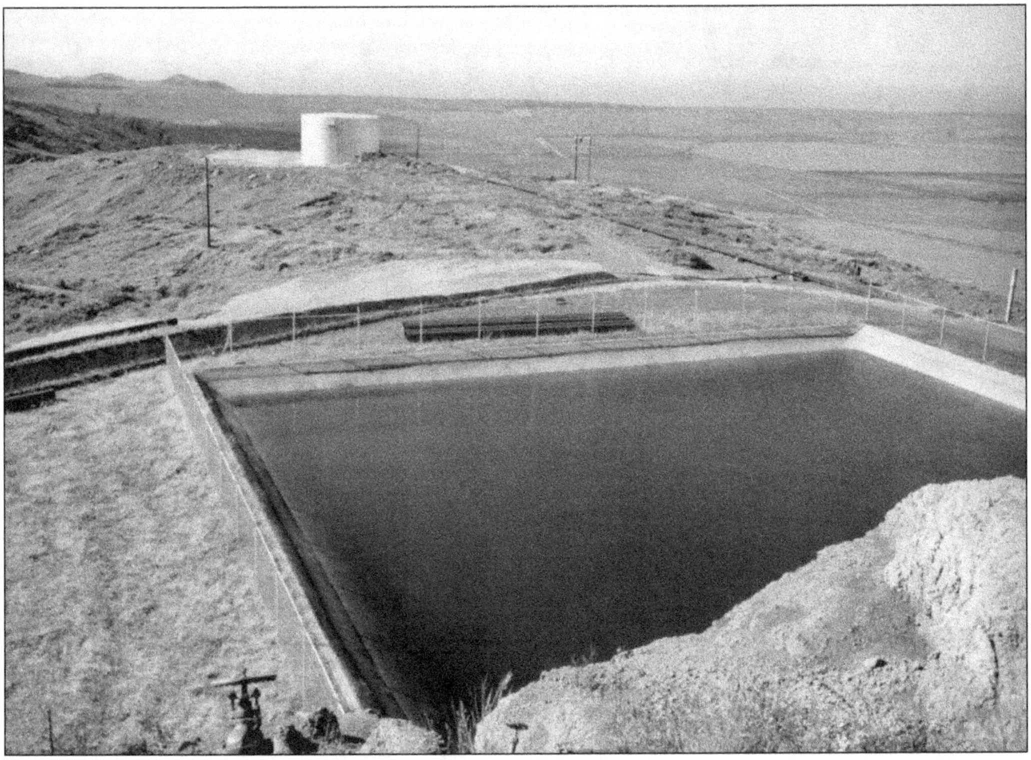

Water drawn from the island's aquifer located deep beneath Lāna'ihale was stored at a reservoir above Pālāwai at Hi'i to provide water for irrigating new fields during the island's dry season. (HAPCo collection.)

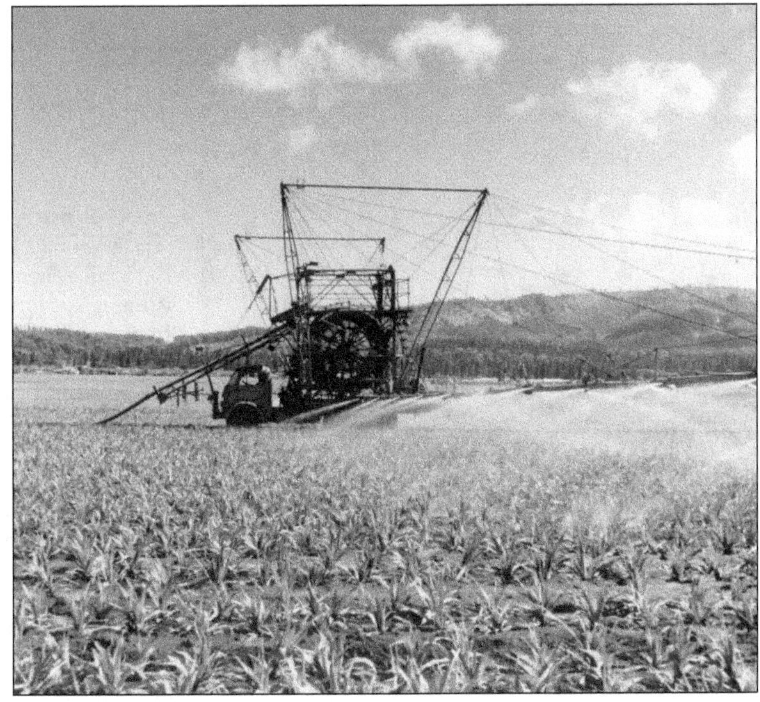

Giant sprinklers with arms stretching out across the top of rows of plants irrigated the fields when needed. Although pineapple can tolerate some drier weather, the island's annual rainfall and field conditions were closely monitored to maximize each field's yield. (HAPCo collection.)

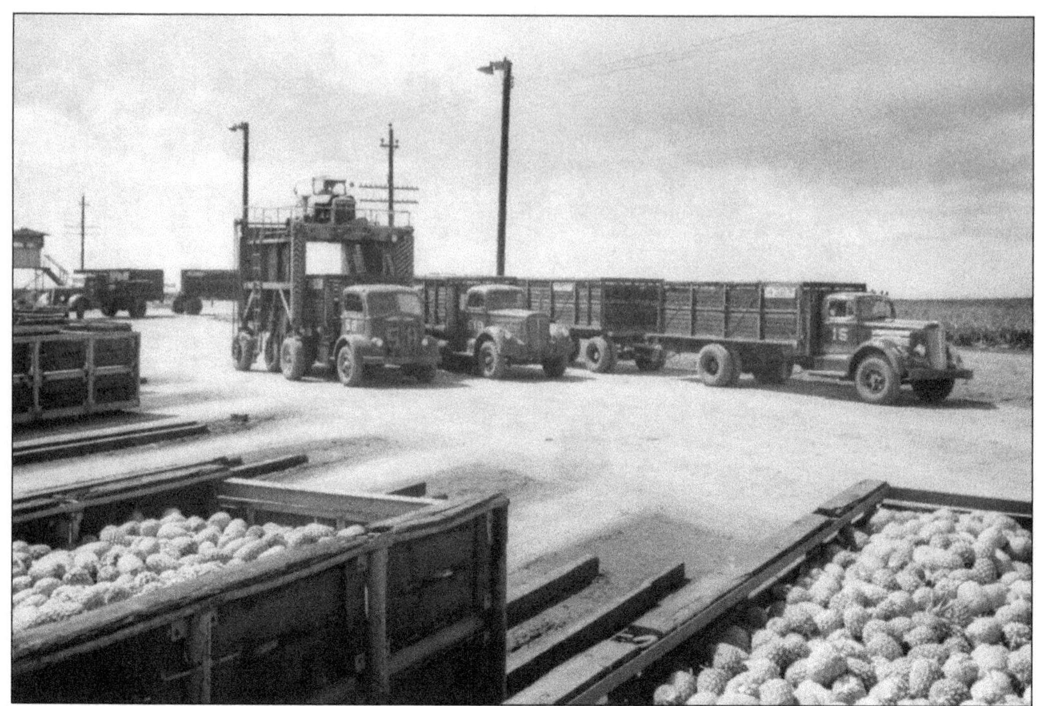

Trucks loaded with bins full of ripe pineapples were off-loaded at the central shuttle station, located on Kaumālapa'u Highway. The bins were moved with a specially designed contraption called a Ross Carrier, named after its designer, Jack Ross. Looking like a giant spider with four legs, its operator sat high on top of it, drove it over the bin on the truck, and could carry the bin off and lower it onto the ground or onto a trailer truck going to the harbor. (HAPCo collection.)

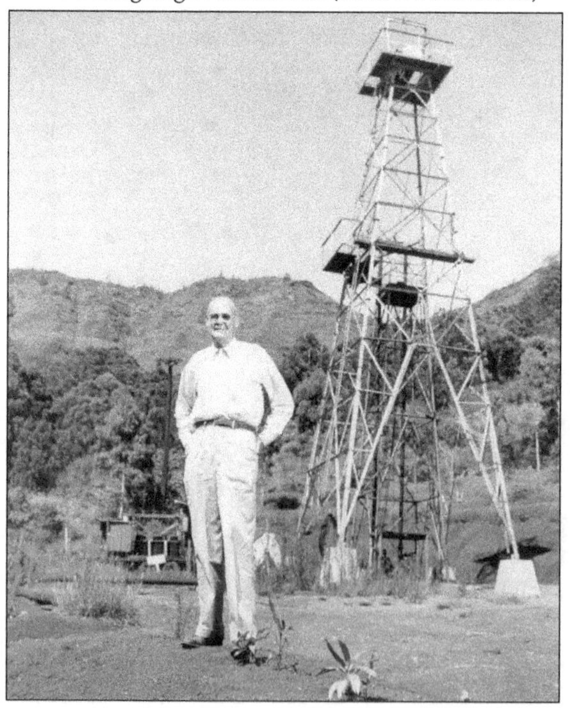

Lāna'i plantation manager William Aldrich stands in front of a new well shaft. Lāna'i does not have ponds, lakes, or running streams. Instead, its water comes from aquifers, pockets of water trapped underground. Fog and low-lying clouds condense into water droplets on the pine needles of the Cook Island pine trees that grow on Lāna'ihale, the island's mountain range, to create a watershed area. The water percolates through layers of earth and collects in the aquifer. During the island's ranching and plantation days, and continuing to the present time, the island's water resources are closely monitored to assure they will be sustainable for future generations. (HAPCo collection.)

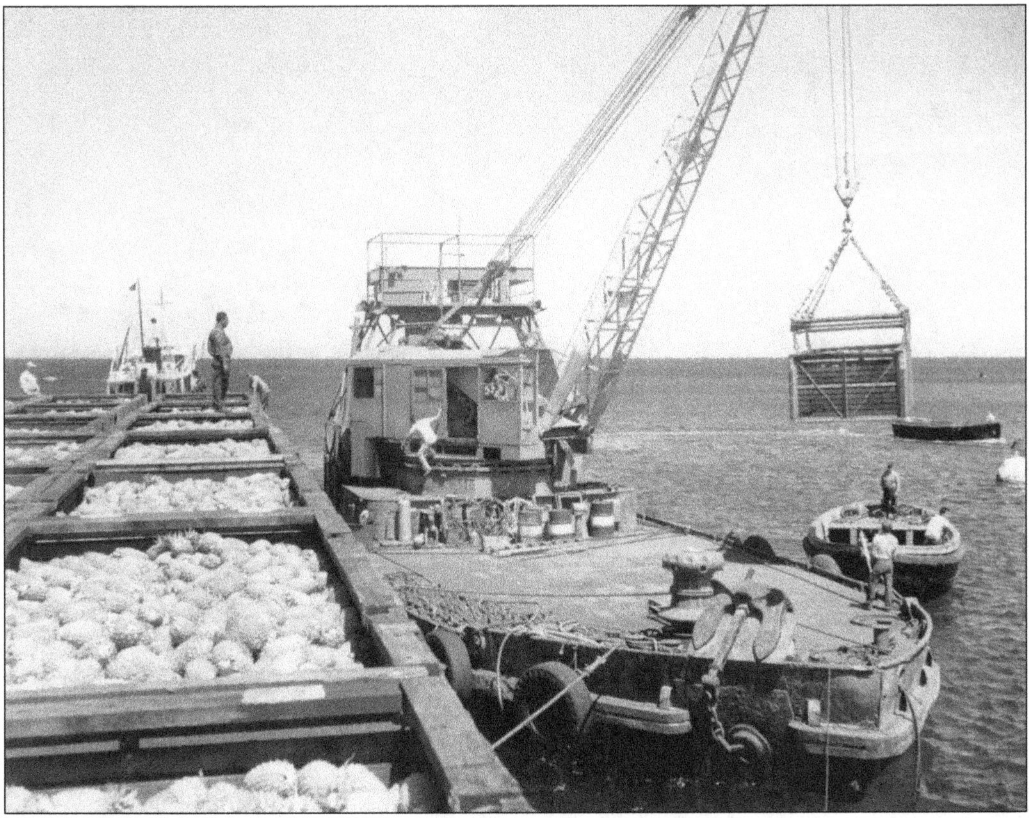

A crane mounted on a boat moves the last empty bins from the barge, which is almost fully loaded with pineapples. The loading and off-loading process was changed when two cranes were mounted onto steel tracks dockside. (HAPCo collection.)

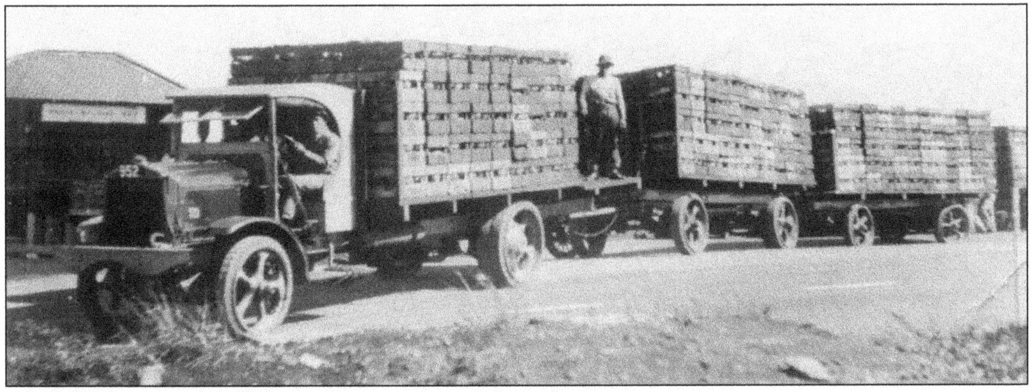

In the plantation's earlier days, pineapples were hand-harvested and carried to the roadside to be packed into wooden crates. The crates were loaded onto trucks manually and then transported to the harbor. (HAPCo collection.)

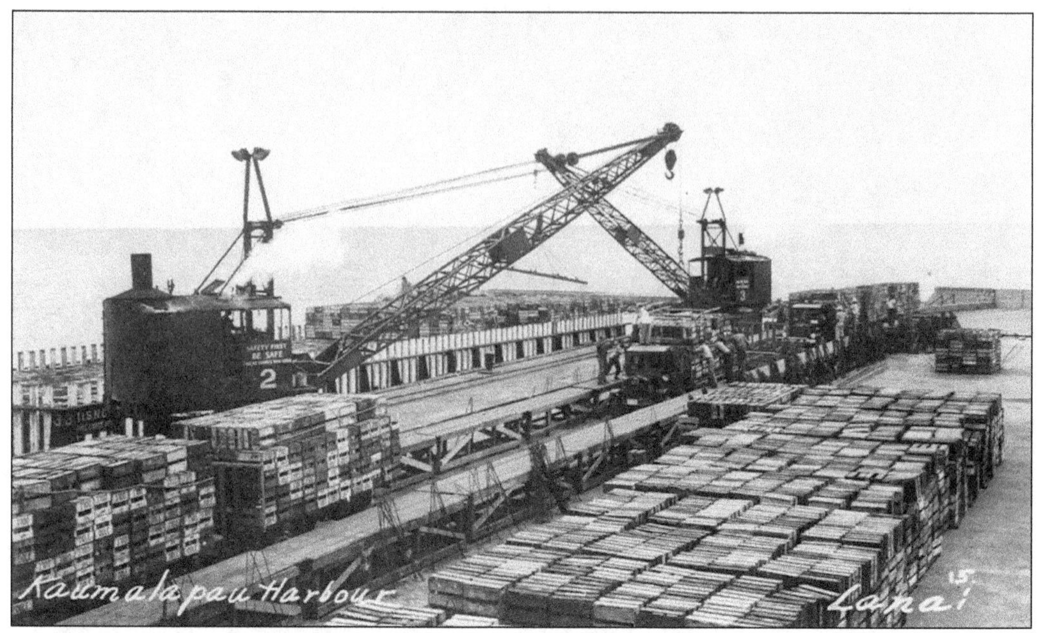

After the loading process was mechanized with steam-powered cranes, trucks arriving at Kaumālapaʻu could be switched over very efficiently. One crane lifted each filled bin and placed it onto the barge. The truck moved farther down a lane, and the second crane took an empty bin off the barge and placed it onto the truck. The cranes were mounted on metal rails and could move back and forth as they worked. (HAPCo collection.)

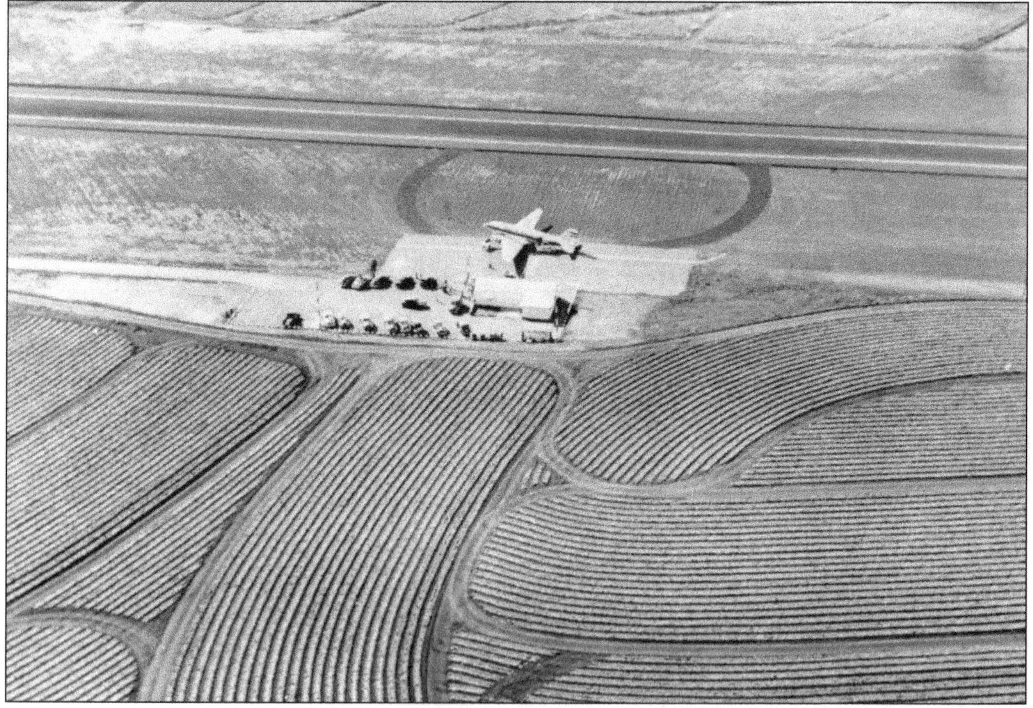

Lānaʻi Airport is surrounded by contoured rows of pineapples. Today, many of the island's fallow fields still bear signs of the roads that traversed the fields. (HAPCo collection.)

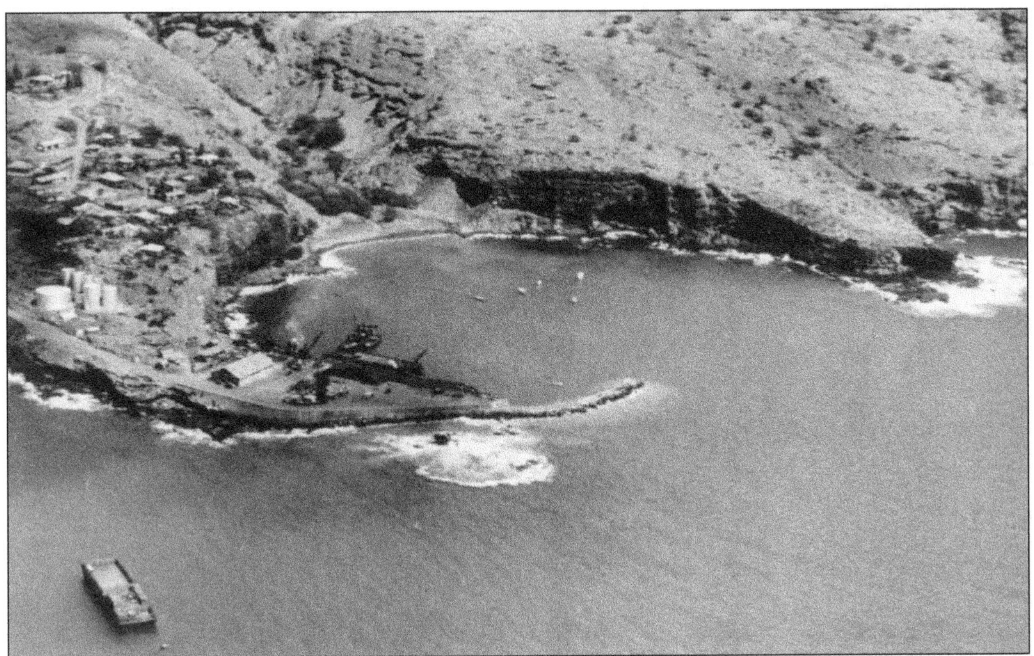

Nestled into the base of the cliff, Kaumālapaʻu Harbor looks serene in this photograph from 1950. The village above it and the fuel tanks are all clearly visible. The blowhole from the legend of Kaʻala is located across from the harbor's breakwater, near the surging foam of the ocean. (HAPCo collection.)

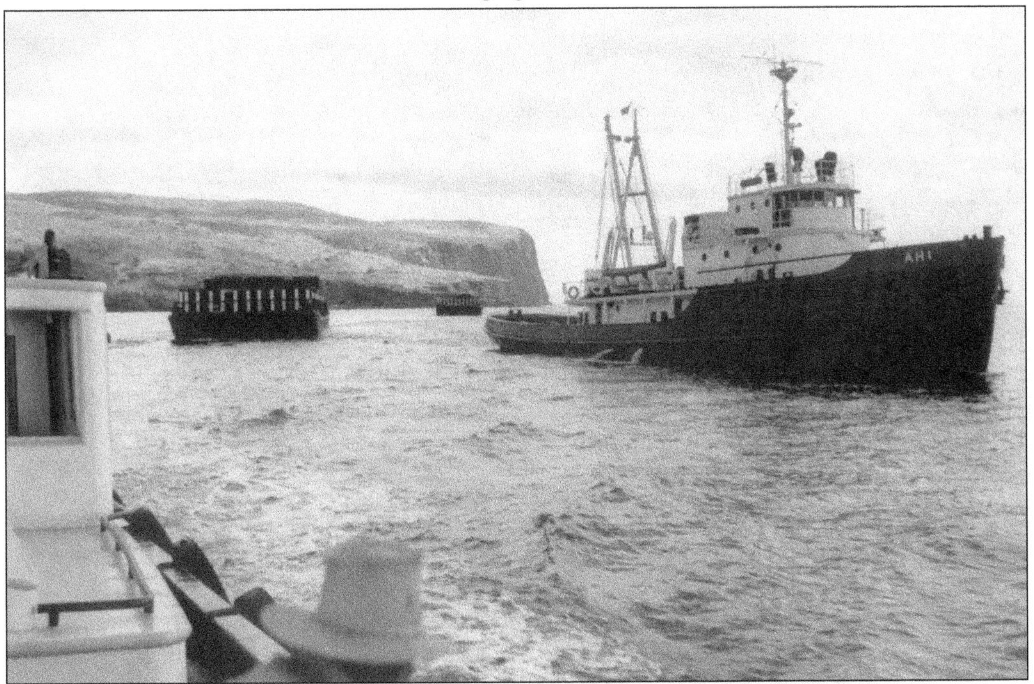

Ahi, an Isleways tugboat, tows a barge into Kaumālapaʻu. One of the narrowest harbors in Hawaiʻi, it takes a skilled harbor pilot to navigate a tug moving a barge safely up against the docks. During the height of the harvesting season, the barges traveled continuously throughout the week to deliver freshly harvested pineapples to the cannery. (Aurelio Del Rosario collection.)

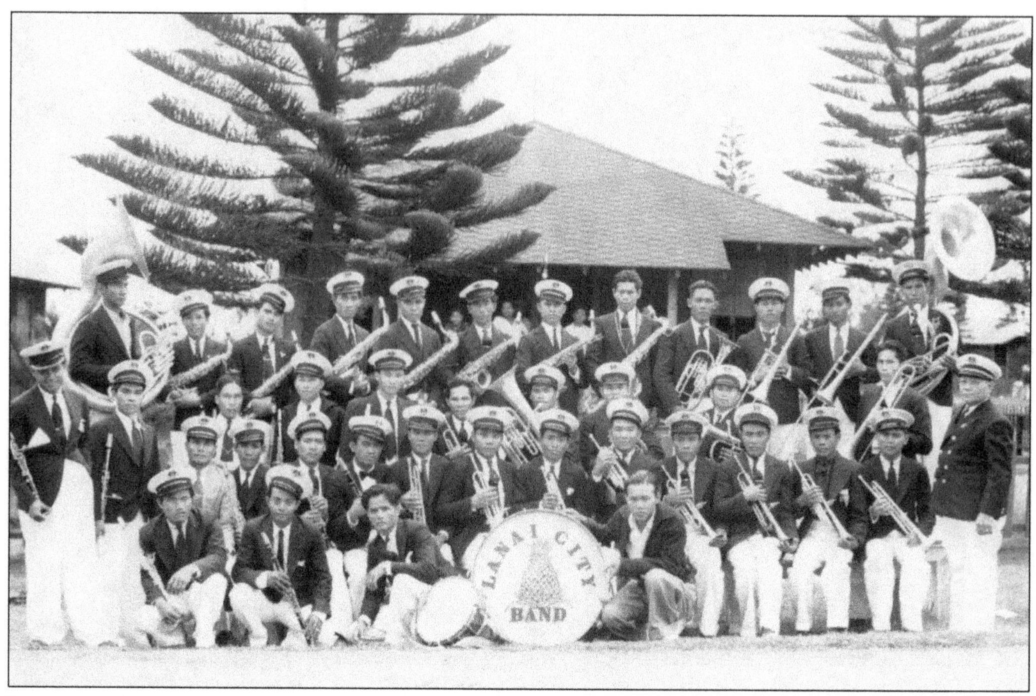

Lāna'i City Band members pose with their instruments and in full uniform in this 1938 photograph. The pine trees behind them are approximately 10 to 12 years old. In addition to the school band, an adult band played regularly at community dances. (Aurelio Del Rosario collection.)

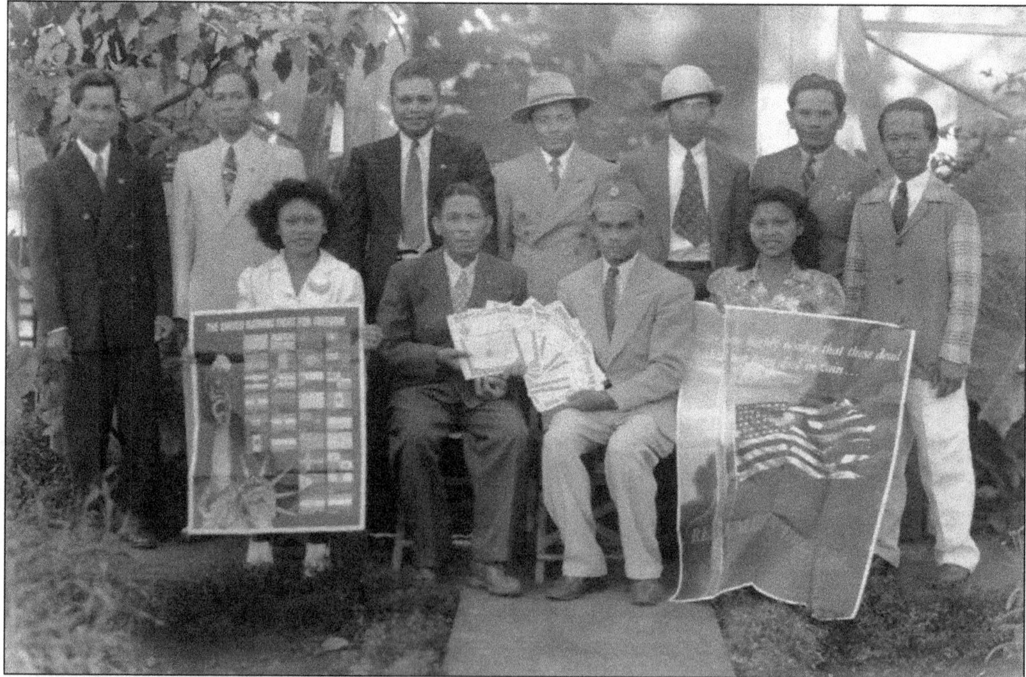

"The United Nations Fight for Freedom," reads the banner held by the young Filipina on the left. Filipino families on the island supported the war bond effort and were very proud of their native countrymen who joined the US armed forces to serve in World War II. (Roberto Hera collection.)

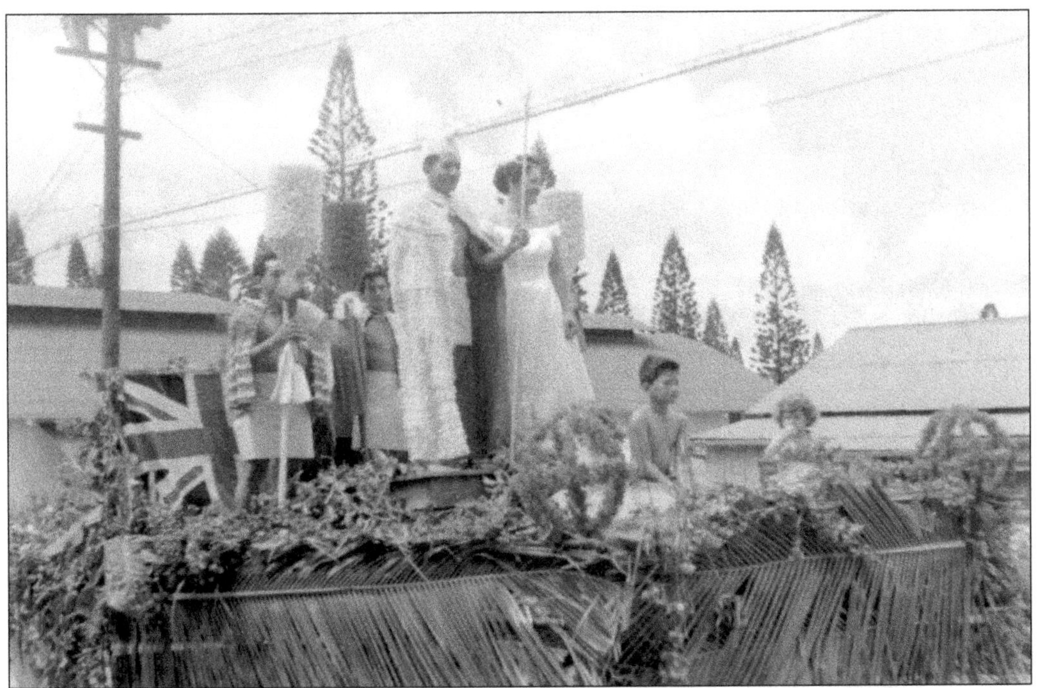

Hawaiian Pineapple Company encouraged residents to participate in community activities such as this parade for May Day in 1961. Sam and Elaine Kaopuiki are the May Day king and queen. Elaine Kaopuiki was a noted *kumu hula* (dance teacher) and taught generations of keiki. (Jack Ross collection.)

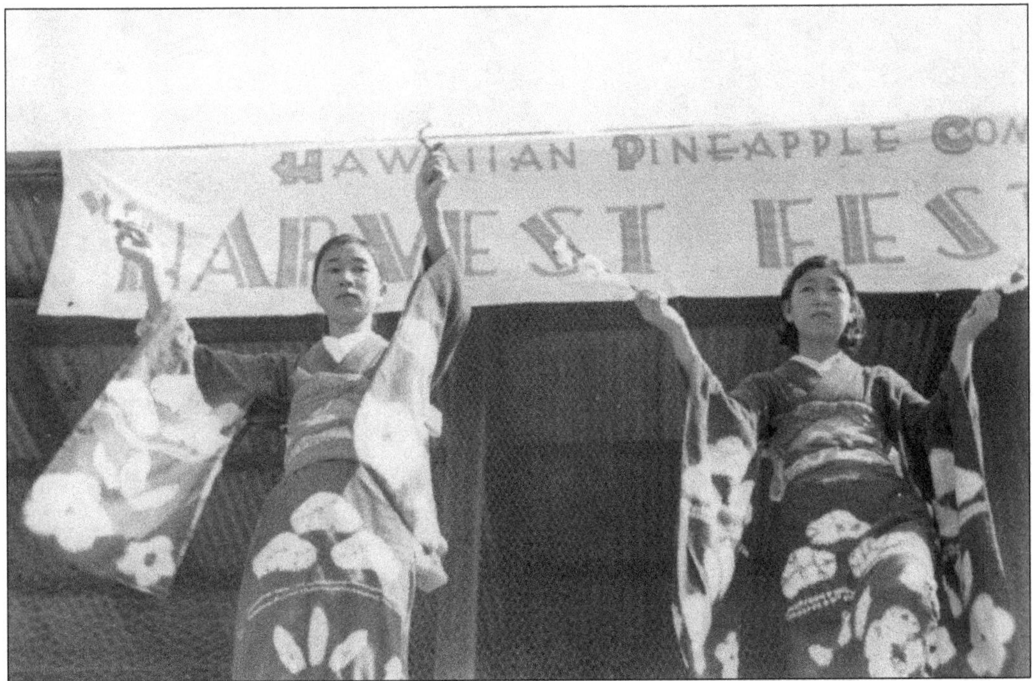

Two young ladies of Japanese ancestry perform at a festival sponsored by the Hawaiian Pineapple Company. Families also sent their children to Japanese language classes after their regular school day. (Matsumoto family collection.)

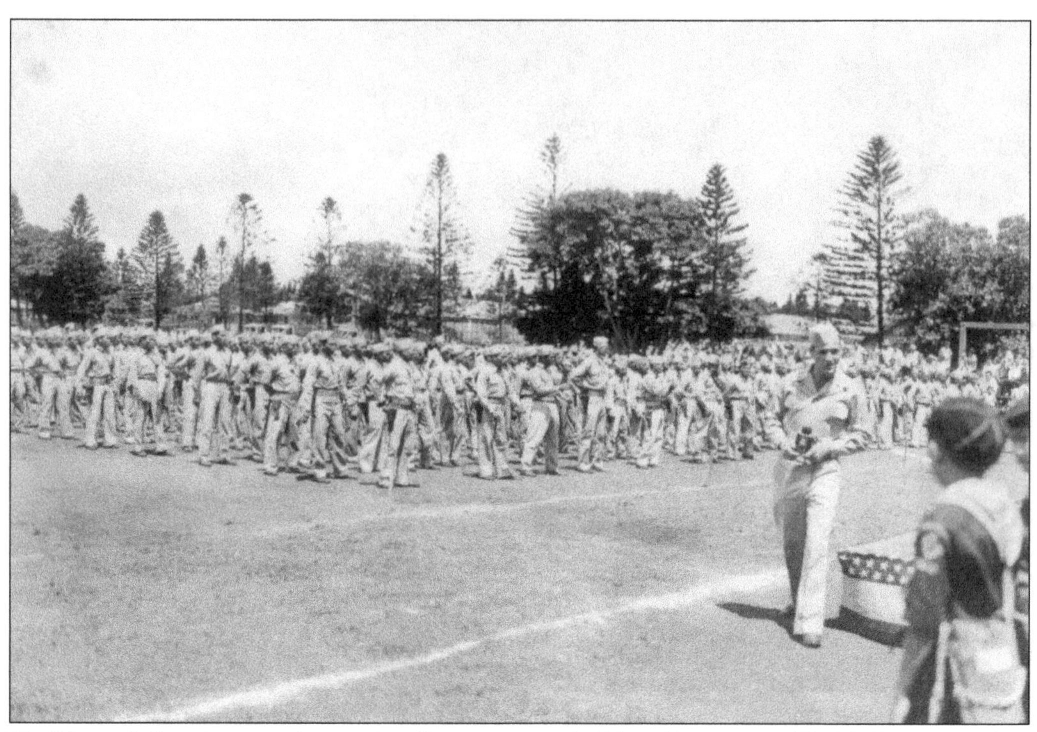

The National Guard recruited many Lāna'i men to join the Maui Unit during World War II to defend Hawai'i if necessary. (HAPCo collection.)

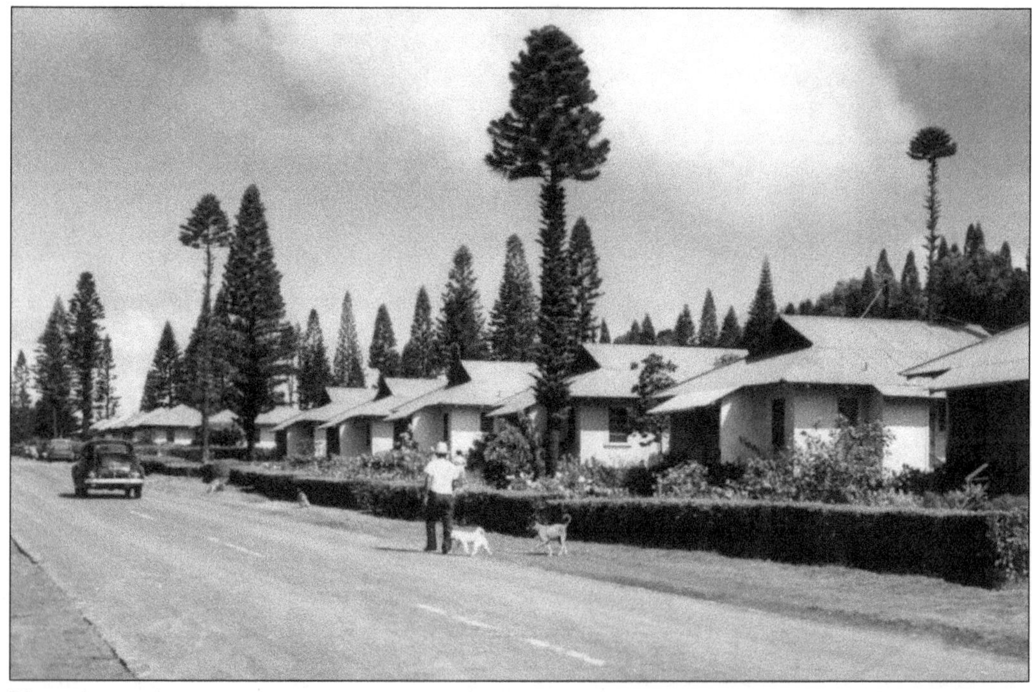

Plantation workers were given the opportunity of purchasing the homes they rented from Hawaiian Pineapple Company following the 1951 strike by ILWU members, which lasted for more than a year. (Richard Fuller collection.)

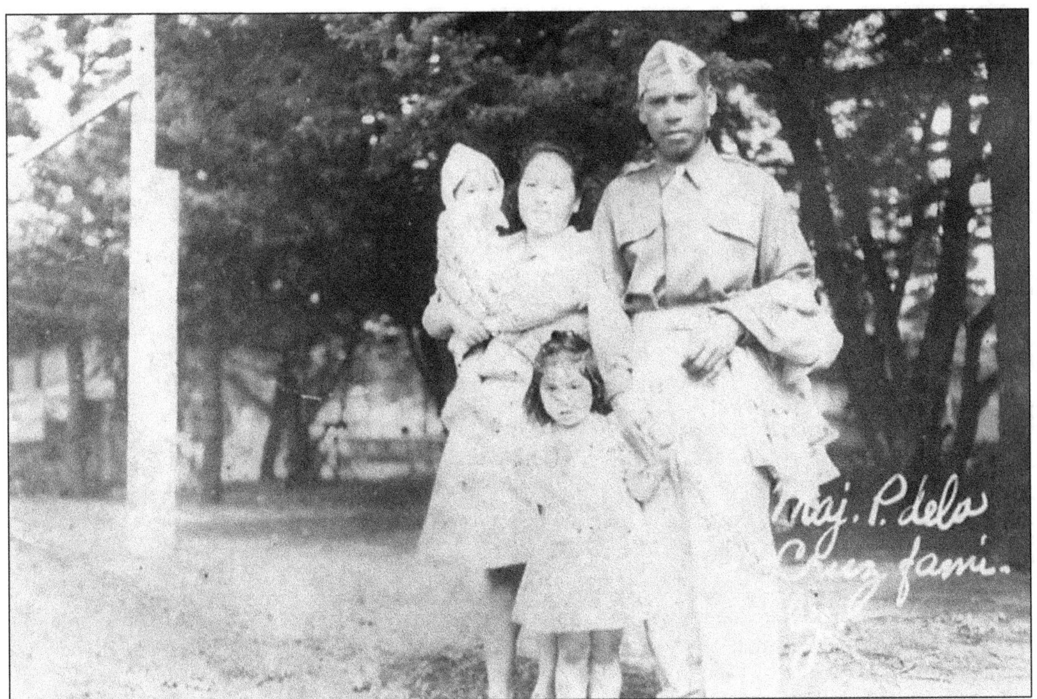

National Guard member Pedro dela Cruz is pictured here with his family: Helen (Kawano), son Alvin in her arms, and daughter Flora. Dela Cruz successfully organized the plantation workers to join the ILWU. He became the first person of Filipino ancestry to become a legislator of the Territory of Hawai'i and later, the state. Lāna'i High and Elementary School's gymnasium bears his name in honor and recognition of his service to the people of Hawai'i. (Andew dela Cruz family collection.)

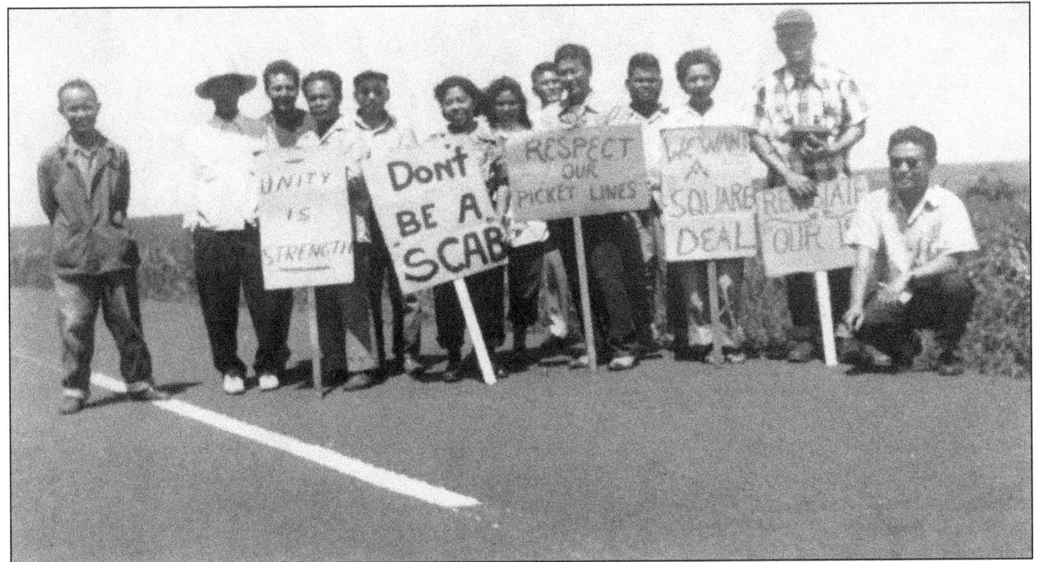

Picketers lined up in front of the Hawaiian Pineapple Company's labor yard during the ILWU strike of 1951. Workers at other plantations were also on strike for better wages and working conditions. The Lāna'i strike lasted the longest, and workers were able to provide for their families by the combined group's efforts to hunt, fish, and farm. (Gregorio Cabuslay family collection.)

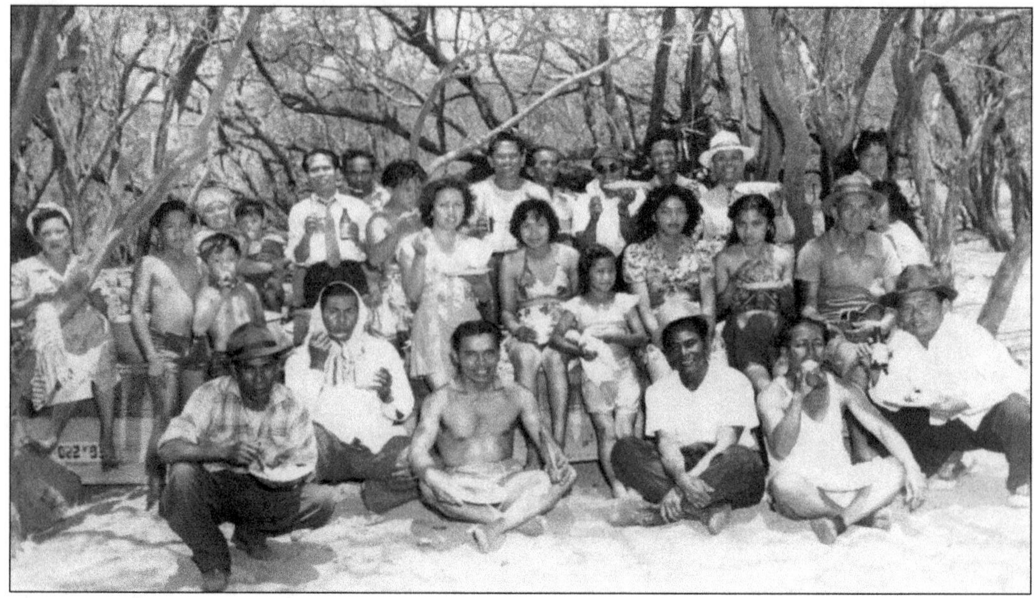

The Costales family and friends gathered for a group photograph by the Cabras Photo Studio at a Hulopo'e Beach picnic. Although plantation work was strenuous, there was time for leisure activities too. (Clarabal family collection.)

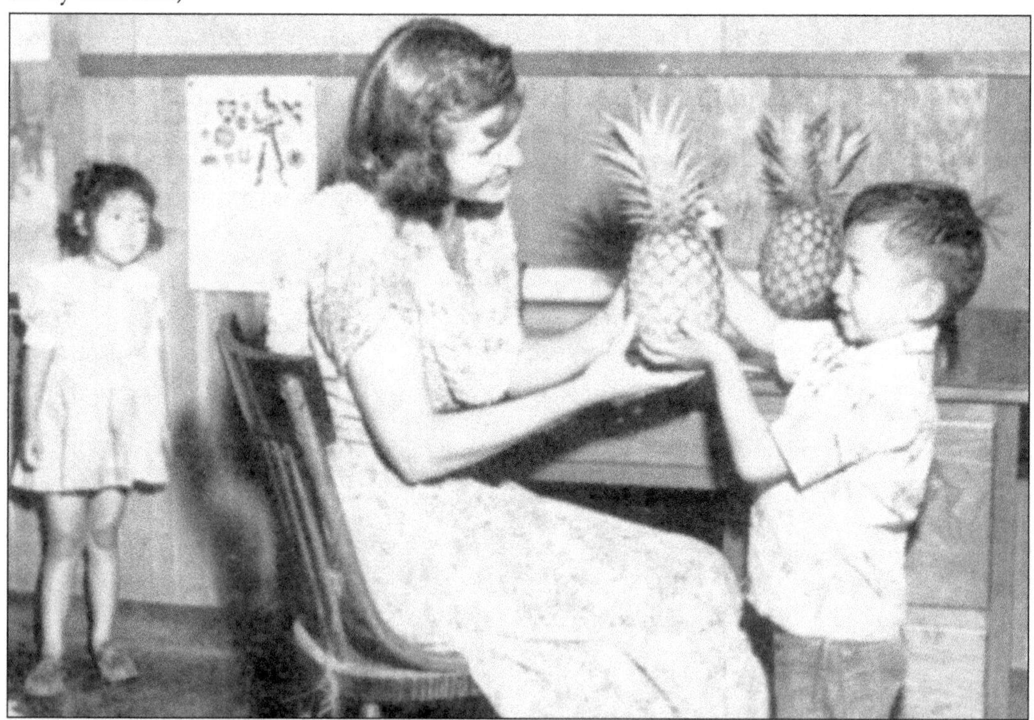

Instead of giving his teacher an apple, Gilbert Suetos hands her a golden pineapple while an unidentified classmate looks on from the side. This 1950 photograph appeared in Hawaiian Pineapple Company's *Pine Parade*, a community newsletter. After he graduated from Lāna'i High and Elementary School in 1963, Gilbert joined the armed forces and lost his life in the Vietnam War. He is buried in the original veterans' section of Lāna'i Cemetery. (HAPCo collection.)

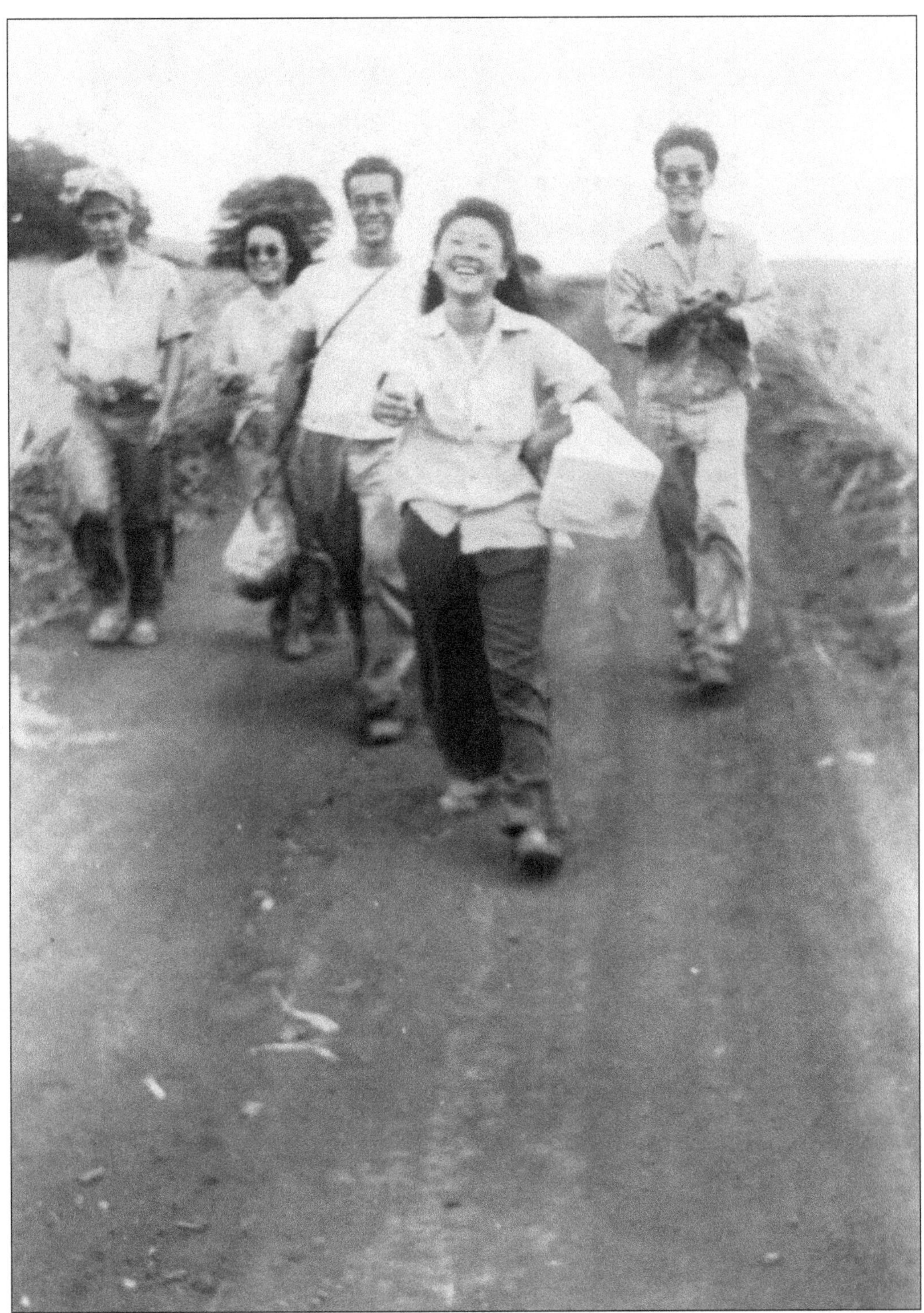

Hiking over Lānaʻihale on the Munro Trail was a tradition students at Lānaʻi High and Elementary School enjoyed as a class before their graduation. Judging from the smiles on their faces, they must have successfully conquered the hale and are homeward bound. (Henry Ahyin Kau Aki collection.)

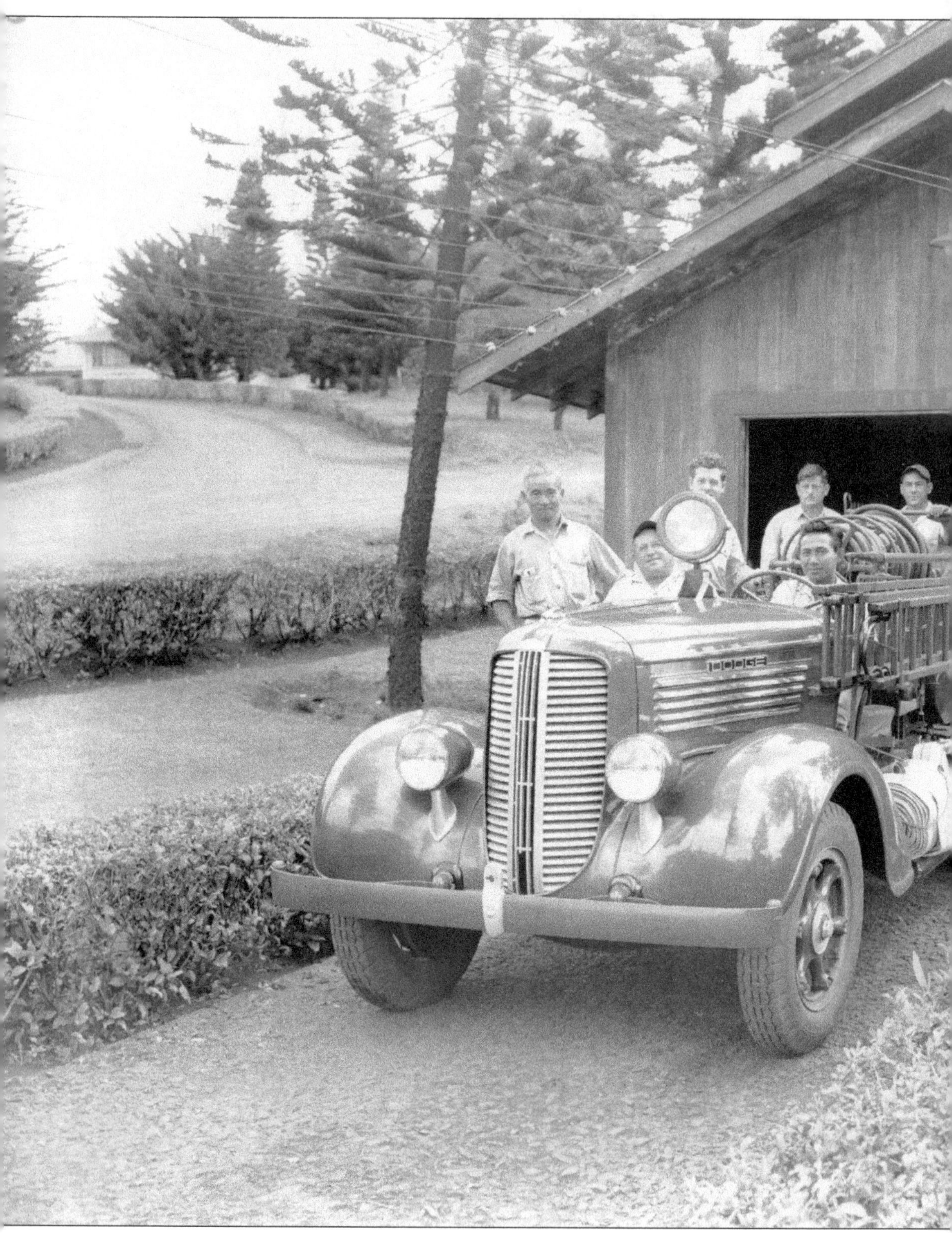
DODGE

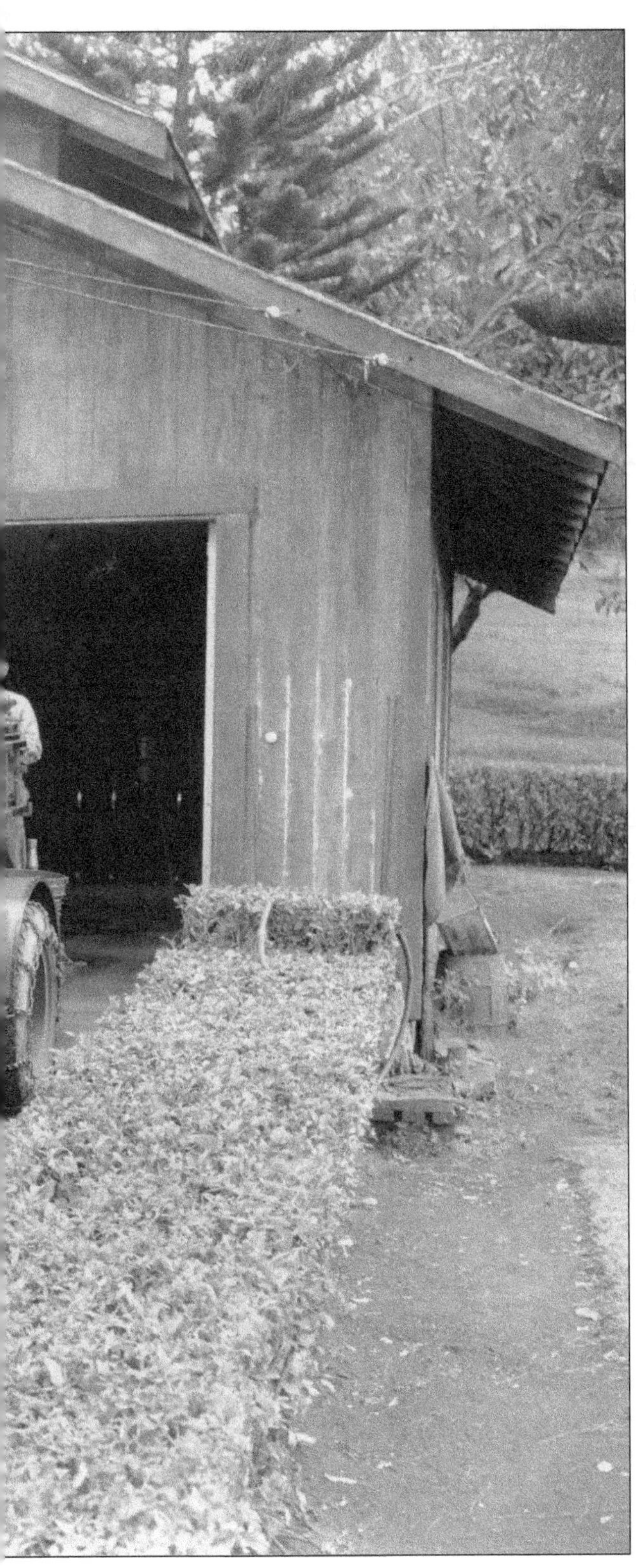

Volunteer firefighters sprang into action whenever they were needed to fight a fire on the island. The fire truck was kept in a garage located on the corner of Lāna'i Avenue and Ninth Street, just below Hotel Lāna'i today. The plantation used the work whistle to call them when they were needed, using a set pattern of blasts to tell them where the fire was located. (HAPCo collection.)

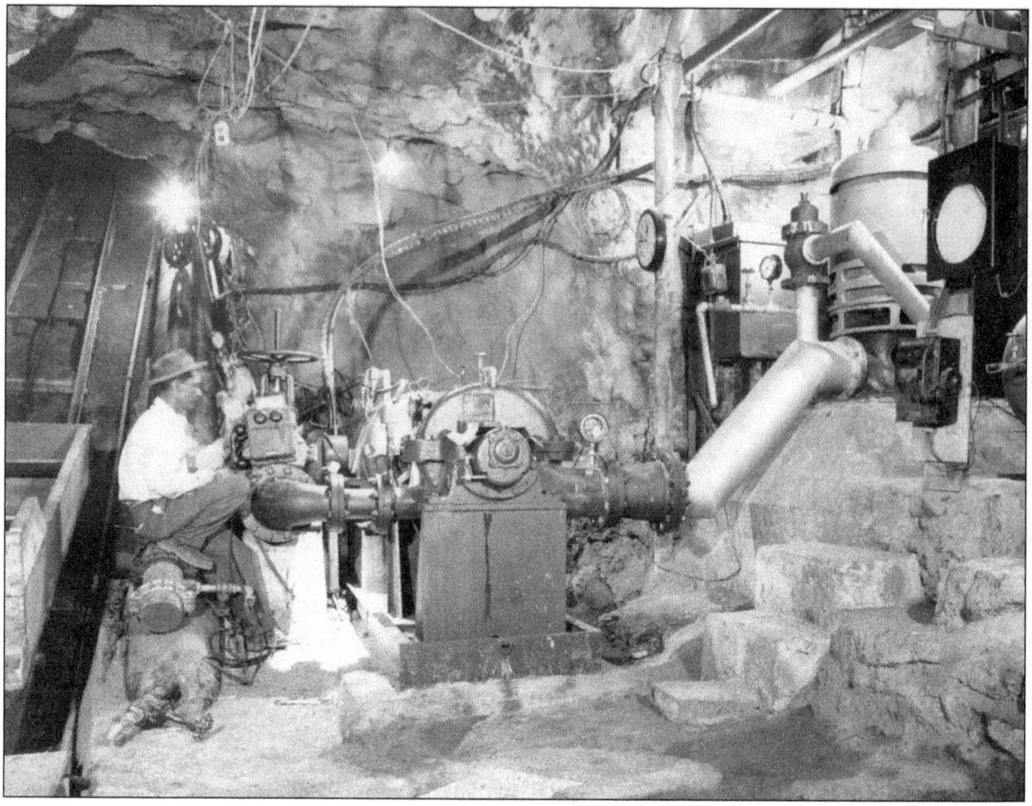

A cable cart set on metal rails carried men and their equipment down a 45-degree shaft to an underground stream set deep inside Lāna'ihale during the plantation days. The shaft's equipment is now monitored remotely. (HAPCo collection.)

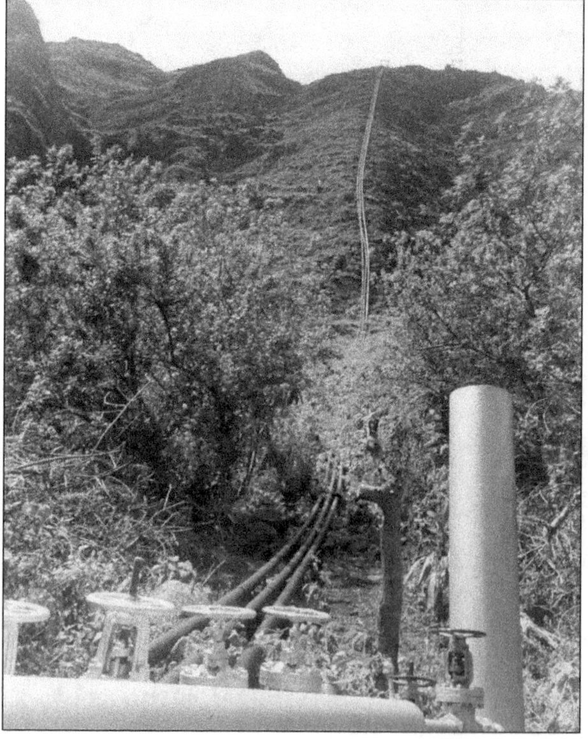

Lāna'i Company dug a tunnel to a depth of 1,100 feet in Maunalei in 1911 and struck water. However, it was not used until 1917, when Harry and Frank Baldwin purchased Lāna'i. The water was piped and pumped up the sides of the gulch and through three tunnels to the two-million-gallon water tank on Nininiwai Hill, behind Lāna'i City. (HAPCo collection.)

Working underground, two men are in one of the tunnels located at the rear of Hi'i Flats, above Pālāwai. (HAPCo collection.)

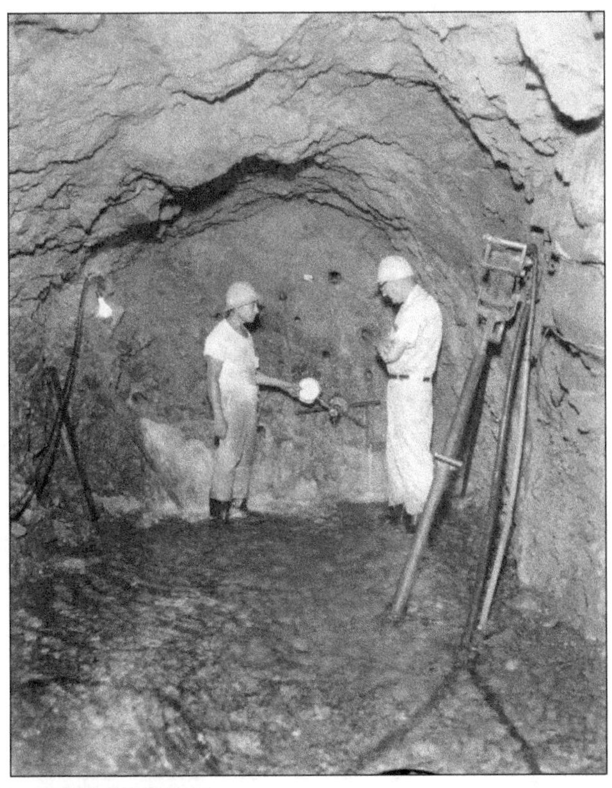

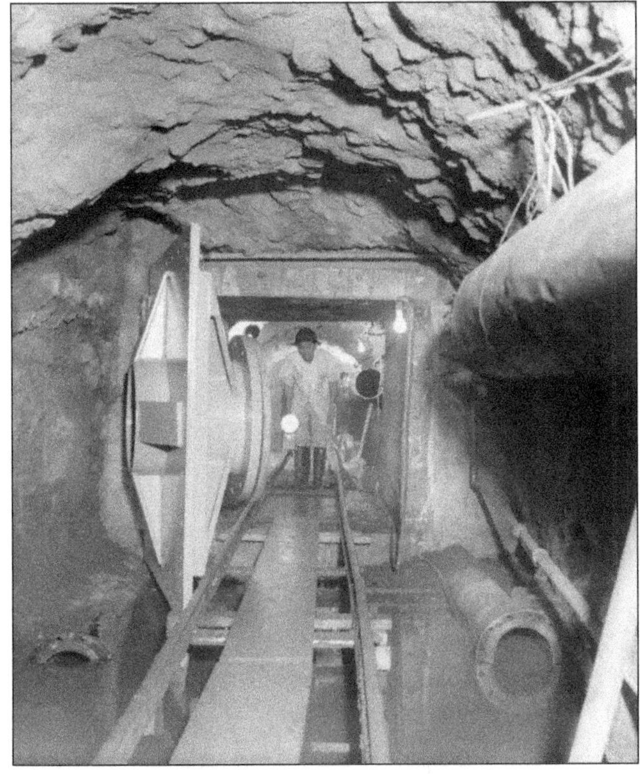

Steel rails guide a cable cart down into the well shaft. Toshi Aoki stands in the entryway to the underground cavern. (HAPCo collection.)

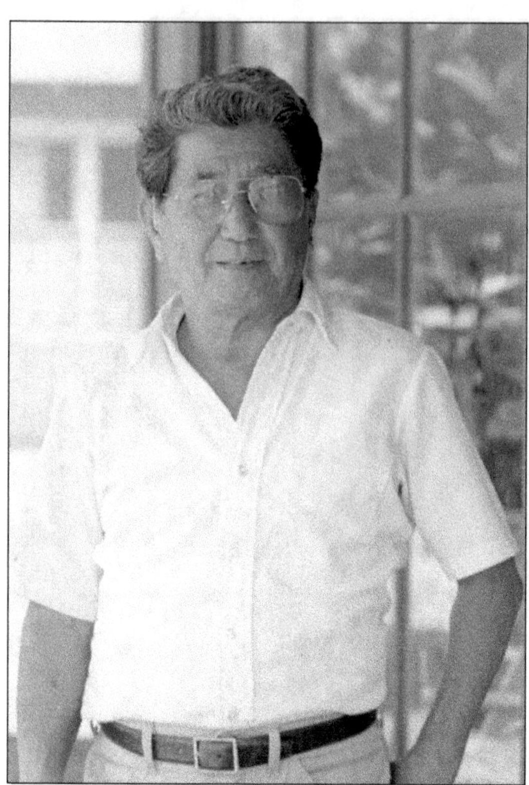

Juichi Nakamoto owned Emura Jewelry, where the Local Gentry is today. (Author's collection.)

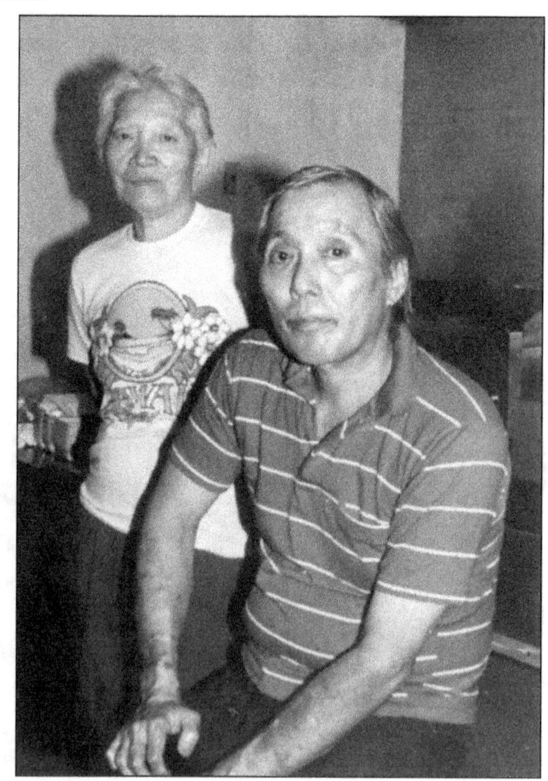

Mother and son, Sumie and Jerry Tanigawa pose at their family's Lāna'i Fountain, where Canoes Restaurant is located today. (Author's collection.)

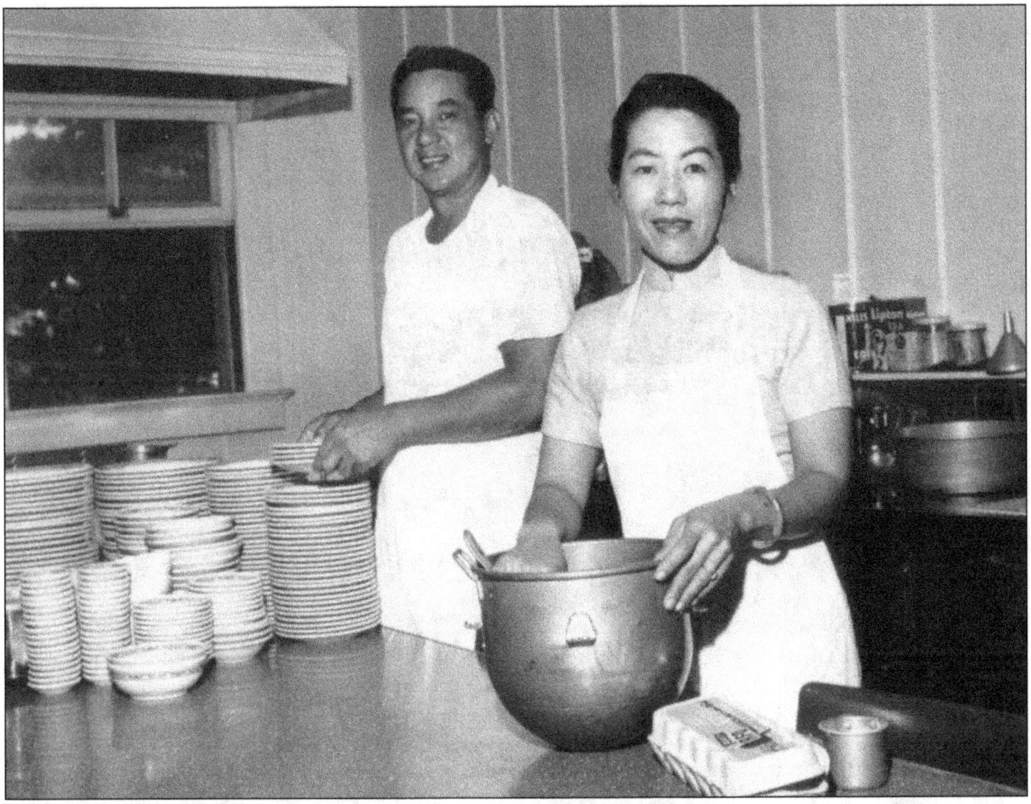

Wallace "Wally" and Ethel Au were the innkeepers at Lāna'i Inn, now Hotel Lāna'i. (HAPCo collection.)

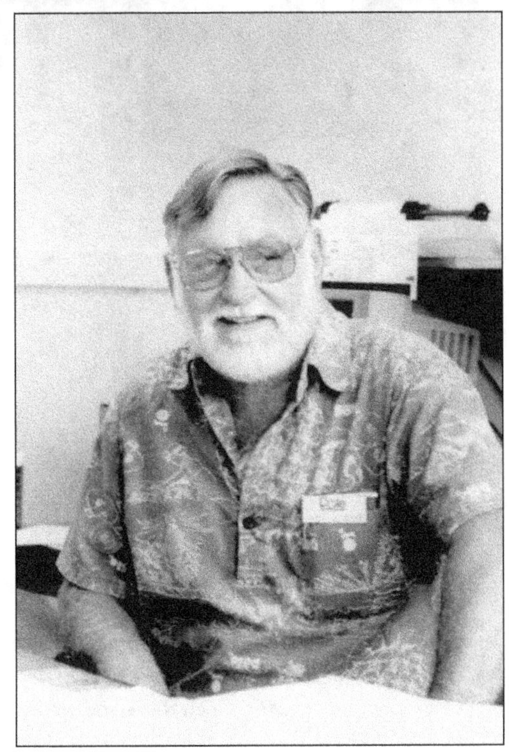

Dole Company's Lāna'i manager Jim Parker was tasked with closing down its Lāna'i plantation in 1992, ending 70 years on Lāna'i. (Author's collection.)

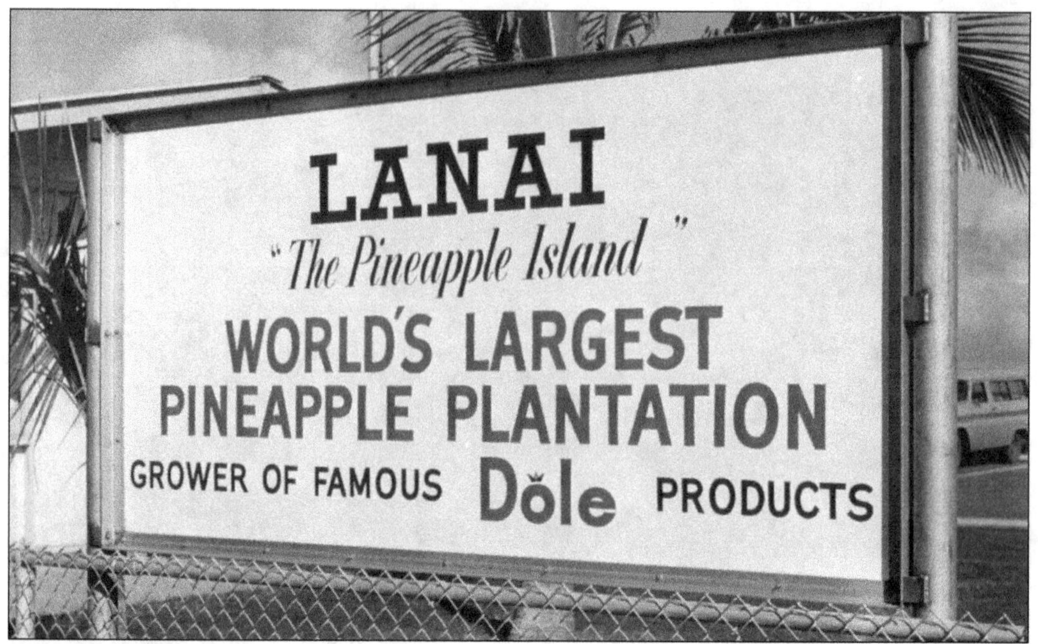

Thousands of visitors used this sign as a backdrop to commemorate their visit to Lāna'i during the island's plantation years. No one can remember when it was first installed at Lāna'i Airport, but after Dole Plantation closed in 1992, the sign was removed. It is now displayed at Lāna'i Cultural and Heritage Center, where visitors continue the tradition of posing in front of it. (Lāna'i CHC.)

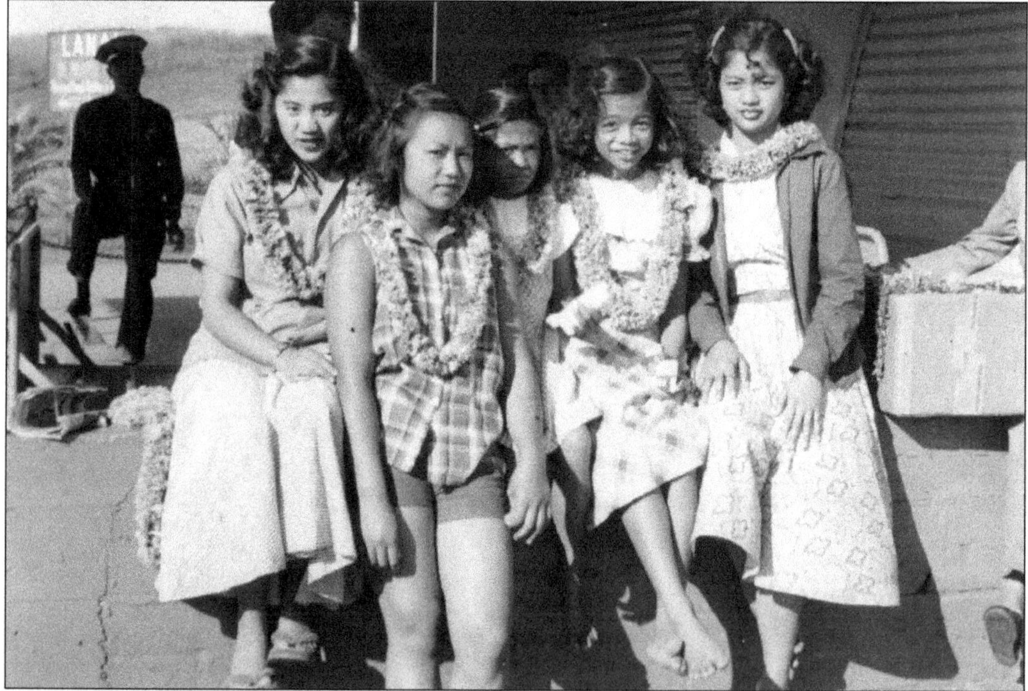

Going to Honolulu was a big event in the lives of these unidentified Lāna'i girls. They are wearing *akulikuli* lei, a lei of ice plant flowers, for which the island was known. Across from Lāna'i High and Elementary School on Fraser Avenue, a Mrs. Lee grew the flowers to make this special lei. (Gregorio Cabuslay collection.)

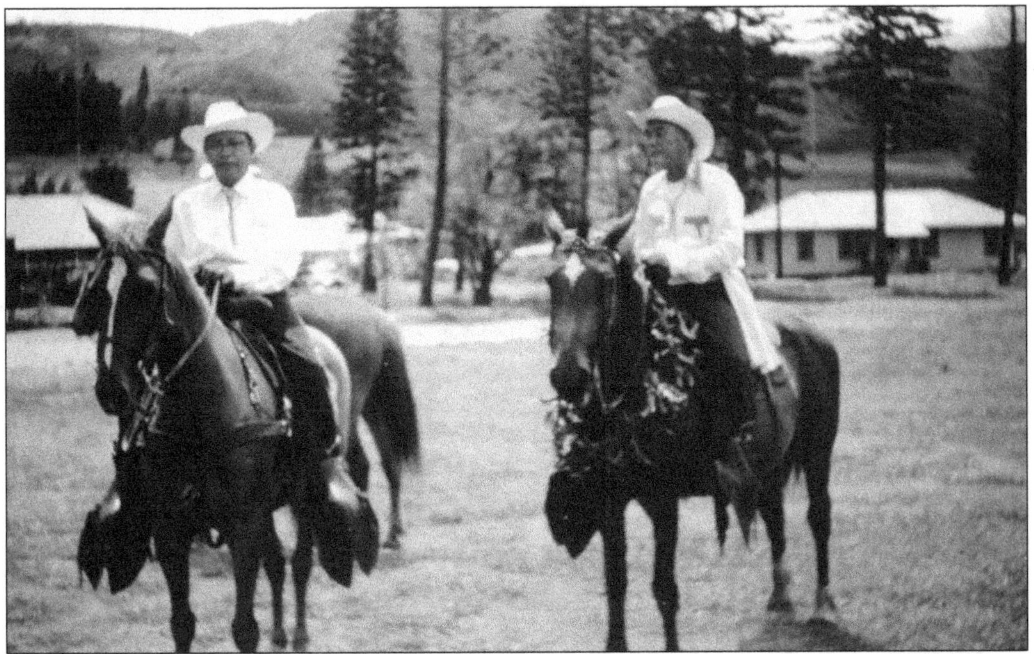

After Lāna'i Ranch closed in 1950, many of its horses were sold to Lāna'i residents, who formed the Lāna'i Horse Club and leased former ranch lands from Hawaiian Pineapple Company for grazing their horses. Pictured on horseback are Dionicio Rabbon (left), who was the proprietor of Rabbon Store, and Teishi Nishiyama. (Jack Ross collection.)

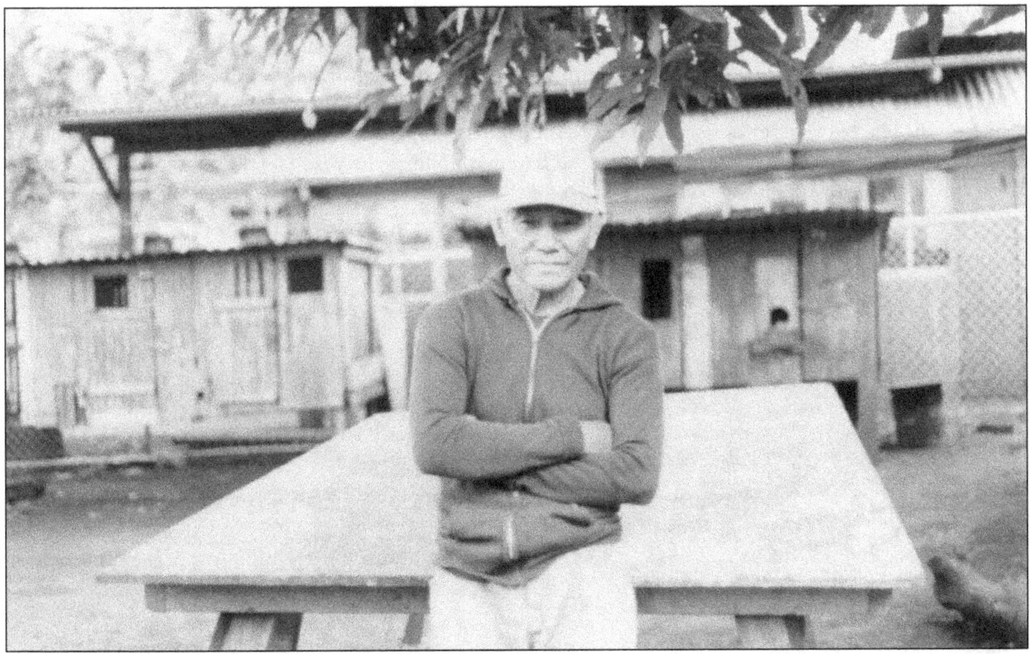

A custodian at Dole's administrative building, Henry Belez raised his two daughters, Nancy and Jean, with the help of his brother Eugene. His son Isaac was raised on the mainland with their mother but returned to Lāna'i to live later. The garden in front of his home on Lāna'i Avenue was always filled with beds of yellow chrysanthemums. (Belez family collection.)

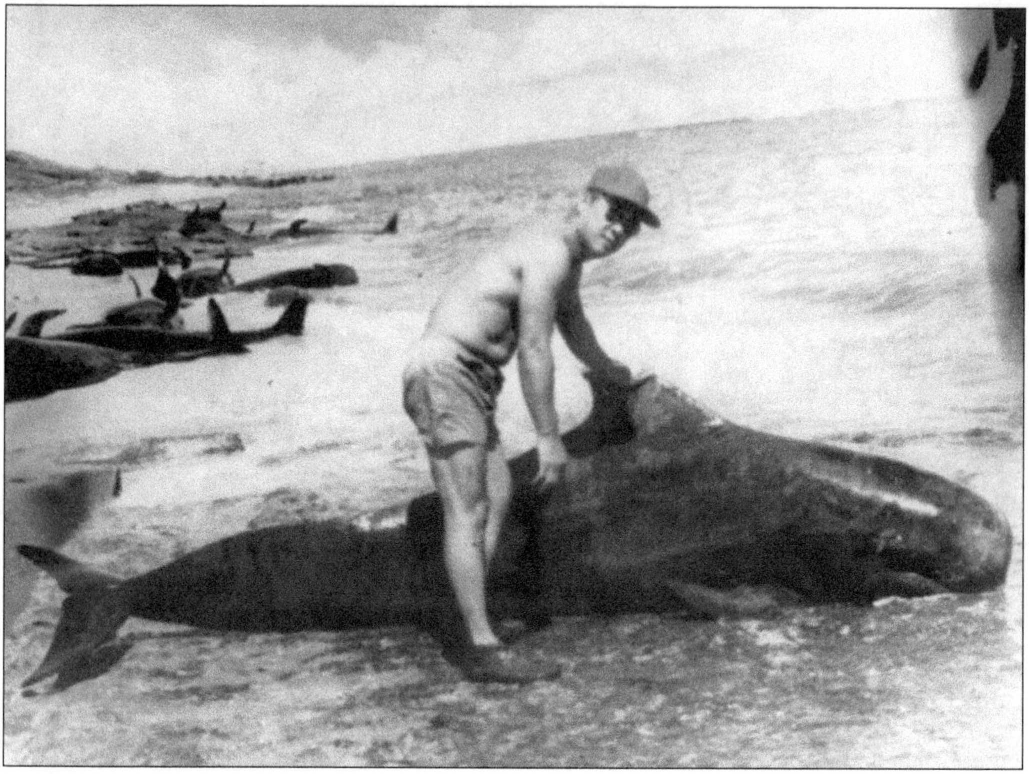

Although there had been accounts of whales beaching themselves on Lāna'i in the late 1800s, in 1959, a pod of more than 16 whales beached themselves in the early morning near Filipino Federation Camp, close to Shipwreck Beach, on the island's north shoreline. By the afternoon, dozens of residents had traveled to the area to see them. Throughout the day, residents tried to push the whales closest to the water back into the sea, but their efforts were in vain. As darkness fell, the whales were left to their fate. Richard Morita Sr., the island's game warden, is pictured here with one of the whales. (Photograph by Fr. Gailen Everest, Richard Morita family collection.)

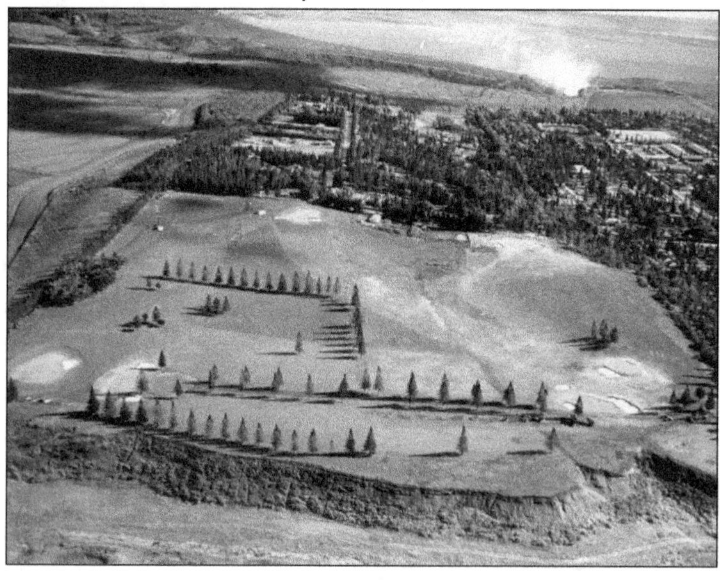

Lanai's residents and their visiting friends could enjoy Cavendish Golf Course, the only free golf course in Hawai'i. The nine-hole course was lined with pine trees and crossed over a gully. Tee boxes set up at different locations for each hole gave golfers an 18-hole game. (Richard Fuller collection.)

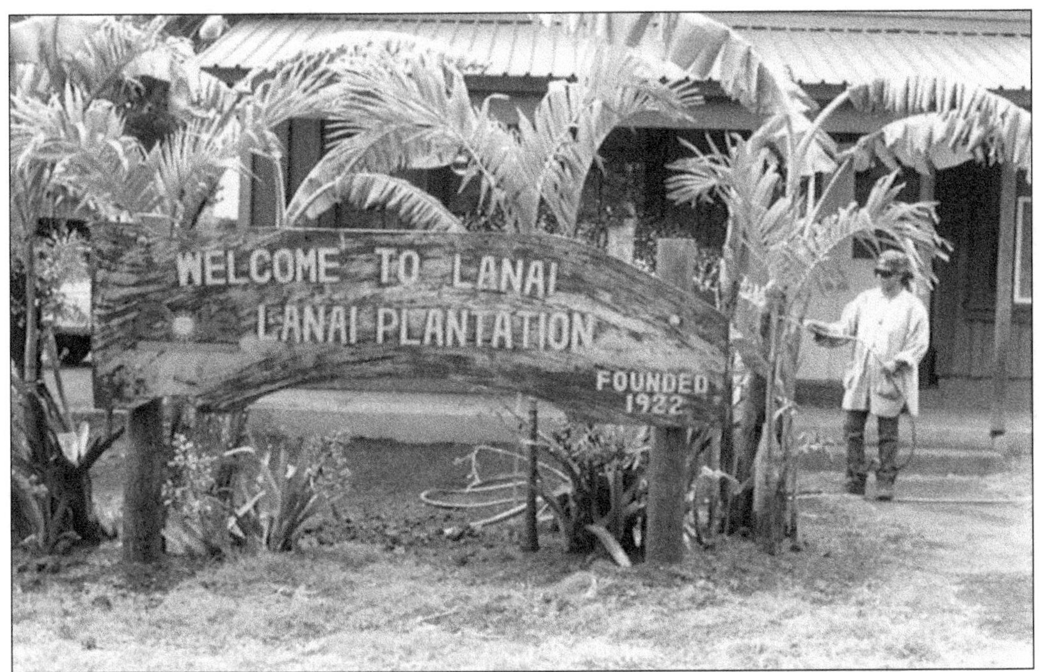

A welcome sign outside a Dole company office is framed by coconut palms. (HAPCo collection.)

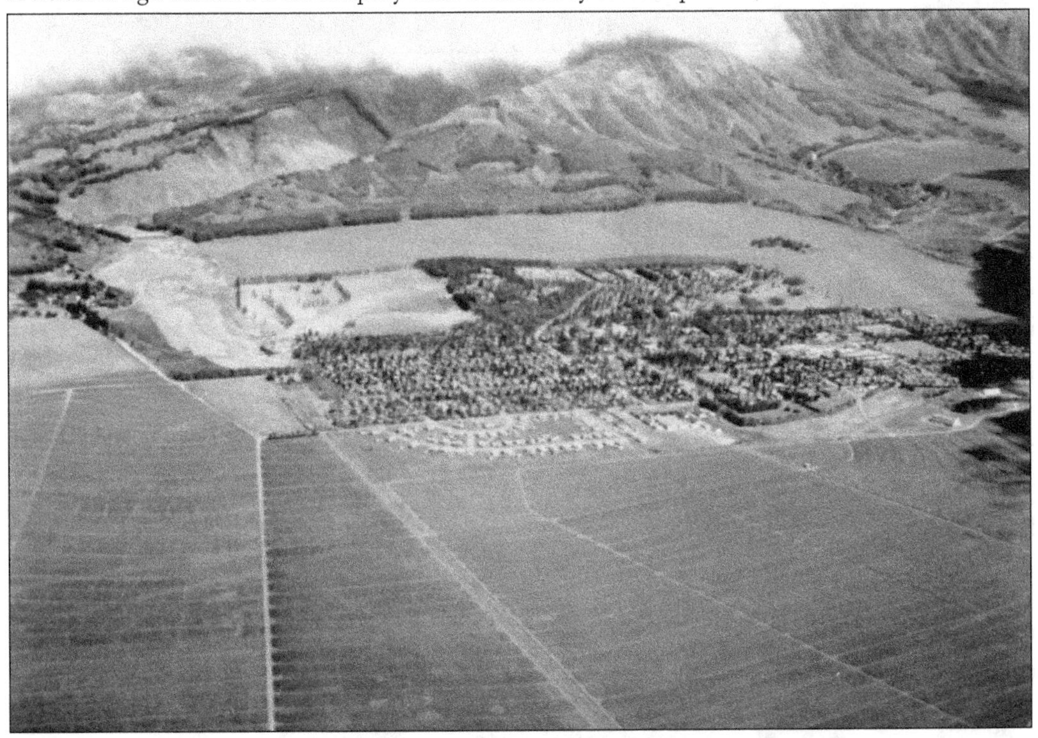

Pineapple fields come up to the western edge of Lāna'i City in this photograph. Mauka, toward the mountains, in the fields at Nininiwai, the small green patches are trees that surrounded Lālākoa, Charles Gay's family home. The Gays planted the island's first pineapples in 1921 in this same location, before James Dole started Hawaiian Pineapple Company. (A. Duane Black collection.)

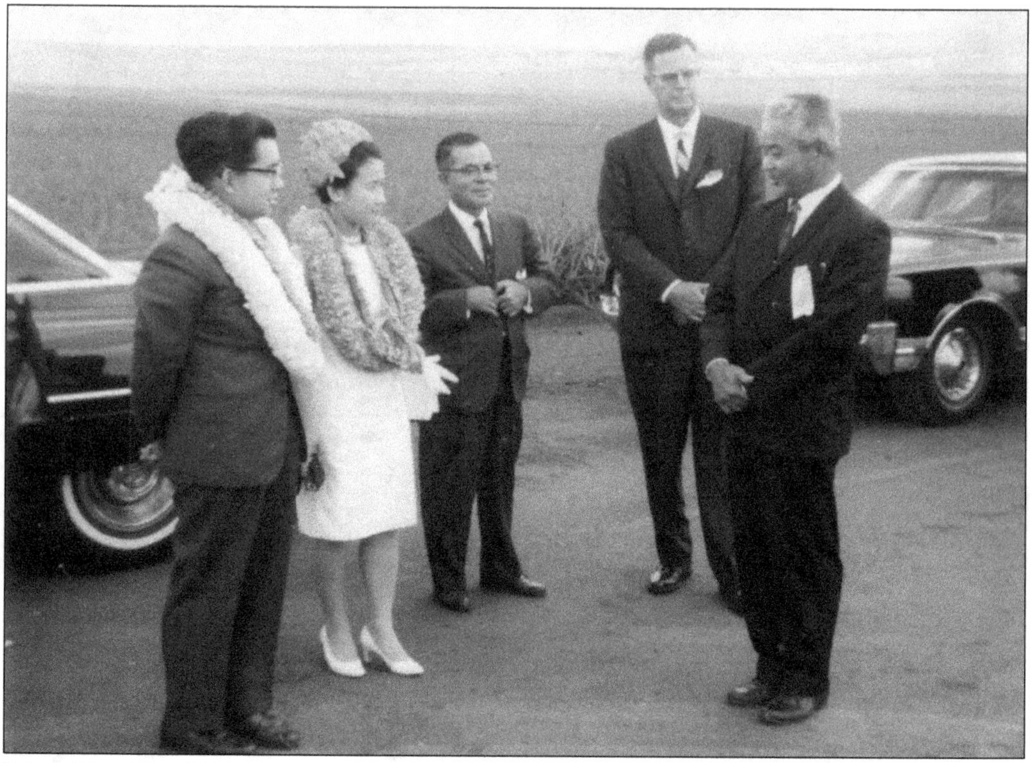

Prince Hitachi and Princess Hanako, members of Japan's imperial family, visited Lāna'i in 1968 and attended a ceremony at Lāna'i Community Hospital to recognize the efforts of community residents who contributed funds to build it. To commemorate their visit, Princess Hanako planted two Australian bottlebrush trees. The royal couple also toured the plantation with Hawaiian Pineapple Company representatives. The two trees were incorporated into a floral garden designed and planted for the hospital's patients in 2015 by the Lāna'i Community Hospital Auxiliary. (A. Duane Black collection.)

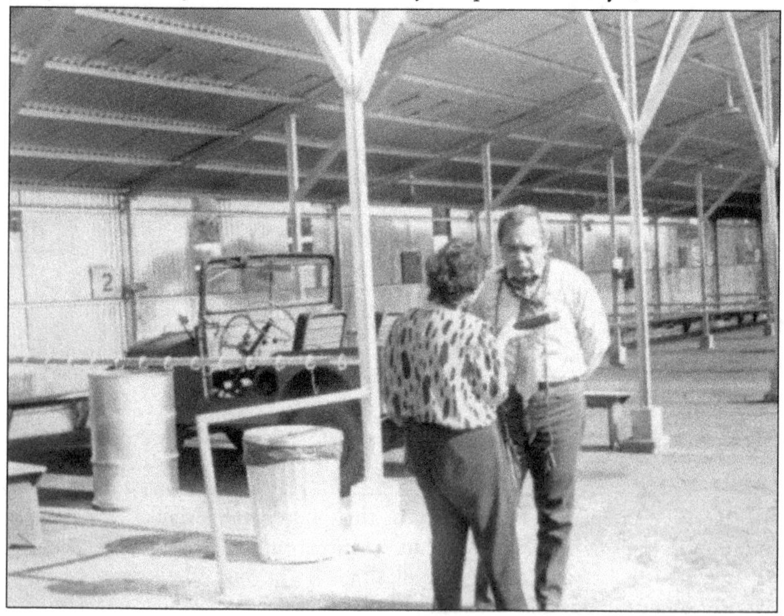

An unidentified news reporter interviews Gov. John Waihee at Dole Pineapple Company's labor yard. Field workers reported to the labor yard each morning before they were transported to their assigned fields and returned to it at the end of the day. (Author's collection.)

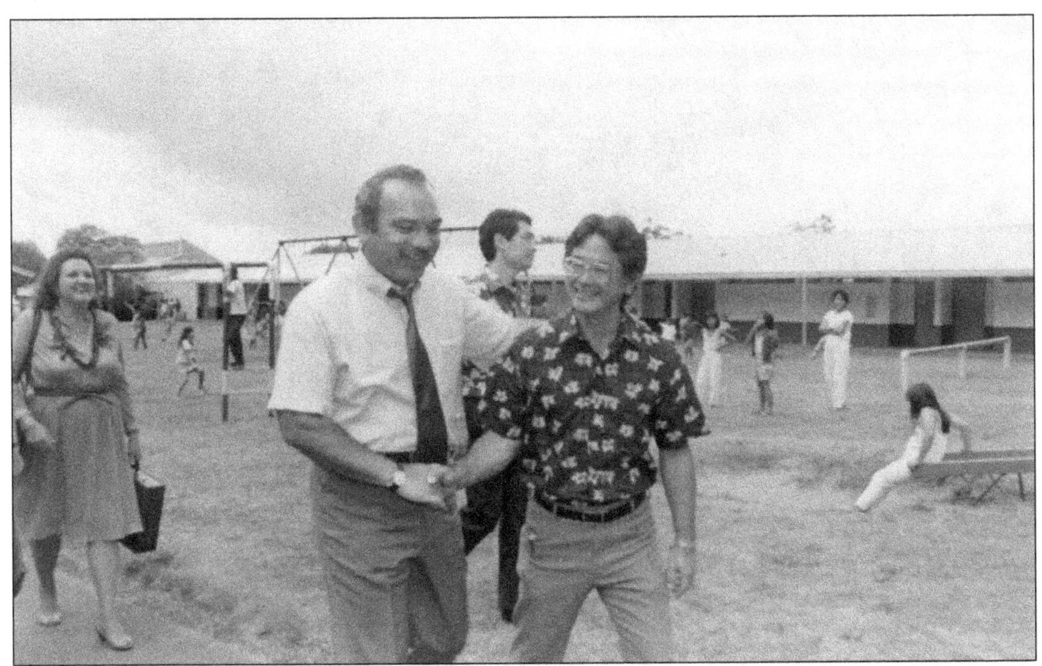

Hawai'i's first governor of Hawaiian ancestry, John Waihee (left), enjoyed visiting Hawai'i's outer islands and declared a "Capital for a Day" trip to Lāna'i in 1990. He is pictured touring Lāna'i High and Elementary School with its vice principal, Dennis Hokama. Walking behind them is Department of Education director Lokelani Lindsay. (Author's collection.)

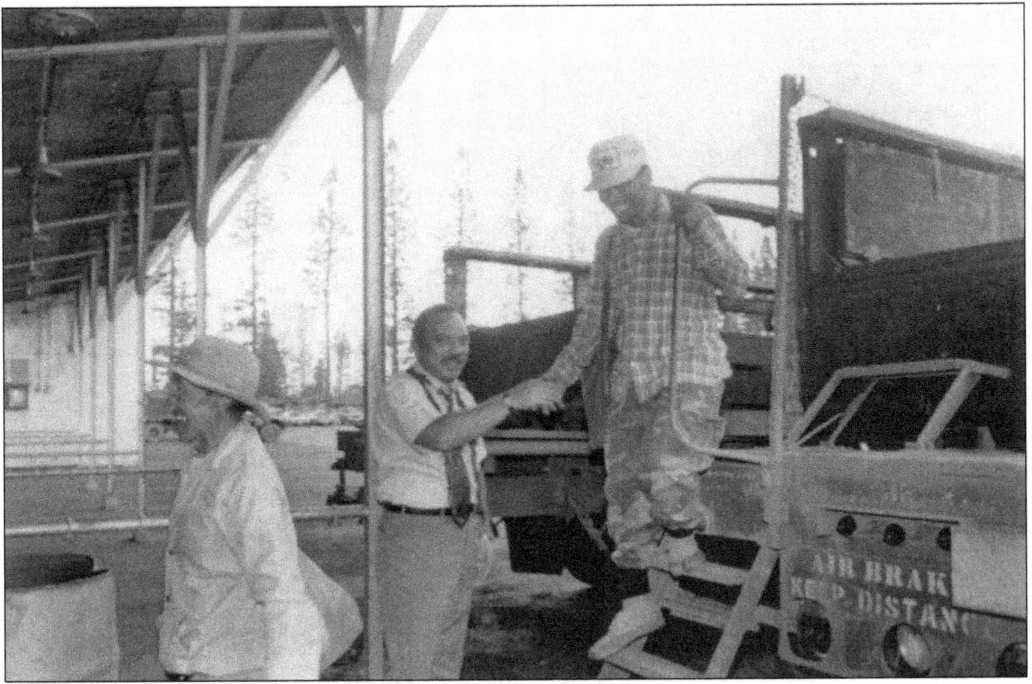

Workers returning to the labor yard after a day of work are greeted by Gov. John Waihee. While being transported to and from the fields, they rode standing up in empty pineapple bins and hung onto the sides. (Author's collection.)

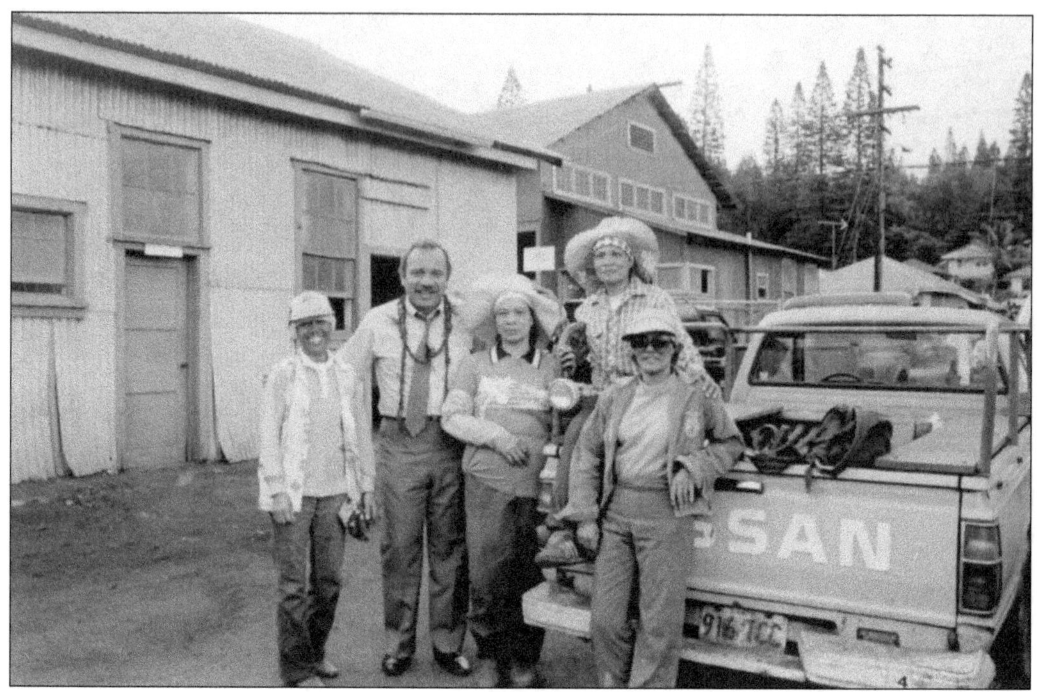

These ladies commemorated Governor Waihee's visit with a photograph. Field workers dressed in long-sleeved shirts and wore broad-brimmed or baseball caps to shade themselves from the sun. In the fields, they donned heavy canvas chaps over their jeans and used a bandana over the lower half of their face. Their eyes were protected from the spiky leaves of the plants with screened goggles or dark glasses, and they also wore gloves to protect their hands. (Author's collection.)

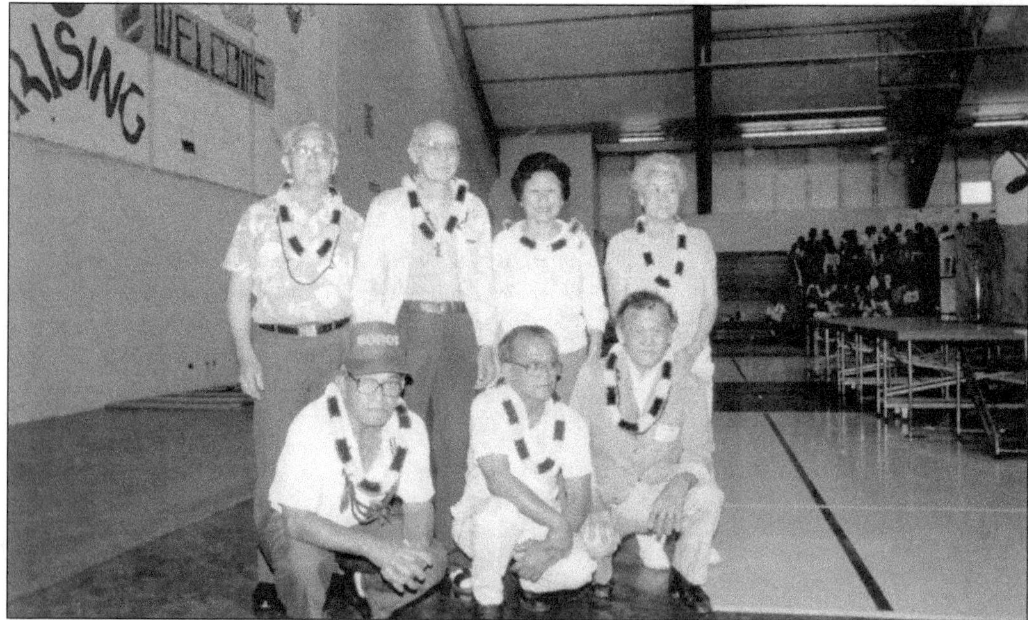

Members of the classes of 1938 and 1939 at Lāna'i High and Elementary School's 50th reunion in 1988 are, from left to right, (first row) Solomon Kaopuiki, Hilio Raquino, and unidentified; (second row) Wallace Nunotani, unidentified, Annie Hahn Ching, and Diane Y.K. Kim. (Author's collection.)

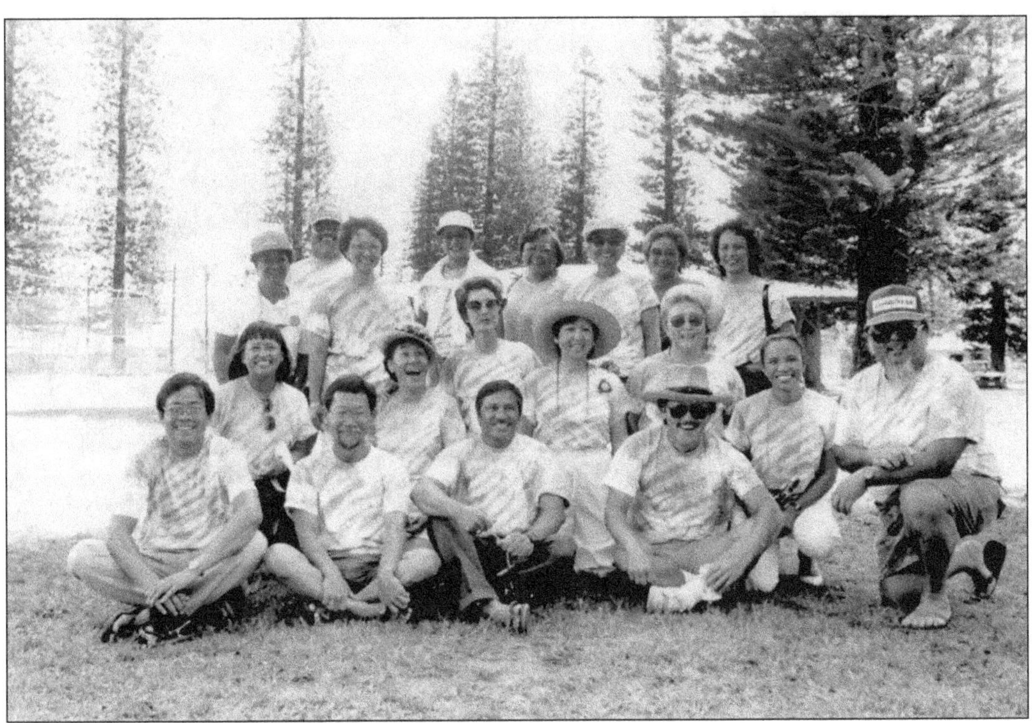

With all of the excitement of seeing their classmates again at the school's 50th reunion, the only class organized enough to sit still for a photograph was the class of 1959. (Author's collection.)

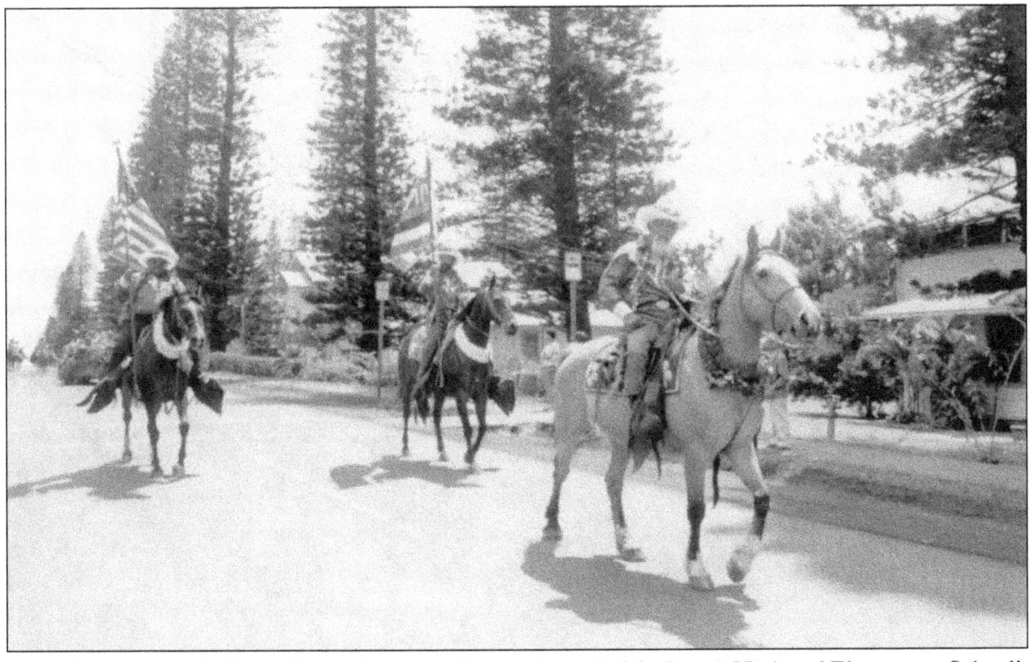

Lāna'i Ranch paniolo Ernest Richardson was the grand marshal for Lāna'i High and Elementary School's 50th anniversary parade. Mounted on his horse Maile, he is followed by his hānai son Albert Morita carrying the Hawaiian flag and mounted on his horse Brandy. Ernest's son Clarence "Hoss" Richardson is to his right carrying the American flag. (Author's collection.)

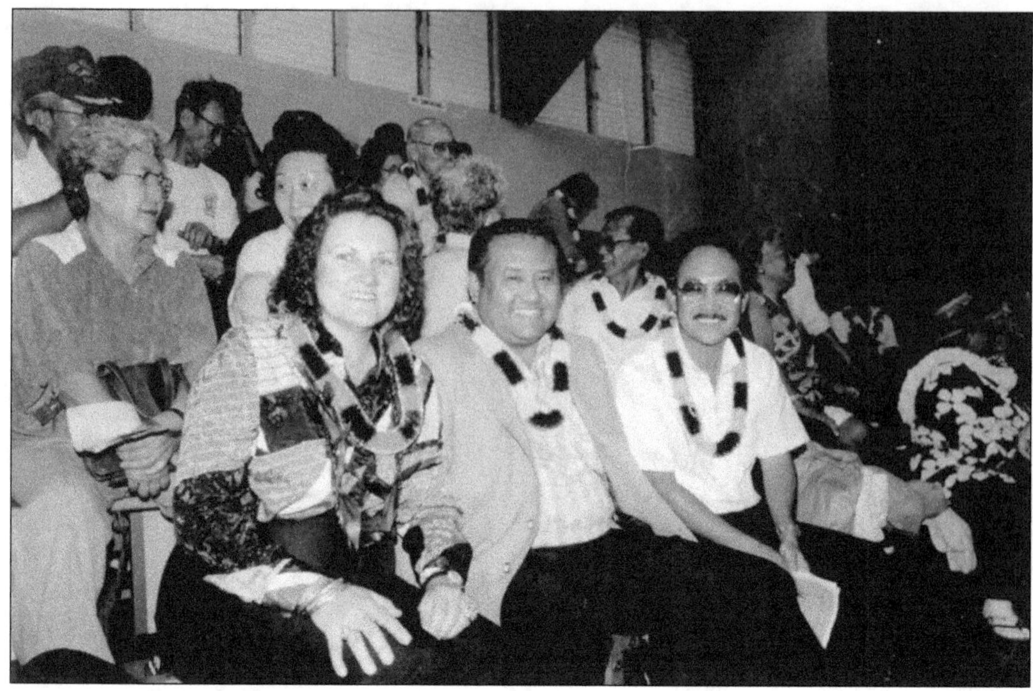

From left to right in the first row, Hawai'i State Department of Education director Lokelani Lindsay and Lāna'i High School class of 1958 graduate Liberto Viduya, also a DOE state official, and school principal Howard Sakamoto are pictured at the reunion assembly in the Pedro dela Cruz Gymnasium. (Author's collection.)

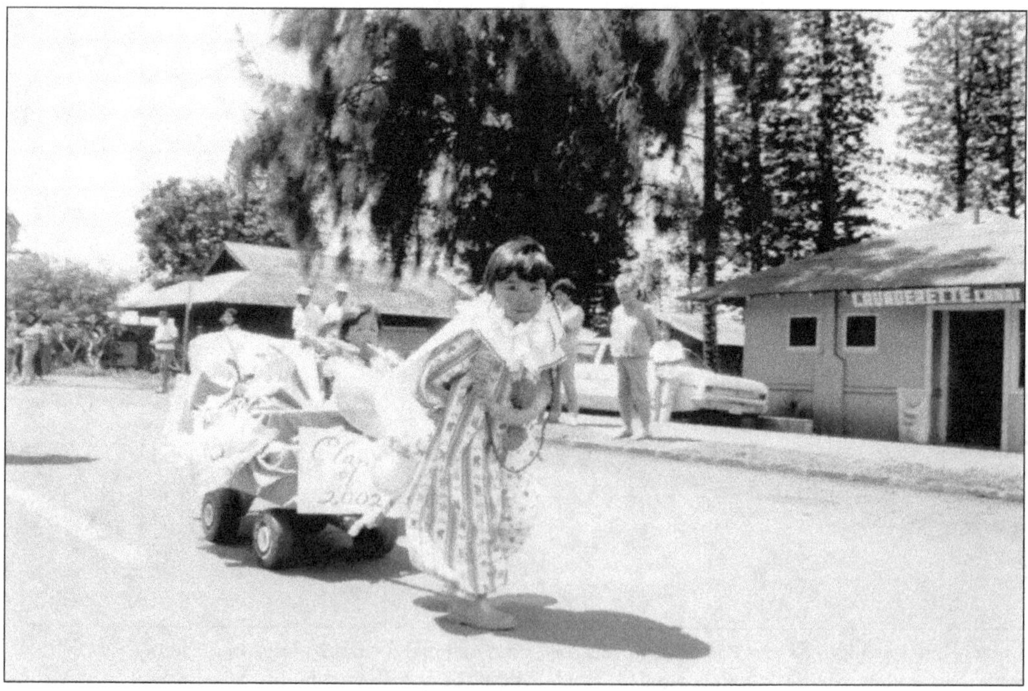

Dressed in a clown's suit, an unidentified child from the class of 2002 pulls his classmate in a decorated wagon behind him in the 50th reunion parade. (Author's collection.)

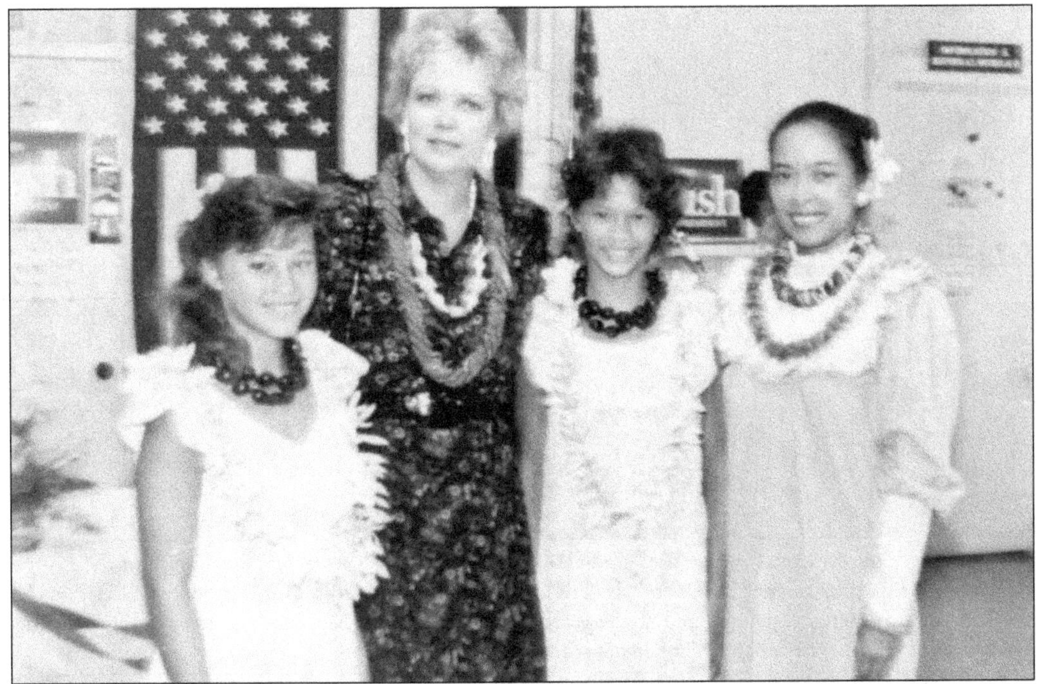

Maureen Reagan appeared on Lāna'i to represent her father, Ronald Reagan, in his presidential campaign. With her are, from left to right, Marissa Hera, Andriana Alonzo, and kumu hula Lehua Matsuoka. The black nut lei the young ladies wear are *kukui* (candlenuts) gathered from Maunalei. The nuts provided early Hawaiians with oil they used in torches at night. (Author's collection.)

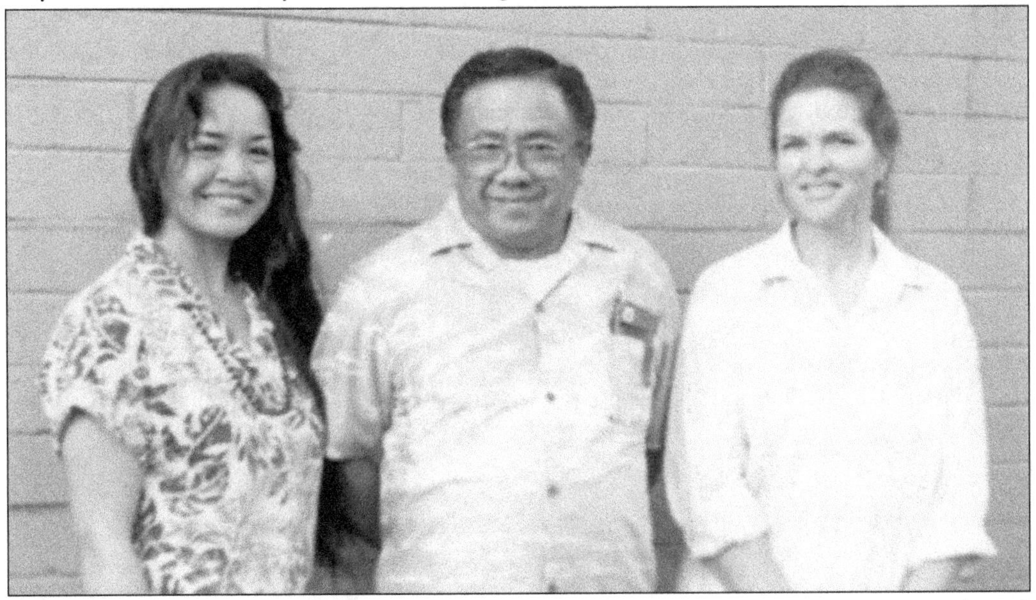

Postal clerks Pauline Richardson (left) and Lorrie Cornish (right) and postmaster Cecil Hera (center) were the last to work at the old Lāna'i Post Office before it was torn down. The concrete-block building was located on Lāna'i Avenue and replaced by a new facility located behind the Mike Carroll Gallery on Eighth Street. It was named for Goro Hokama, who served as a County of Maui councilmember for 33 years before retiring. (Author's collection.)

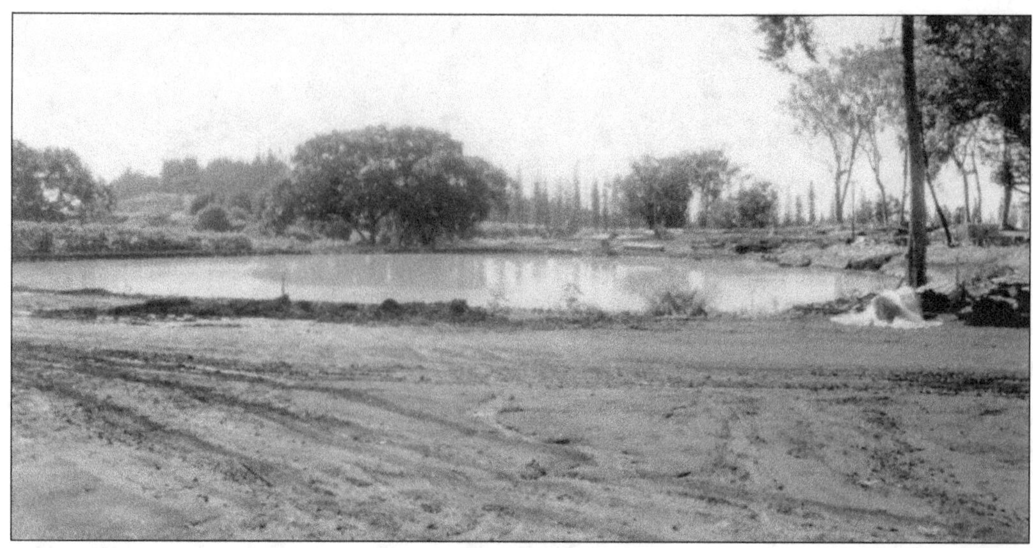

Lāna'i Ranch's reservoir was turned into a reflecting lake to become the central focal point of the Lodge at Kō'ele's gardens. It was originally built by Frederick Hayselden to store water for domestic use at the ranch. Migratory birds often stopped at the reservoir in later years. Many of the trees planted during Kō'ele's early years as the ranch headquarters still stand today. (Author's collection.)

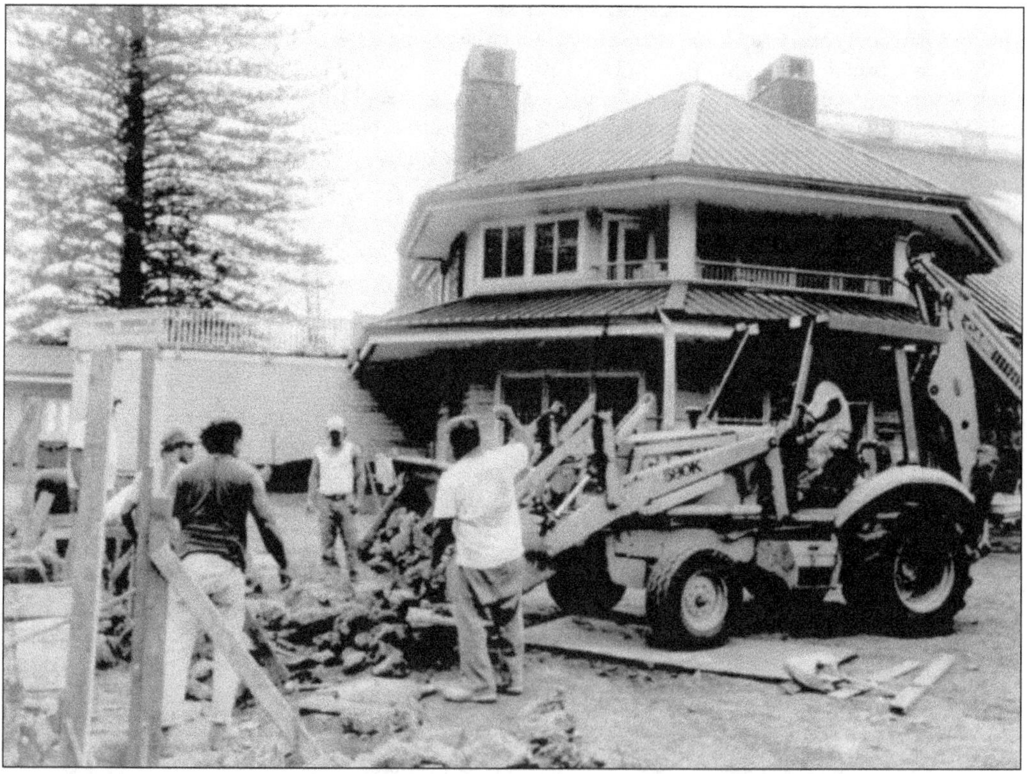

Men direct heavy equipment at the Lodge at Kō'ele's south wing. In the background is Kō'ele's original Norfolk pine tree. During the construction of the lodge, every effort was made not to compact the root zones of the property's existing trees. A croquet court is now located in this section of the lodge's gardens. (Author's collection.)

Six

Tourism

A New Direction

Pineapple was king and the Territory of Hawai'i's second largest industry in 1915. Castle & Cooke, an island company started by missionary descendants in 1851, acquired a 21-percent interest in James D. Dole's Hawaiian Pineapple Company in 1932 and began to use Dole's name on its canned pineapple and juice products. In 1961, Dole merged with Castle & Cooke, retained Dole's label, and began a plantation in Mindanao in the Philippines under the name Dolefil. By 1982, Dole bought out food producers in several countries and became the largest supplier of bananas to the American market.

In 1985, Castle & Cooke was nearly bankrupt when David H. Murdock acquired a majority interest in the publicly traded corporation, which included Dole Food Company, and began the island's transition from growing pineapples to providing luxury accommodations for Hawai'i's visitors. In 1986, construction of two resorts, the 102-room Lodge at Kō'ele, the former ranch headquarters of previous owners, and the 203-room Mānele Bay Hotel, overlooking Hulopo'e Beach, began.

Two golf courses, Challenge at Mānele and Experience at Kō'ele, more than 300 affordable homes for the resorts' workers, and three multifamily apartment-rental complexes came next. Luxury homes and condominium townhouse complexes were also constructed at Mānele and Kō'ele for upscale buyers, and the infrastructure to support the resorts followed. The Lodge at Kō'ele opened in 1990, and the Mānele Bay Hotel opened in 1992. Four Seasons Resorts assumed the management of both properties in 2005.

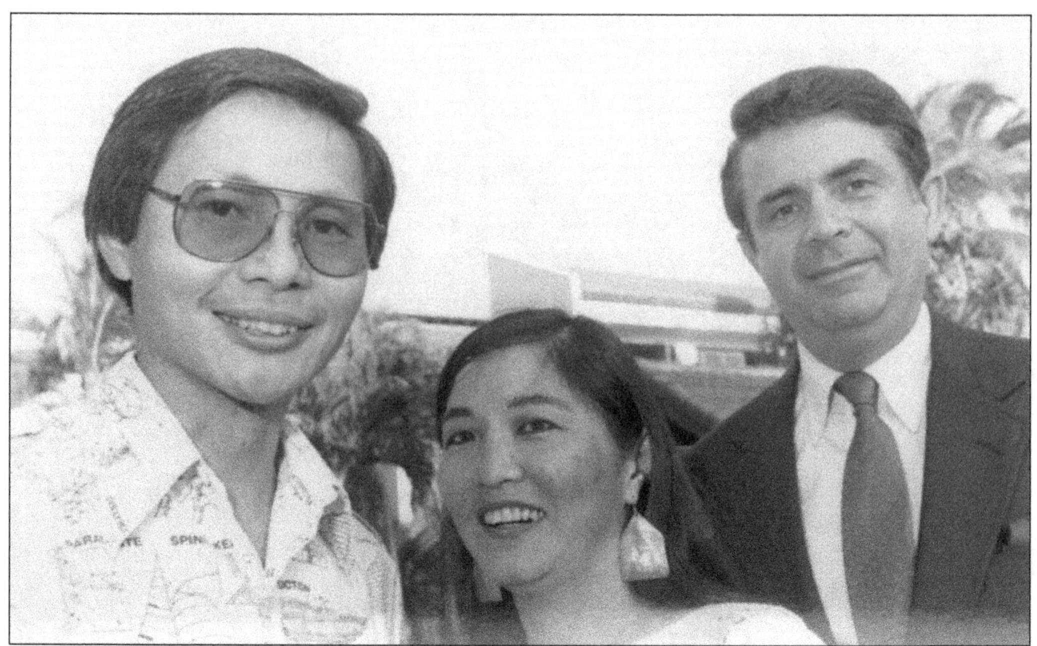

The architects who worked on the Lodge at Kō'ele were Francis Oda, from Group 70, one of the leading architectural firms in Hawai'i, and Arnold Savrann, senior vice president of architecture at Castle & Cooke Inc. With them is landscape architect Juli Kimura Walters. (Author's collection.)

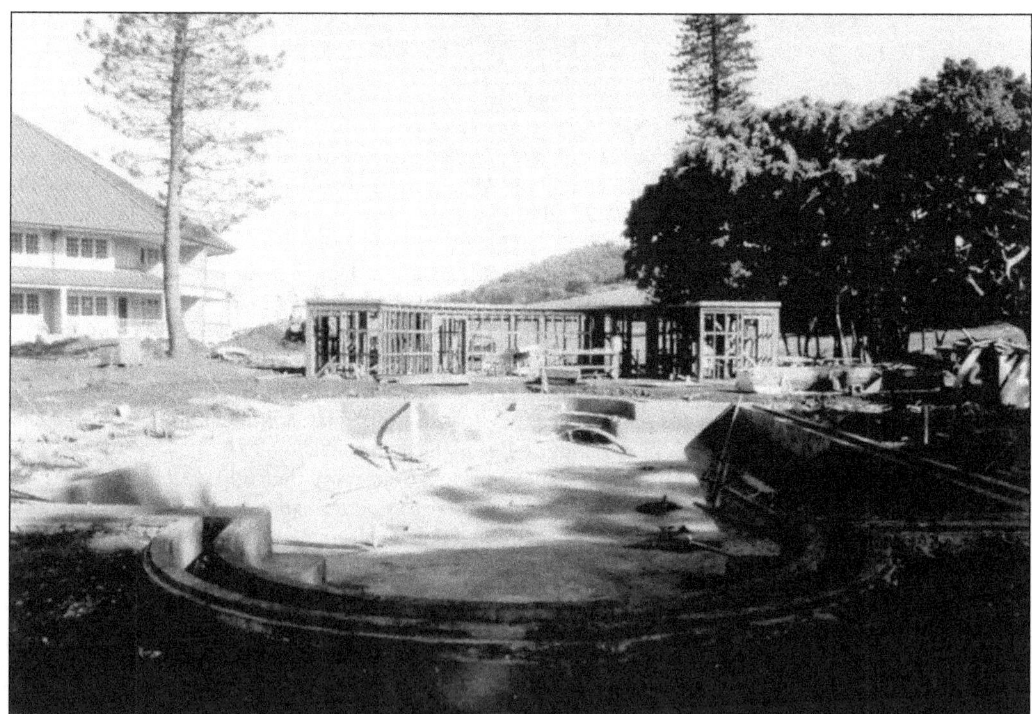

Kō'ele's church was moved to a location alongside Keōmoku Road, and in its place, the lodge's swimming pool and bathhouse emerged. Set at the rear of the west wing of the lodge, the pool's garden views extend beyond the reflecting lake to the hillside behind the lodge. (Author's collection.)

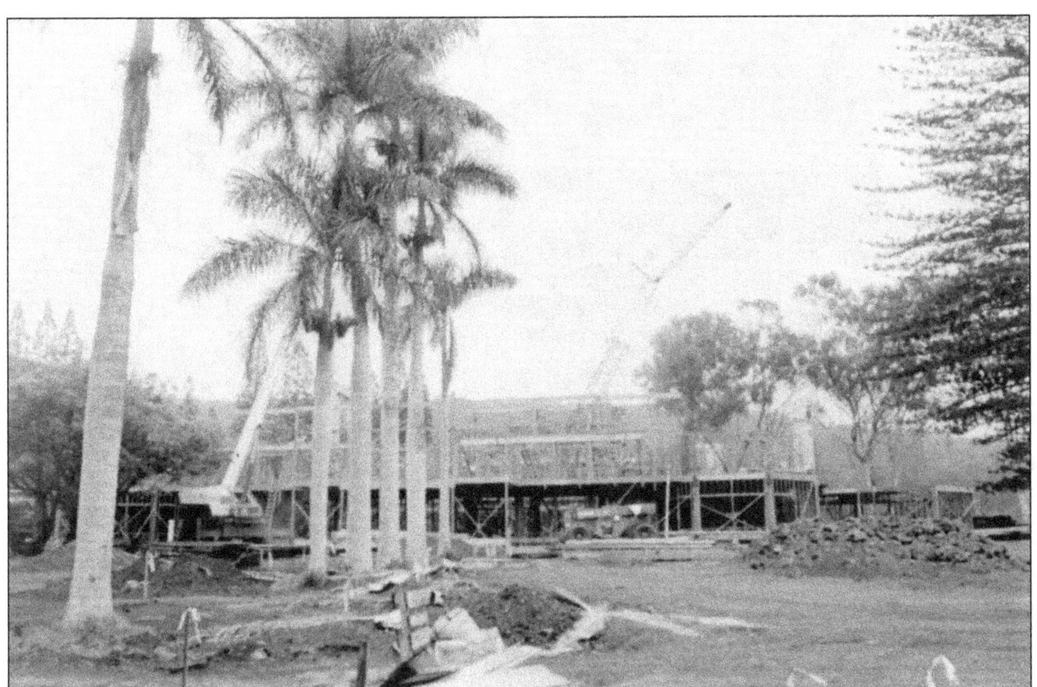

Royal palm trees were planted along the original entry to the ranch manager's house. The palms were to be moved to a location where they would be silhouetted against the sun setting in the west, but they were replanted against the hillside instead. The palms were moved with a helicopter, and only one did not survive being transplanted. (Author's collection.)

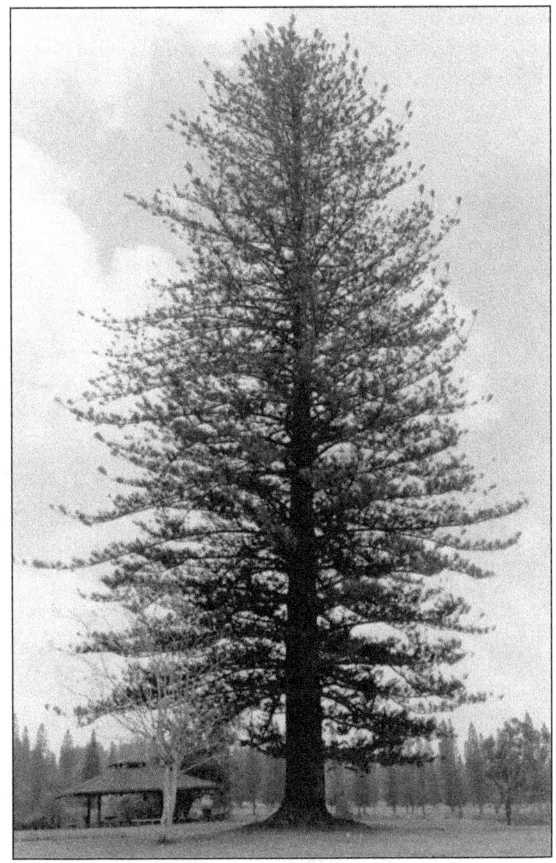

On a summer day in the 1960s, Jimmy Gibson, a grandson of Walter Murray Gibson, and Richard Morita Jr., the son of Lāna'i's game warden, became the only two boys ever known to climb Kō'ele's giant Norfolk pine tree. They left a white flag draped in its uppermost branch as proof of their accomplishment. Walter Murray Gibson was given two seedlings by King David Kalākaua in 1875, but only one tree survived. The pavilion pictured here near the tree was built by Dole Company and used as a refreshment stop on their island tour for day visitors. (Author's collection.)

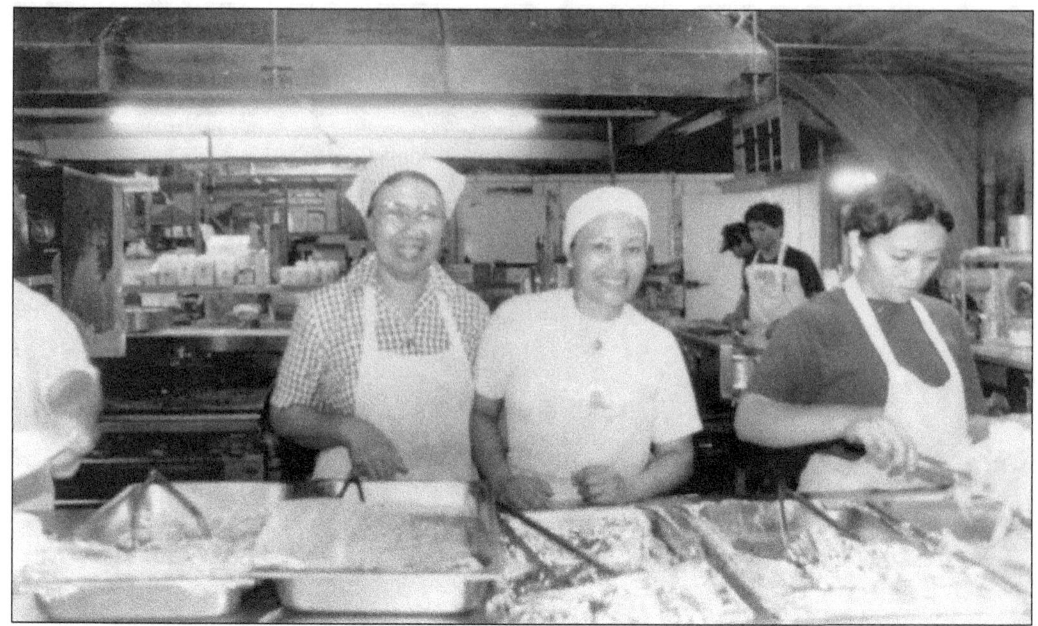

Construction workers brought in from other islands to work on Lāna'i stayed in Dole's "log cabins," dormitory buildings previously used to house seasonal workers. A food hall kept the crews well fed and was staffed by Lāna'i residents such as Midy Eharis, Basilia Castillo, and Jojo Urpanil. Eharis was known for her delicious cakes and made sure there were always enough desserts to feed more than 500 workers each weekday. (Author's collection.)

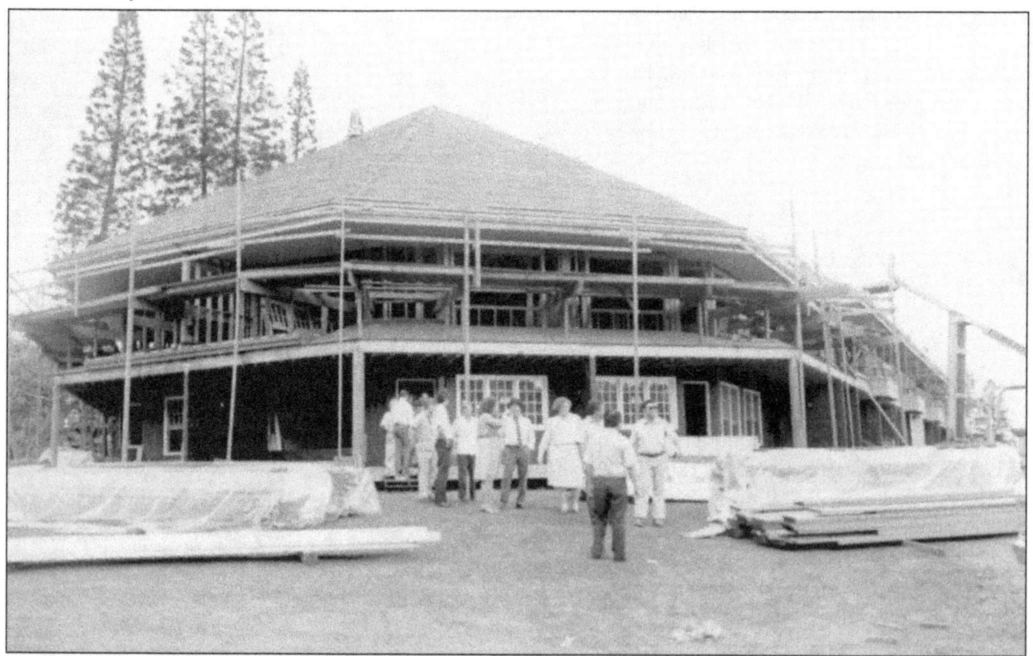

An after-work tour of the Lodge at Kō'ele's construction site gave Castle & Cooke visitors a chance to see part of the work being done. The two wings and the central building of the lodge are the largest wooden buildings in Hawai'i. The trees surrounding the buildings added to the lodge's charm, which looks as if it has always been there. (Author's collection.)

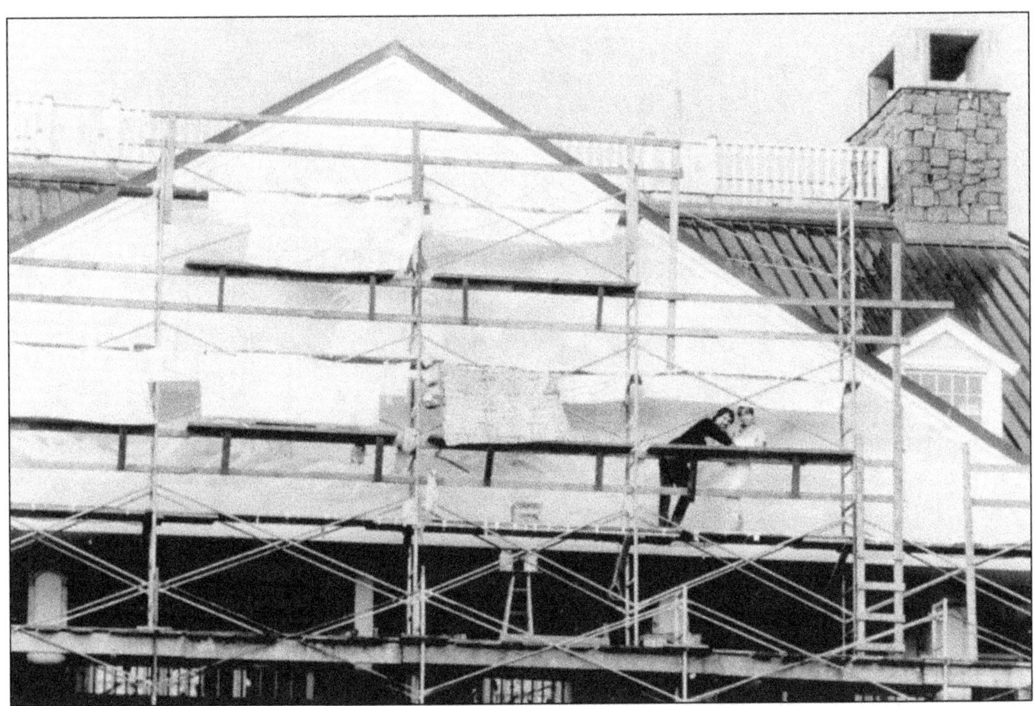

Scaffolding was set to paint a pineapple design with a kauna'oa lei over the lodge's entrance to welcome guests into the building. Kauna'oa is the flower of Lāna'i. It is a member of the laurel family and grows along the seashore and in the mountains on top of other plants. Directly inside the foyer, on the ceiling, is a map depicting Kō'ele as being the center of the island and world. (Author's collection.)

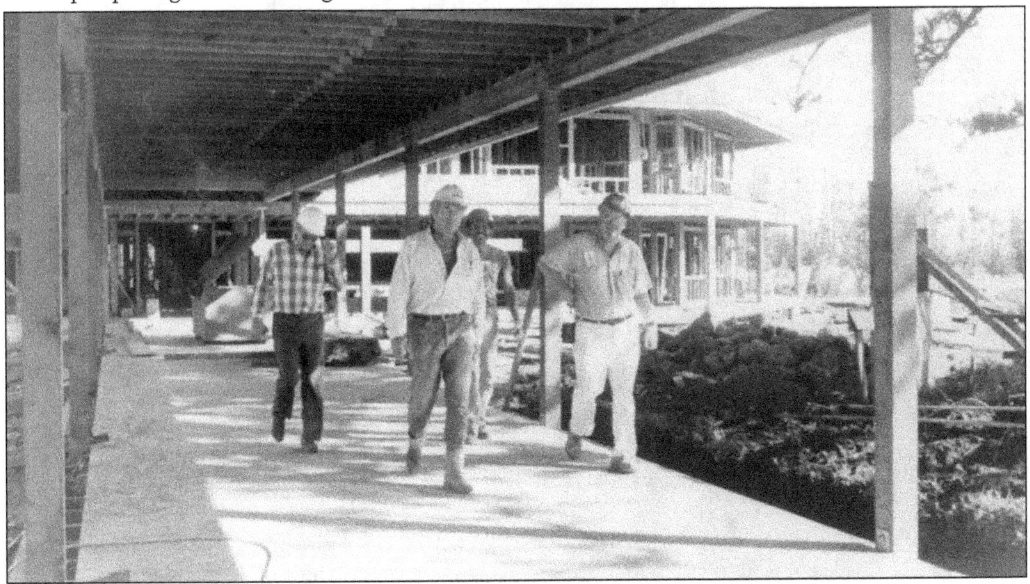

Covered walkways connect the two wings of the lodge to its central building. After construction was completed, wicker chairs with hand-quilted Hawaiian cushions were placed on them. The cushions were quilted by Lāna'i residents who also assisted artist John Wullbrandt with completing the fine details on stenciled designs of Hawaiian birds, plants, and flowers on guest room doors. The Lāna'i Art Center was created to help develop Lāna'i artists for this project. (Author's collection.)

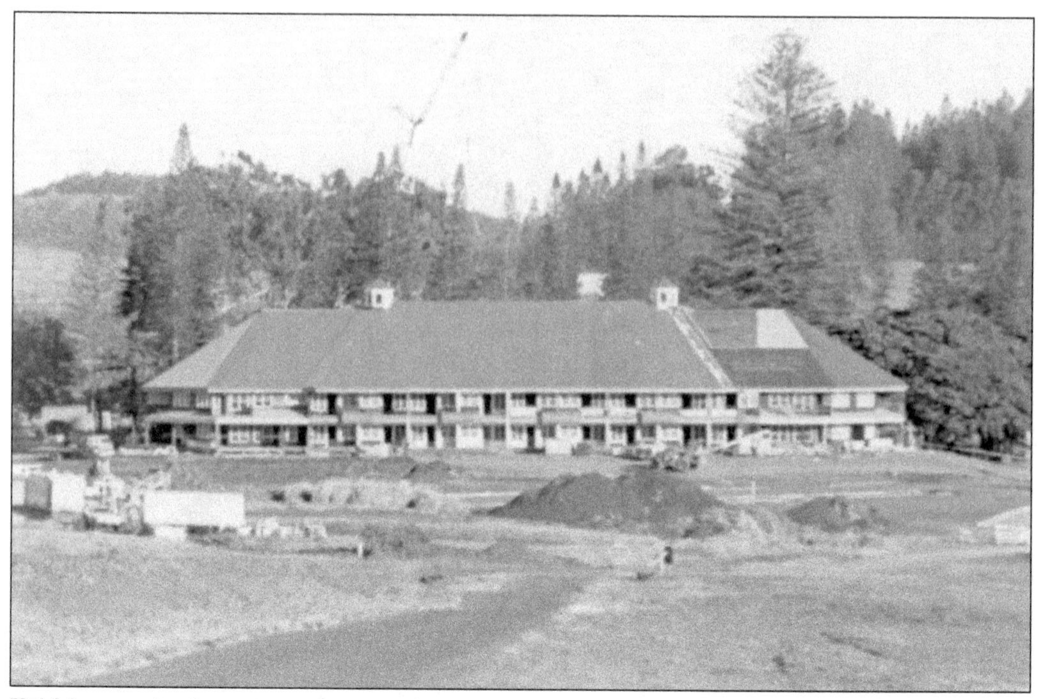

Kōʻele's west wing has sunset views stretching out to the ahupuaʻa of Kaʻa. At night, when Kōʻele may be shrouded in fog, the building disappears, leaving only the dim glow of its outdoor lights visible. During the ranching days, this area housed a blacksmith shop, stock pens for separating livestock, and high, round corrals with wooden sides used to train horses. (Author's collection.)

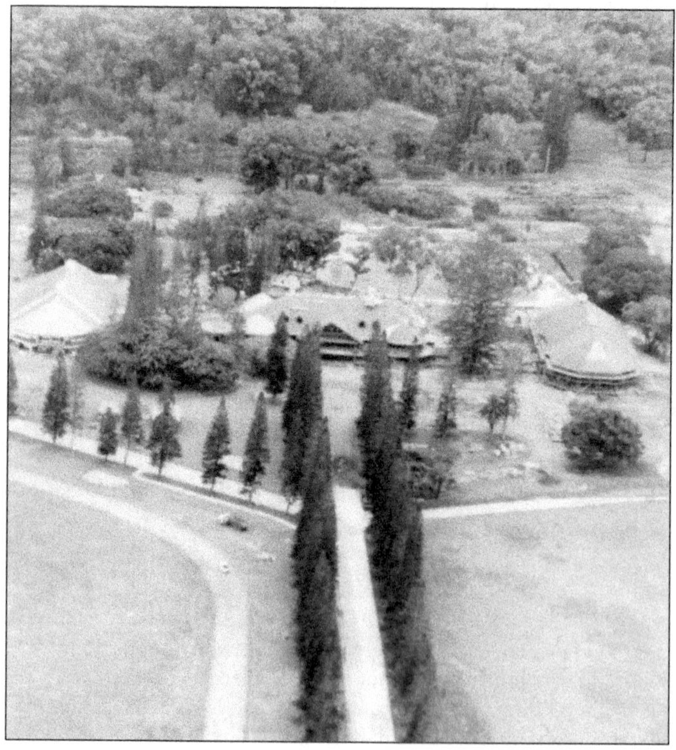

This aerial view from a helicopter in 1988 shows stately rows of Cook Isle pine trees leading to the lodge's front entrance. To the side, branching off beside the Keōmoku road, are younger pine trees. The banyan tree on this side of the lodge is pruned back now to allow grass and other plants to grow under it, but during the 1960s, its branches draped all the way to the ground. (Author's collection.)

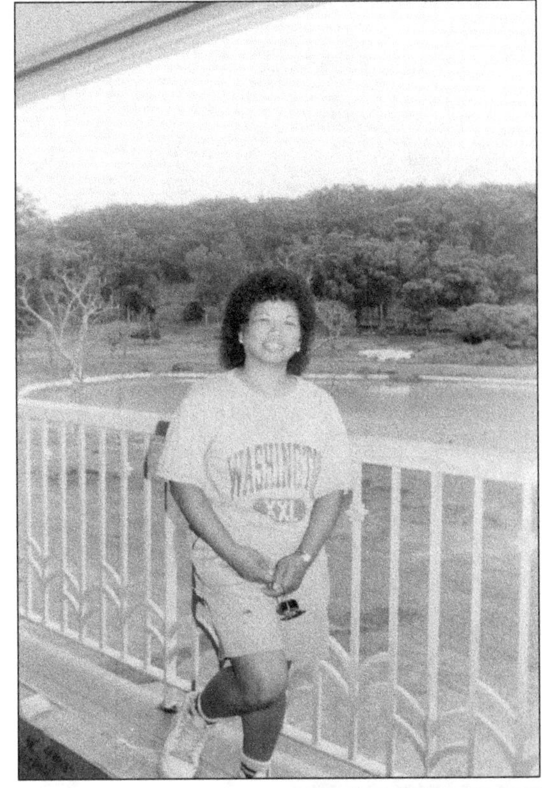

Former resident and class of 1963 Lāna'i High School graduate Barbara Masicampo Kuhr was able to get a sneak preview of the lodge before it opened. Behind her is the reflecting lake, but the wedding gazebo had not yet been built. The tree-covered hillside is very different than it appears in the ranch's early photographs from the 1920s. (Author's collection.)

The transplanted royal palms sit on the hillside behind the John Richardson house, which was removed from the site and stored elsewhere in hopes it could be restored by a community group. Containers filled with building materials sit in the fields formerly used for an arena by Lāna'i Horse Club members. (Author's collection.)

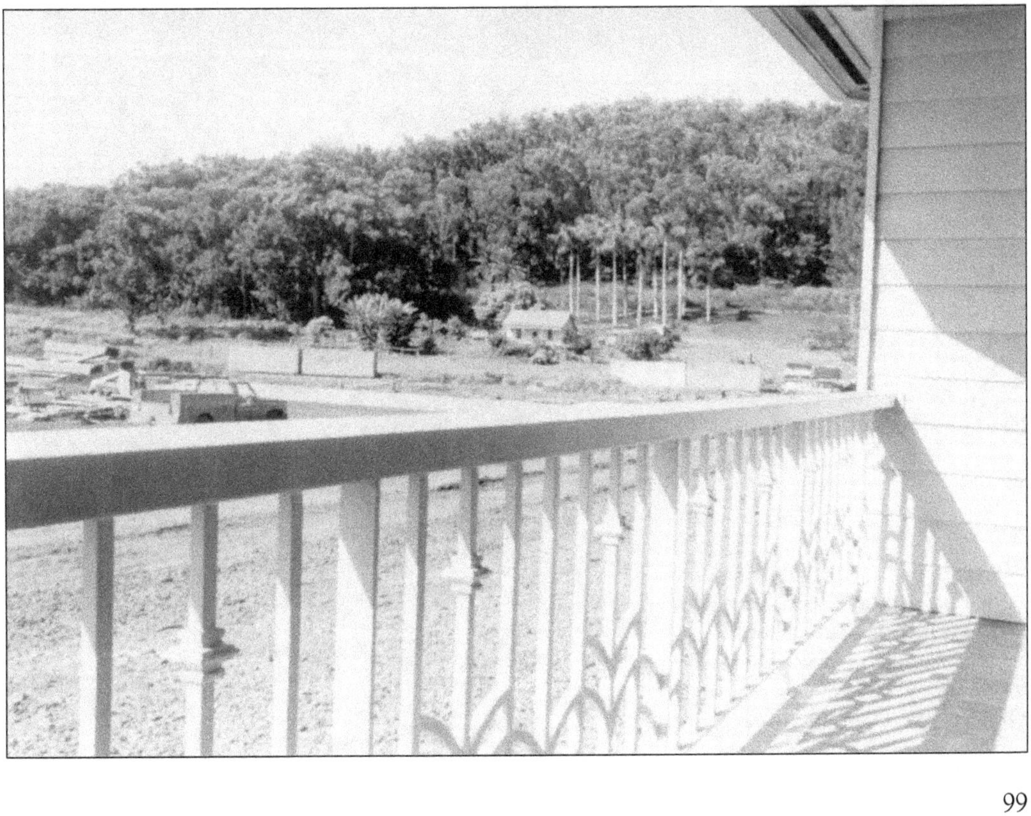

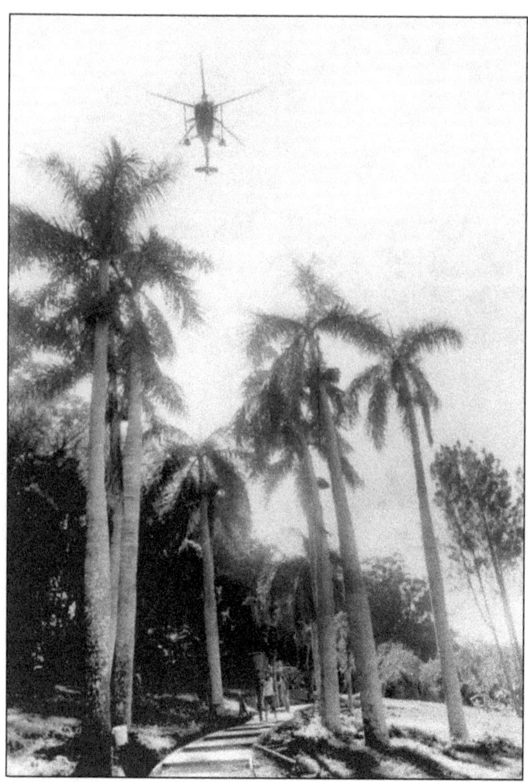

A helicopter hovers above a pathway with a load of wet concrete to pour. All of the pathways were done this way to minimize soil compaction from heavy equipment and trucks moving around the jobsite. Special care was used to protect all of Kō'ele's older trees. (Author's collection.)

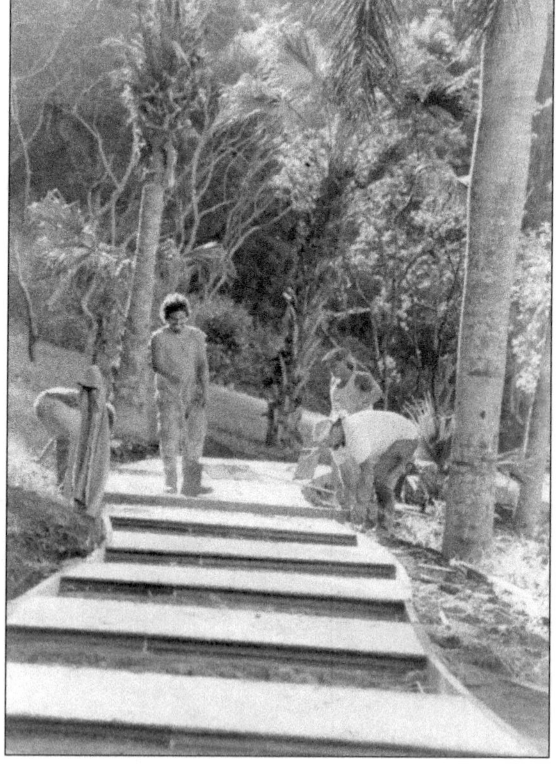

Workmen put finishing touches onto a garden pathway at Kō'ele. Surrounding them is a diverse mix of plants and trees blended together to contribute to the feeling it had been planted at different times over many years, instead of all at once. (Author's collection.)

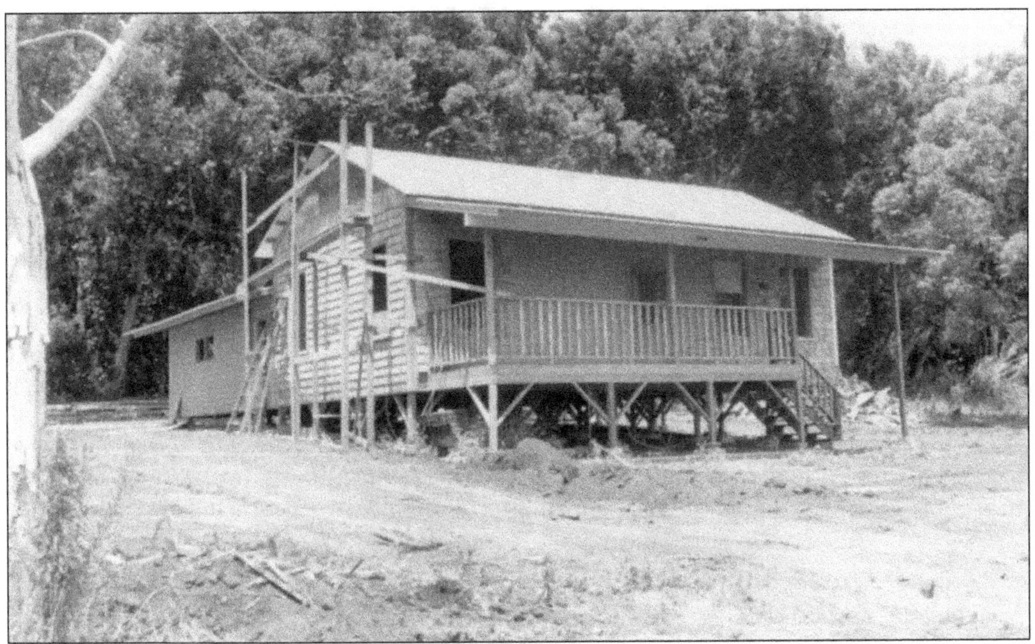

This house was originally located where the hostess stand is in the lodge's terrace dining area. During George Munro's years at Lānaʻi Ranch, it was occupied by Helen "Nell" Forbes and her three children, Mary, Jean and Douglas, after the death of her husband on Oʻahu. The ranch's bookkeeper, she also read the rain gauge and kept track of accumulated rainfall. After the house was moved, it became the home of the John Richardson family. (Author's collection.)

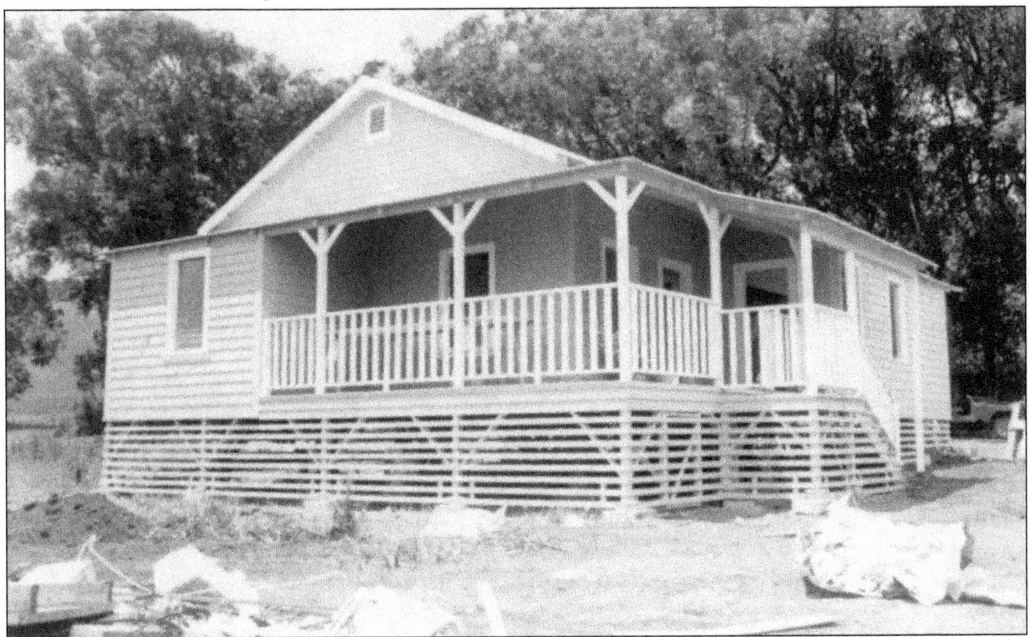

This house was located next to the jacaranda tree beside the lodge's entryway. After the ranching days, it was occupied by William and Eva Kwon and their children. William and Eva grew up in Keōmoku village. He is pictured as a toddler on page 22. Eva is pictured fishing on page 122. After the house was moved, it became the home of her sister and brother-in-law Rebecca and Ernest Richardson. (Author's collection.)

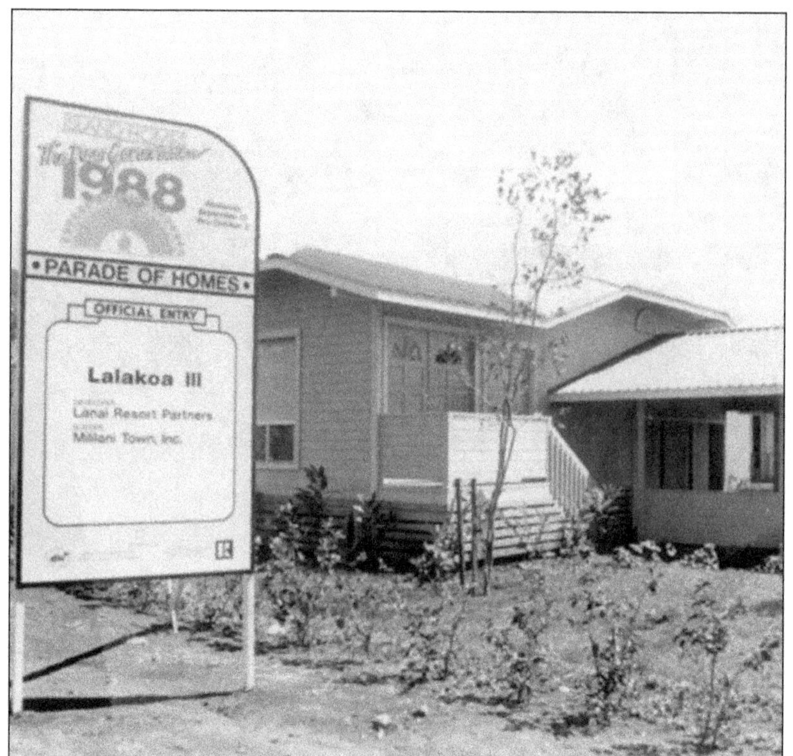

New homes were being built concurrently with the resort project. Lālākoa III is located below the former estate of the Charles Gay family at Nininiwai. Lāna'i residents were able to attend workshops on home ownership and how to apply for a home mortgage. *Lālākoa* means strong limbs; Lāna'i City was growing and extending strong limbs outward to provide homes for its residents. (Author's collection.)

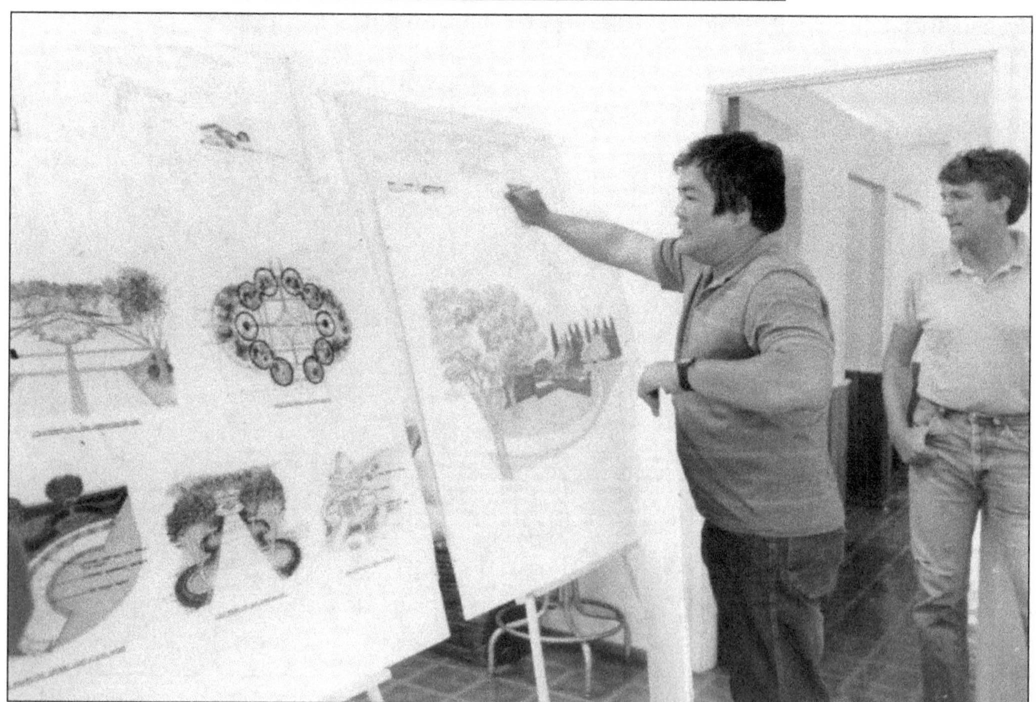

A Castle & Cooke representative prepares display boards for the Lālākoa III project prior to a community meeting. In the years before the resorts opened, Castle & Cooke prepared for the island's transition to tourism by providing educational opportunities and job training for residents. (Author's collection.)

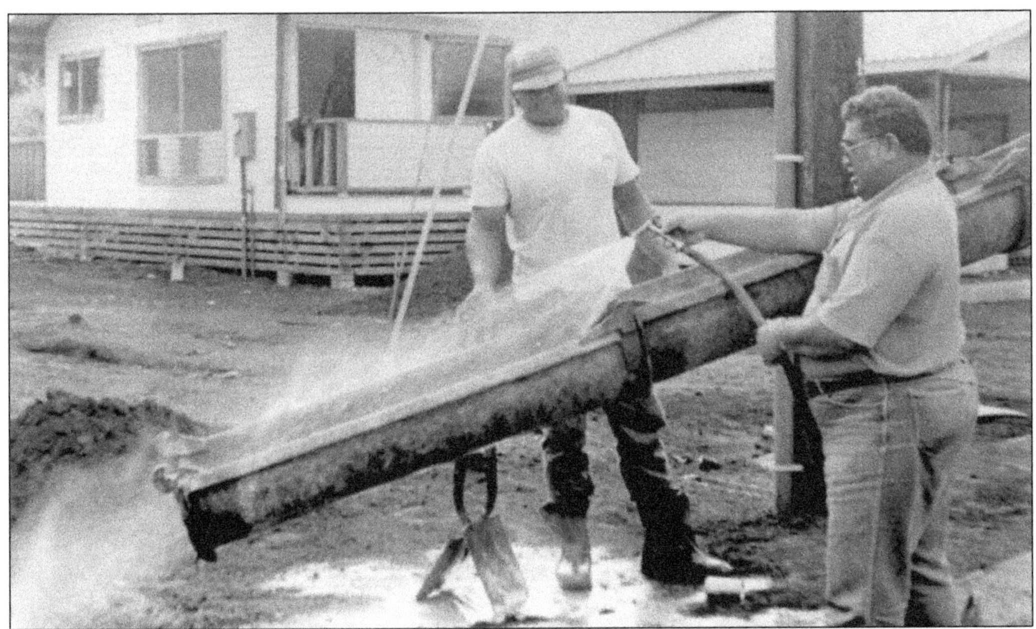

Clarence "Hoss" Richardson washes down his truck's concrete chute after pouring a driveway at a new home at Lālākoa III. His helper stands by to assist him. All of the driveways were installed by Lāna'i Rock and Concrete, a division of Castle & Cooke's Lāna'i operations. Hoss lived almost his entire life at Kō'ele where his father, Ernest Richardson, was one of the island's ranch paniolo. His passing was mourned by hundreds of residents who attended a service for him at Kō'ele. (Author's collection.)

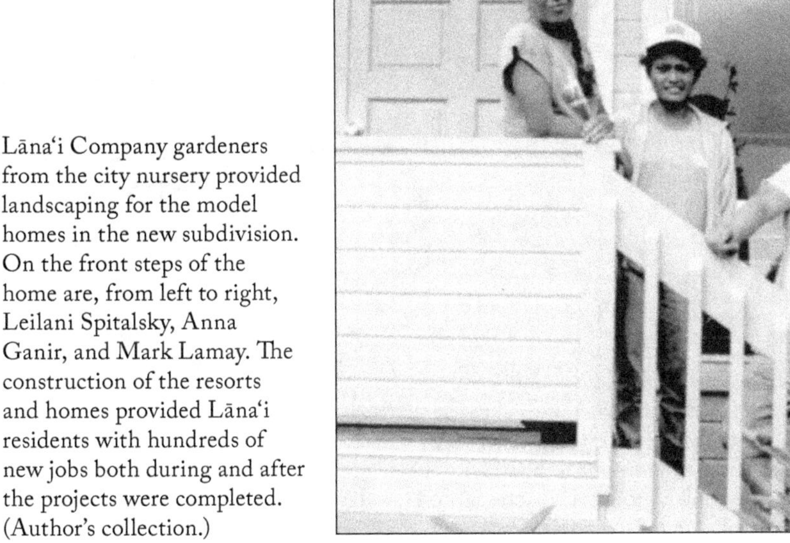

Lāna'i Company gardeners from the city nursery provided landscaping for the model homes in the new subdivision. On the front steps of the home are, from left to right, Leilani Spitalsky, Anna Ganir, and Mark Lamay. The construction of the resorts and homes provided Lāna'i residents with hundreds of new jobs both during and after the projects were completed. (Author's collection.)

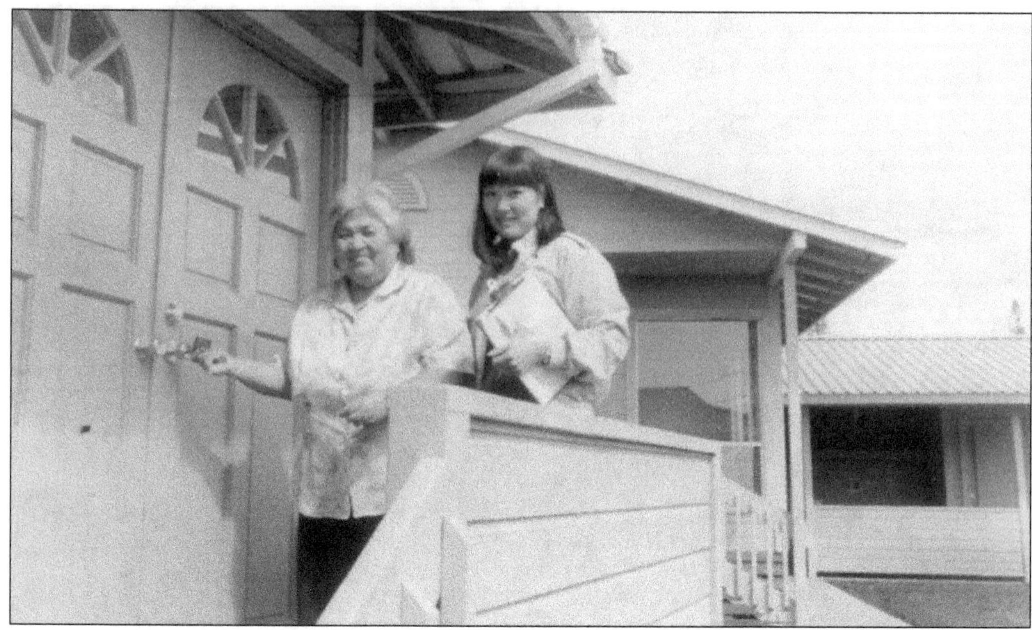

Josephine "Aunty Pine" Reinicke Kawanaole raised her family at Kaumālapa'u village, and after health and transportation issues required her to live in Lāna'i City, she became one of the first residents of Lālākoa III. She is pictured here with Castle & Cooke representative Kathy Inouye (right), who presented her the keys to her new home. "Aunty Pine" made the best biscuits on the island and enjoyed sharing them with her family and friends. (Author's collection.)

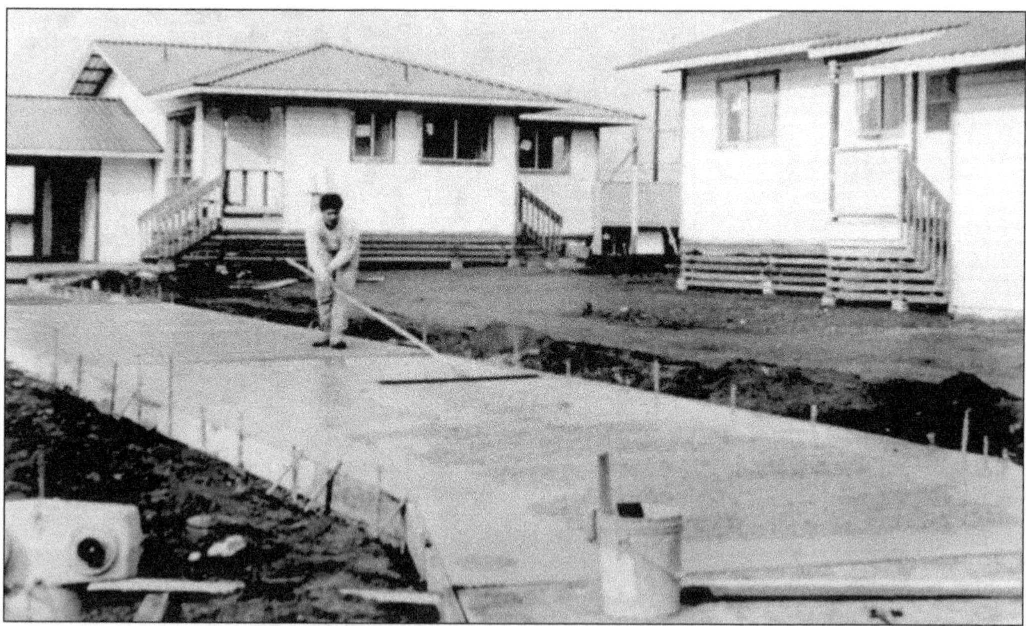

Taking pride in his work, an unidentified worker finishes the driveway to a new home. In addition to the homes at Lālākoa III, Castle & Cooke built three other apartment complexes: Lāna'i City Apartments, Iwiole, and Kānepu'u, and more single family homes in the Olopua Woods subdivision. David H. Murdock also donated 50 acres of land to the Department of Hawaiian Homelands for a subdivision for native Hawaiians. (Author's collection.)

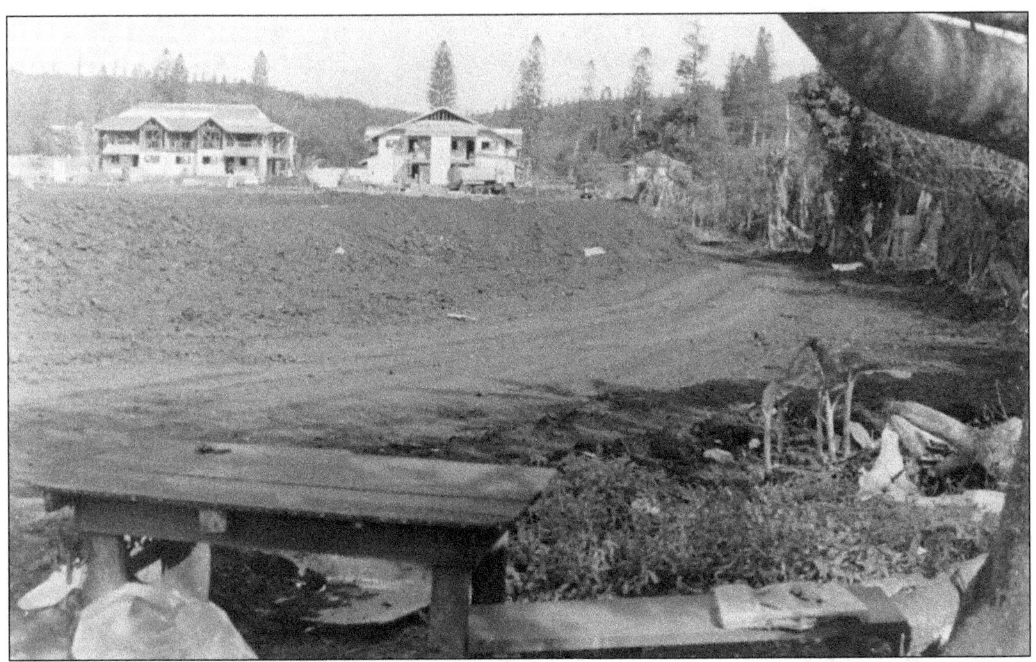

Iwi'ole Apartments is located on the northwestern edge of Lāna'i City, across from the eighth fairway of the Cavendish Golf Course. The two-story buildings on the right side of the complex offered tenants views of the sunset across the fields to Ka'a and the north end of the island. *Iwi'ole* is a kind of adze that may have been found in this ahupua'a. (Joana Varawa.)

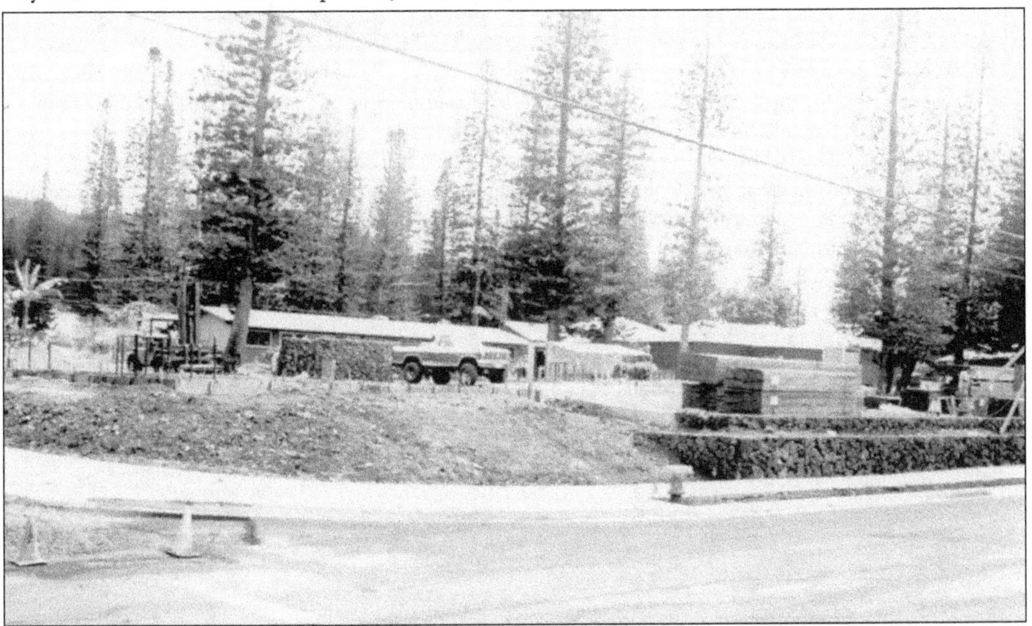

Lāna'i City Apartments is located next to the Lāna'i Senior Center, and when it was built, several of its units were handicapped accessible, as it was originally thought senior residents would find it a convenient place to live. However, Hale Kūpuna, a senior-housing project with a live-in manager, was built a few blocks away on Ilima Avenue. Lāna'i City Apartments was sold by Castle & Cooke in 2012 and turned into condominium units by its buyer. (Author's collection.)

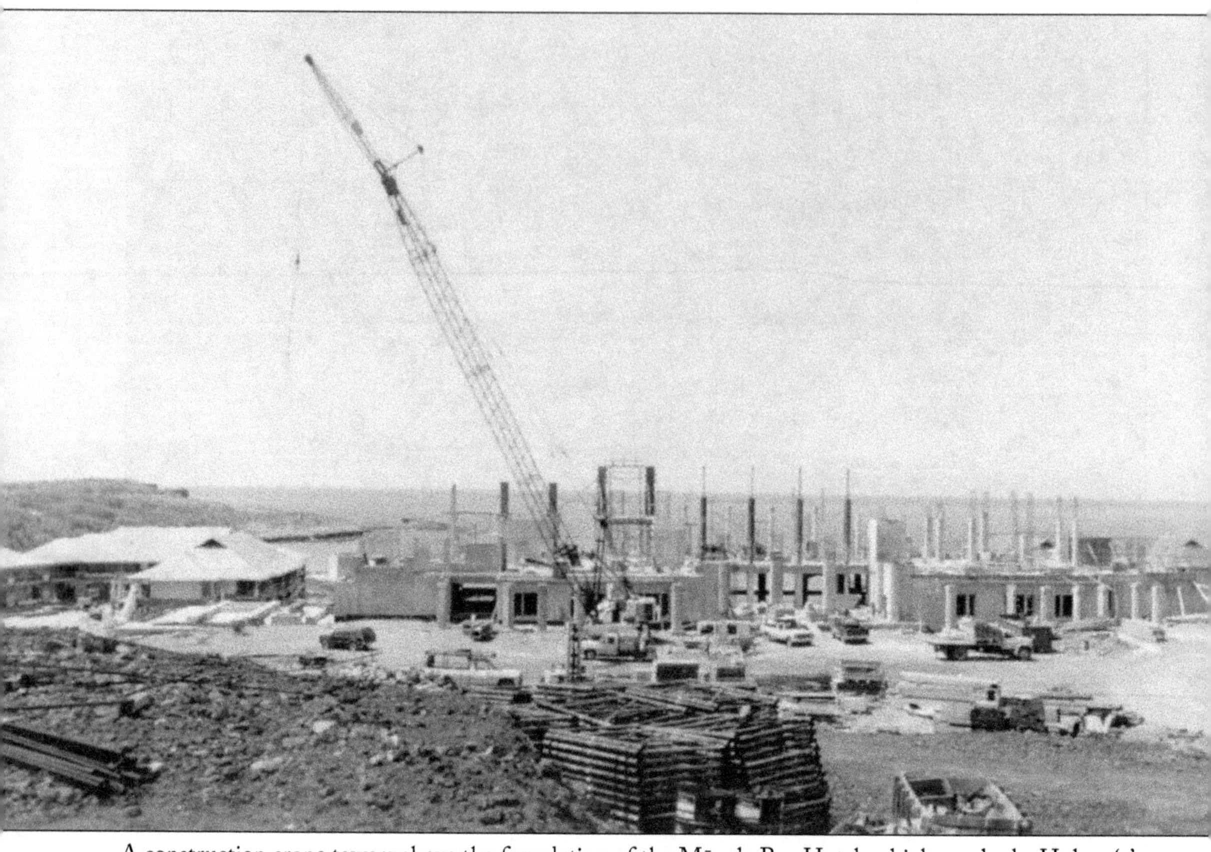

A construction crane towers above the foundation of the Mānele Bay Hotel, which overlooks Hulopo'e's white sand beach. During the ranching days, a freighter anchored in Mānele Bay and waited for pipi to be brought out to it by paniolo. It would have provided a fascinating spectacle for today's visitors lounging under beach umbrellas. In the 203-room hotel's lobby, a mural of Lāna'i's legendary hero, Kaululā'au and the bonfire he set on the beach, welcome guests. In the legend, Kaululā'au tricked all of Lāna'i's demon spirits to their deaths, except for their chief, who fled to Kaho'olawe. Kaululā'au is credited with making the island safe for humans to inhabit. The ruins of a Hawaiian village sit near the pathway to the beach. (Author's collection.)

An unidentified construction worker waits for more materials to reach him as he perches on top of the building forms. The construction crew for Mānele was housed in a tent city set up for them at a nearby site with complete services, including air-conditioned bedrooms shared by two people. (Author's collection.)

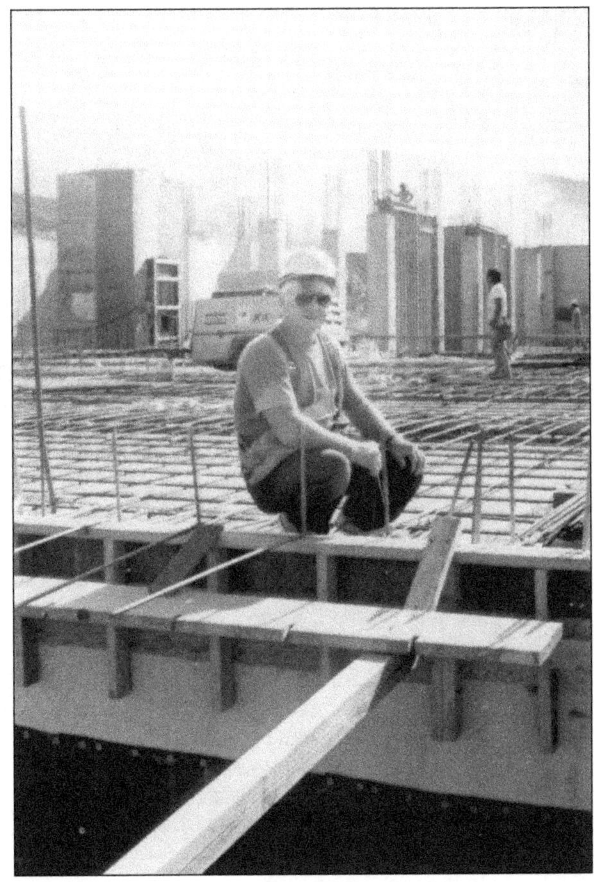

With its first floor in place, one of the hotel's guest wings waits for its second story to be built. Behind the hotel, the hillside covered with short grasses is the terrain the crews on board Capt. James Cook's ships *Discovery* and the *Endeavor* saw when they passed by Lāna'i in 1779. (Author's collection.)

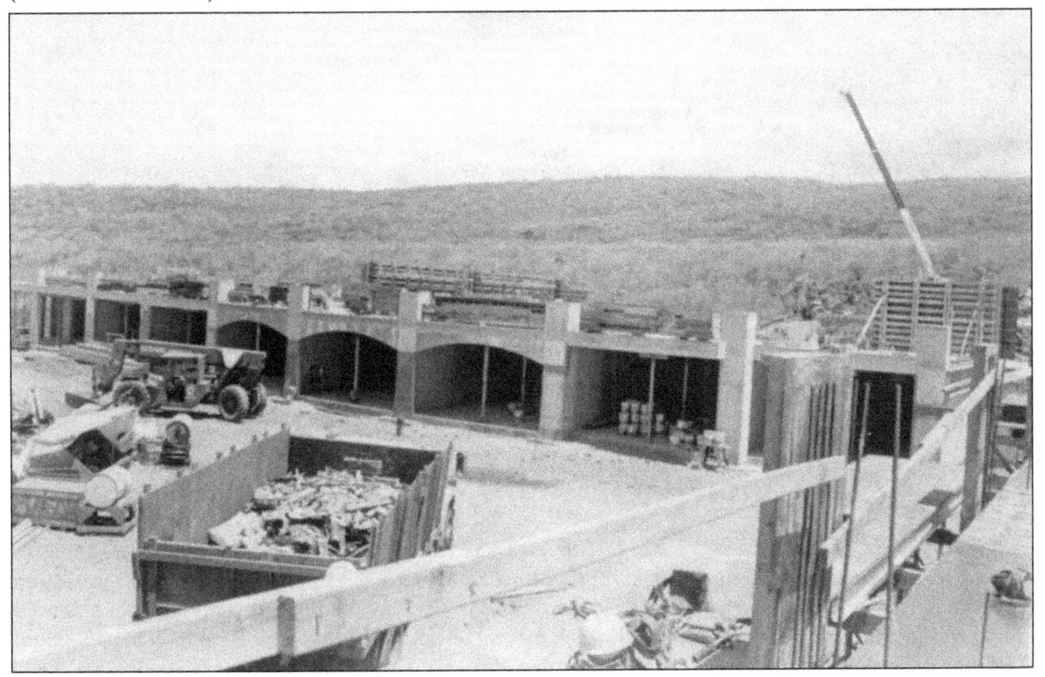

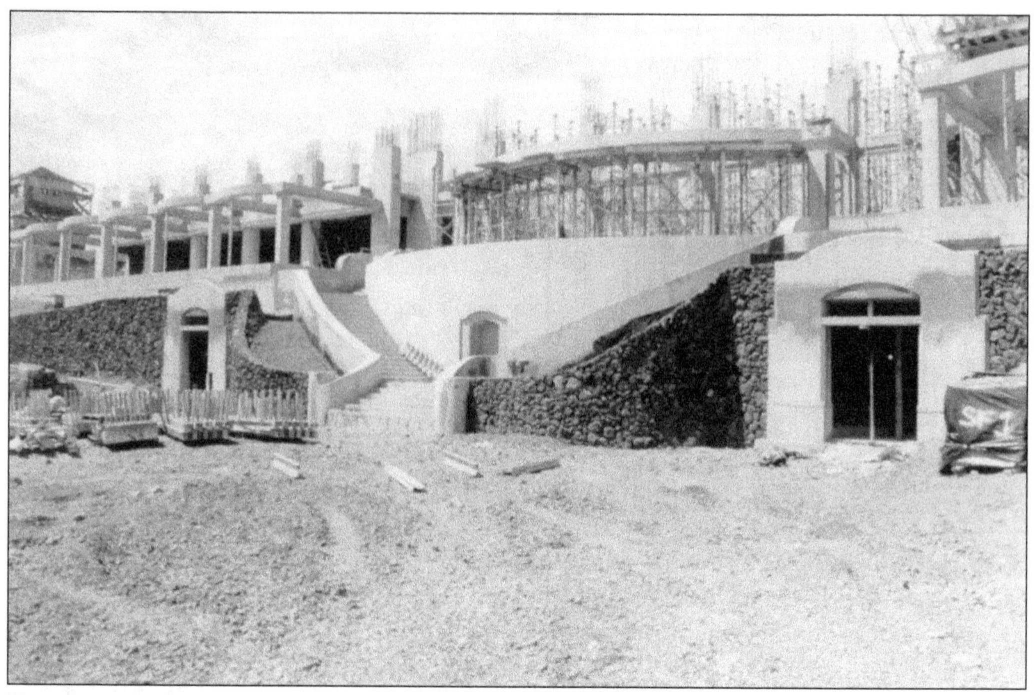

The curved staircase from Mānele Bay Hotel's lower lobby to the swimming pool takes shape. On both sides of the staircase are entryways to the basement level, which leads to the resort's spa facilities and elevators to the lobby levels. (Author's collection.)

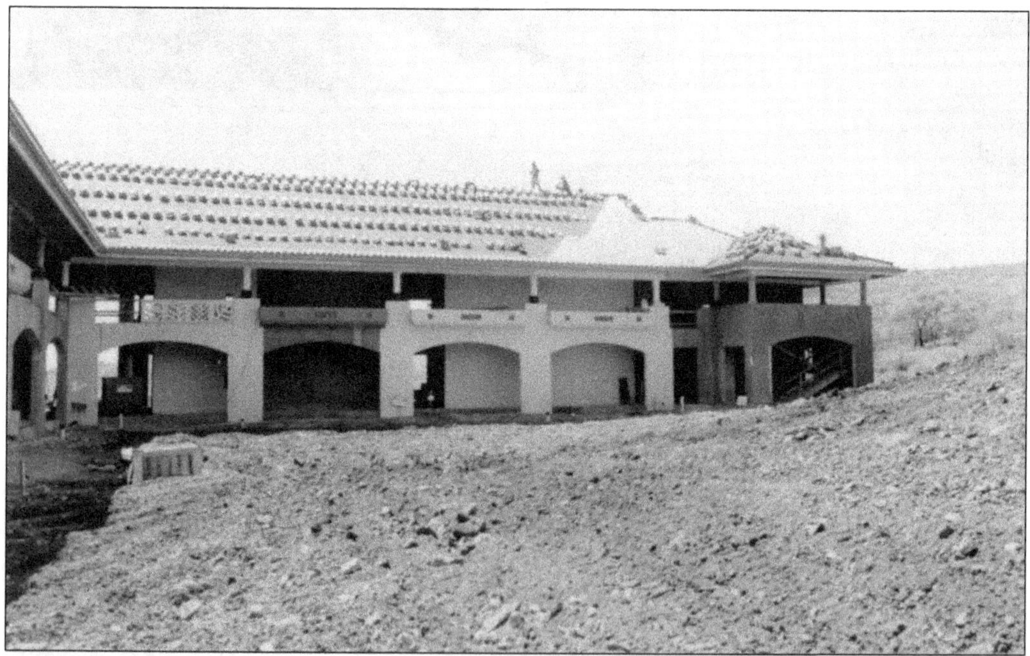

Green tiles similar in color to the leaves of native ilima plants are stacked on the rooftop of this wing in preparation for installation. In 2015, all of the buildings in the hotel's complex were repainted a neutral brown with red undertones to blend into Mānele's natural terrain. The landscaping around the oceanfront buildings was replanted with drought-tolerant native grasses and shrubs. (Author's collection.)

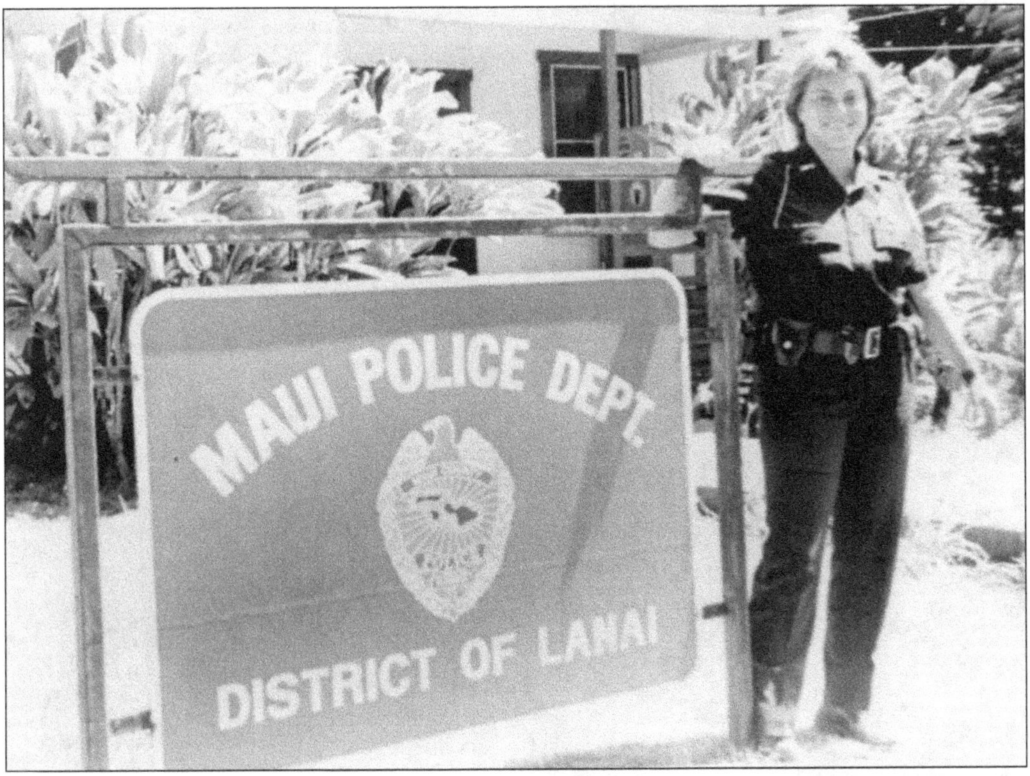

Maui Police Department (MPD) officer Molly Cameron was one of the last officers to occupy the Lāna'i police station located on Eighth Street. The police department occupied half of the wooden building that also served as the district courthouse for the island. A new facility was opened in 2004 on Fraser Avenue. (Author's collection.)

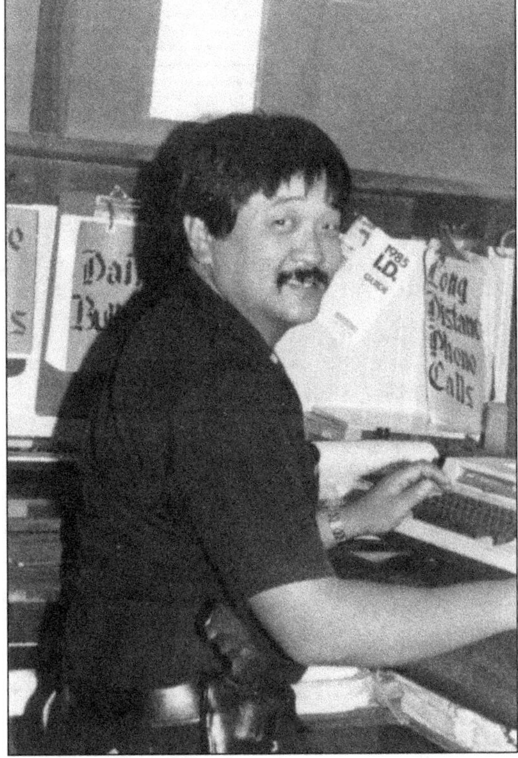

MPD officer Waldo Fujie was born and raised on Lāna'i, where his father worked on the Dole Plantation and his mother taught Japanese, Spanish, French, music, and art at Lāna'i High School. (Author's collection.)

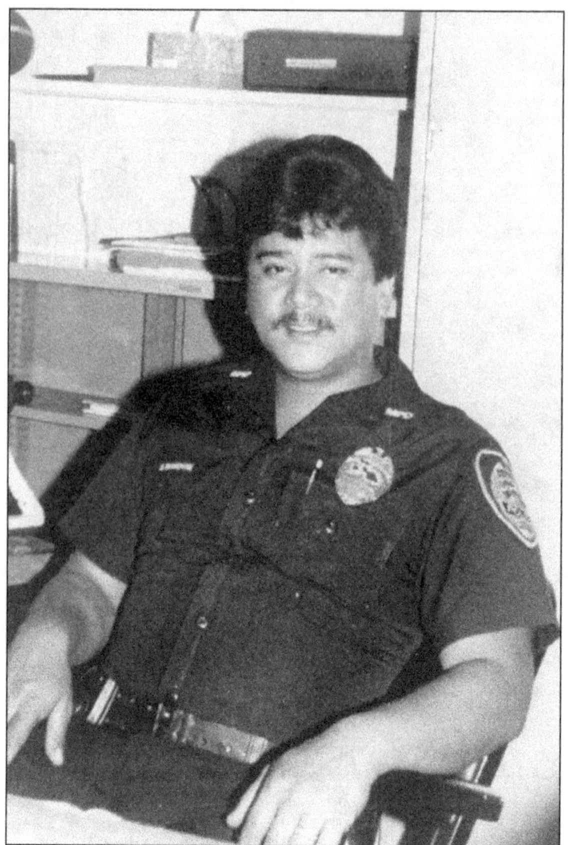

Sgt. Ben Samonte was also one of the last officers at the old station. As the station was very small, a holding cell with a high chain-link fence enclosing a yard at its front was nearby. It was nicknamed the doghouse. Detained individuals were kept there until they could be transported to Maui. The doghouse is one of the most photographed buildings in Lānaʻi City today. (Author's collection.)

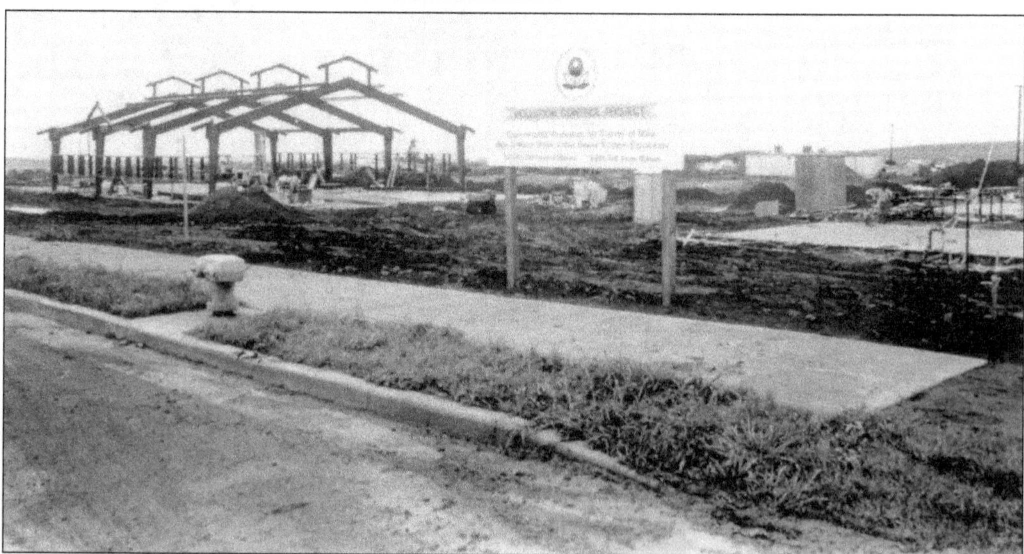

When the hotels were under construction, support facilities had to be built concurrently. At the south end of Fraser Avenue, three large structures were constructed: central, for administrative offices; a laundry; and sharing a long building, a warehouse for distributing supplies and a bakery. The sign in this photograph is for a sewer treatment facility being built by the County of Maui outside of the city. (Author's collection.)

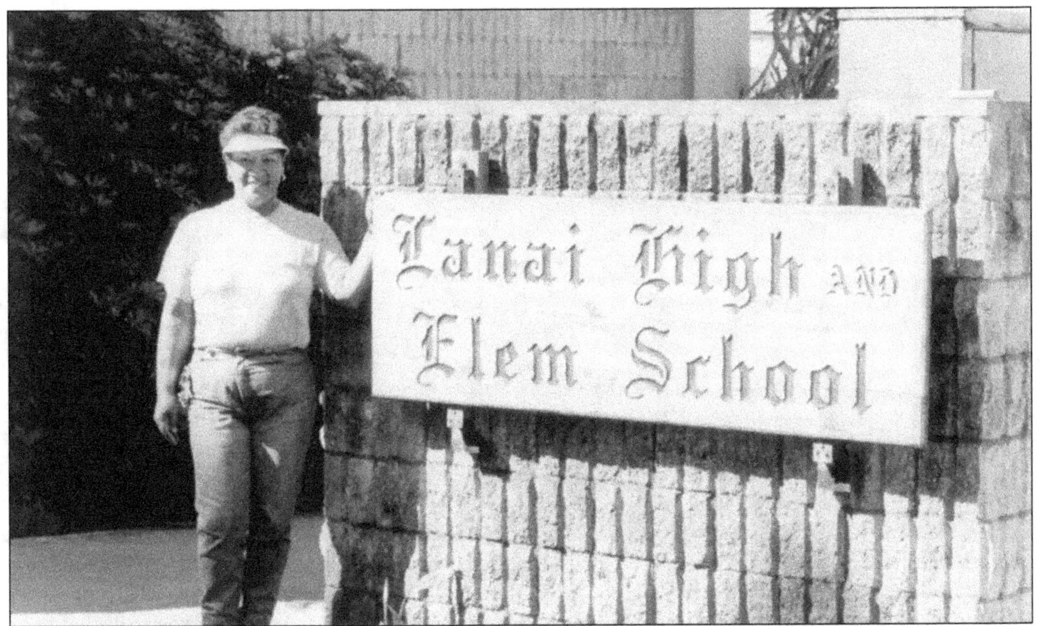

In addition to the jobs being created by Lāna'i's construction projects, many Lāna'i residents were employed in government jobs at the county, state, and federal levels. Lavern Kekahuna Benanua's family members are old-time residents dating back to the Keōmoku village in the 1900s. A custodian at Lāna'i High and Elementary School, she enjoyed taking care of the school's campus where she had been a student too. (Author's collection.)

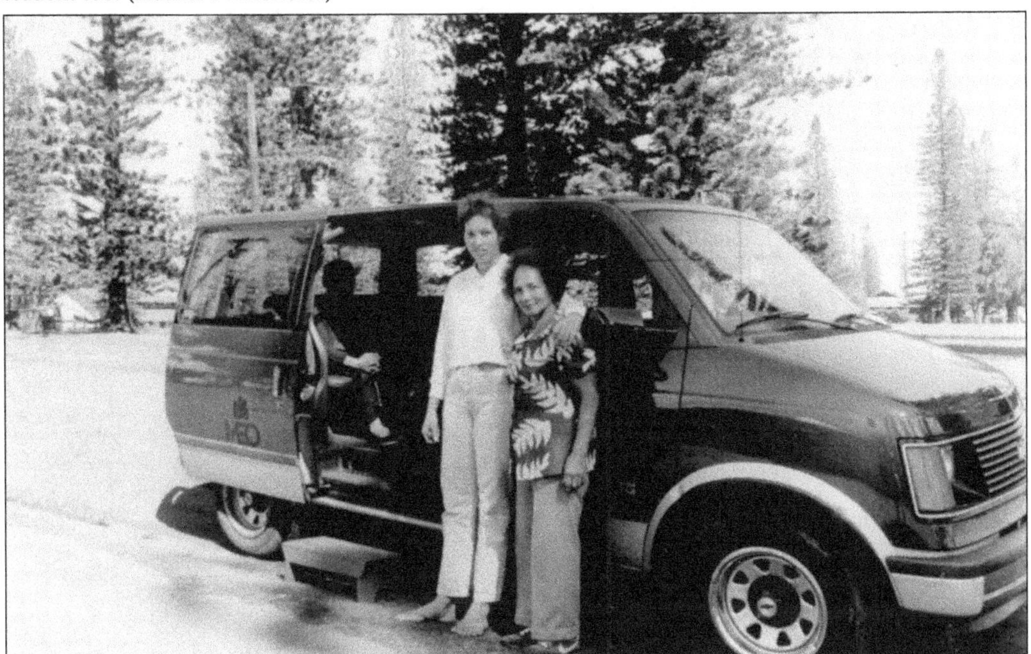

At Lāna'i Senior Center, Cherly Kaiaokamalie, whose family history dates back to the early days at Kaumālapa'u Harbor, is providing a ride home to Rose Pajente. Rose moved into a new plantation house in 1927 with her husband, raised her family, and lived in it until the 2000s. When she moved to O'ahu to live with her family, her home was demolished and replaced with a new house. (Author's collection.)

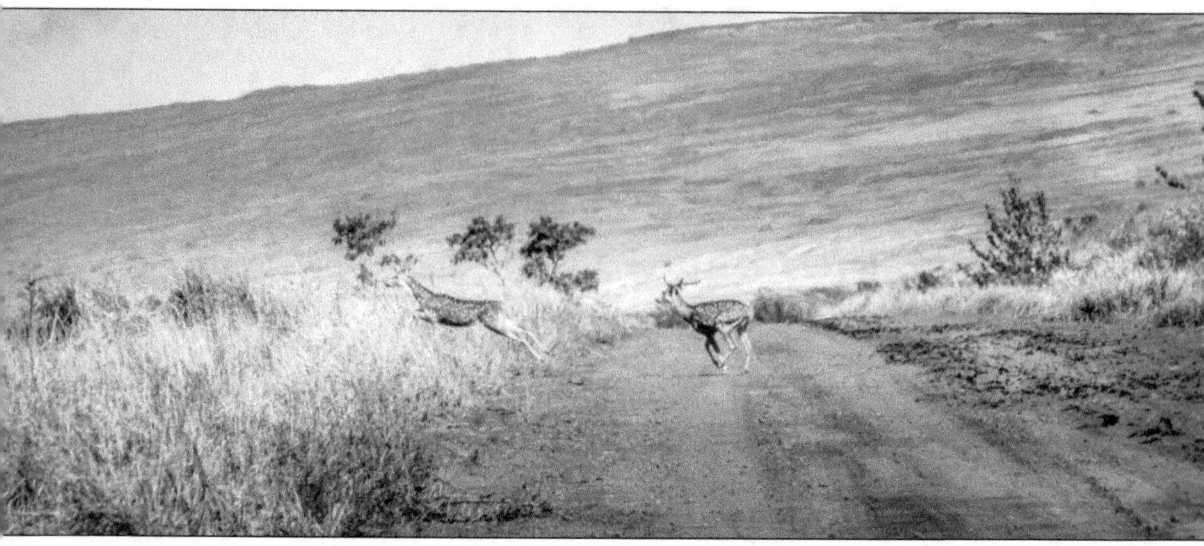

Foreign governments frequently sent gifts to maintain the goodwill of the ruling monarch in the Hawaiian kingdom. King Kamehameha V, who reigned from 1863 to 1872, received a gift of axis deer, four bucks and four does, from the Hong Kong consulate. Captured above the upper Ganges River in India, they were shipped from Calcutta to Hong Kong. Although several of the deer died before reaching Hong Kong, they were replaced and transferred to the *Loch Na Garr* bound for Hawai'i and arrived in December 1867. In January 1868, they were shipped to Moloka'i and released. In 1920, a dozen deer were transferred to Lāna'i at George Munro's suggestion to Frank and Harry Baldwin, owners of the island at that time. At Mānele Bay, the deer were released on the boat and swam to shore. They settled in the cactus patches in the Pālāwai. When the plantation began to remove cactus to cultivate pineapples, the deer migrated to the fringe of the forest. The pineapple company managed to control the deer population by allowing its employees to hunt them. Although later efforts were made to eradicate the deer entirely, they were not successful. Today, the watershed has been enclosed by fencing to protect it from deer. During droughts, the ungulates move into Lāna'i City and have been seen grazing at night in Dole Park. (Russell de Jetley photograph.)

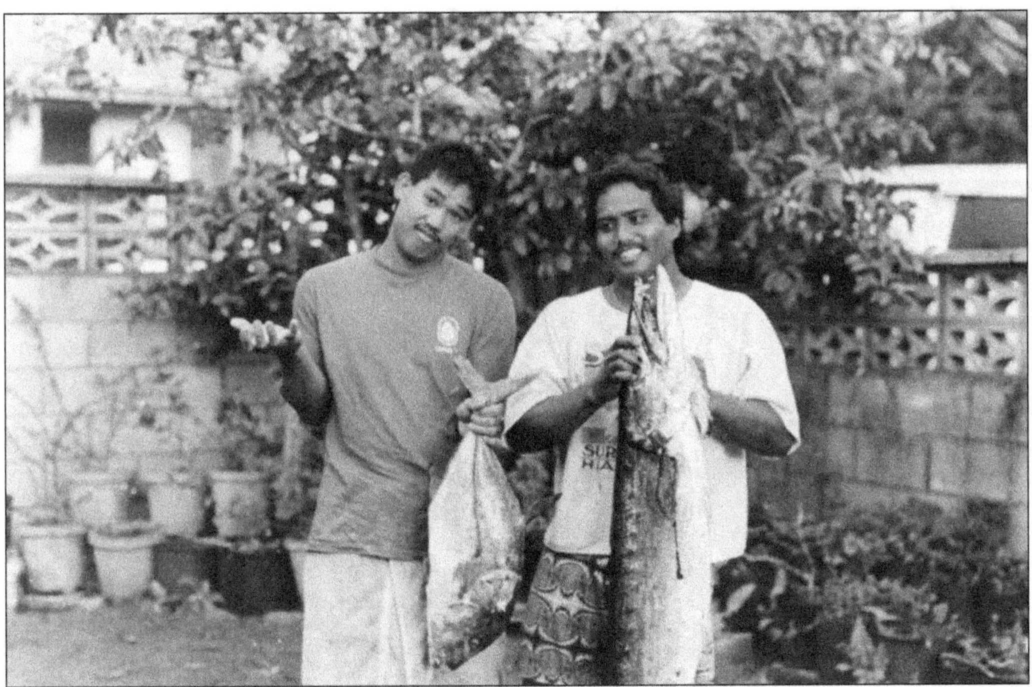

Living off the bounty of the sea and land is important to many Lāna'i residents. Many continue to provide for their families by fishing and hunting. Returning home from a fishing trip, Aurelio "Sonny" Batoon and Lyndel Cabuta show off their catch. (Joana Varawa collection.)

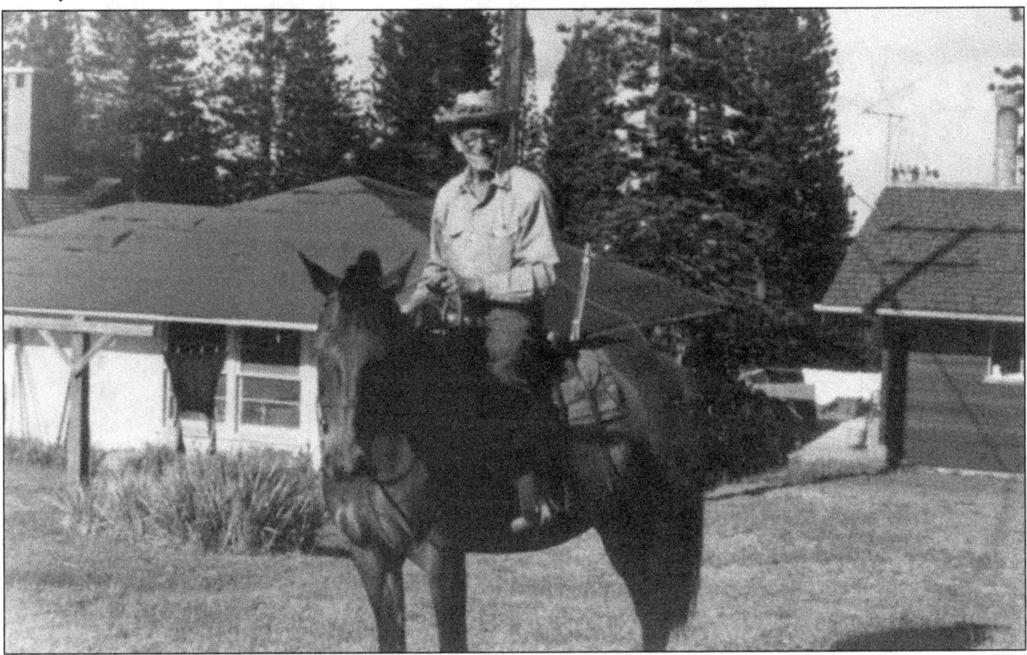

Dr. Kenneth P. Emory continued to visit Lāna'i and shared his knowledge of the places he had surveyed in his book *The Island of Lāna'i, A Survey of Native Culture*, with the island's younger residents and historians. Images of a younger Emory climbing to the top of Pu'upehe contrast sharply with this photograph of him on horseback in later years, but the memories of his excursions never faded. (A. Duane Black collection.)

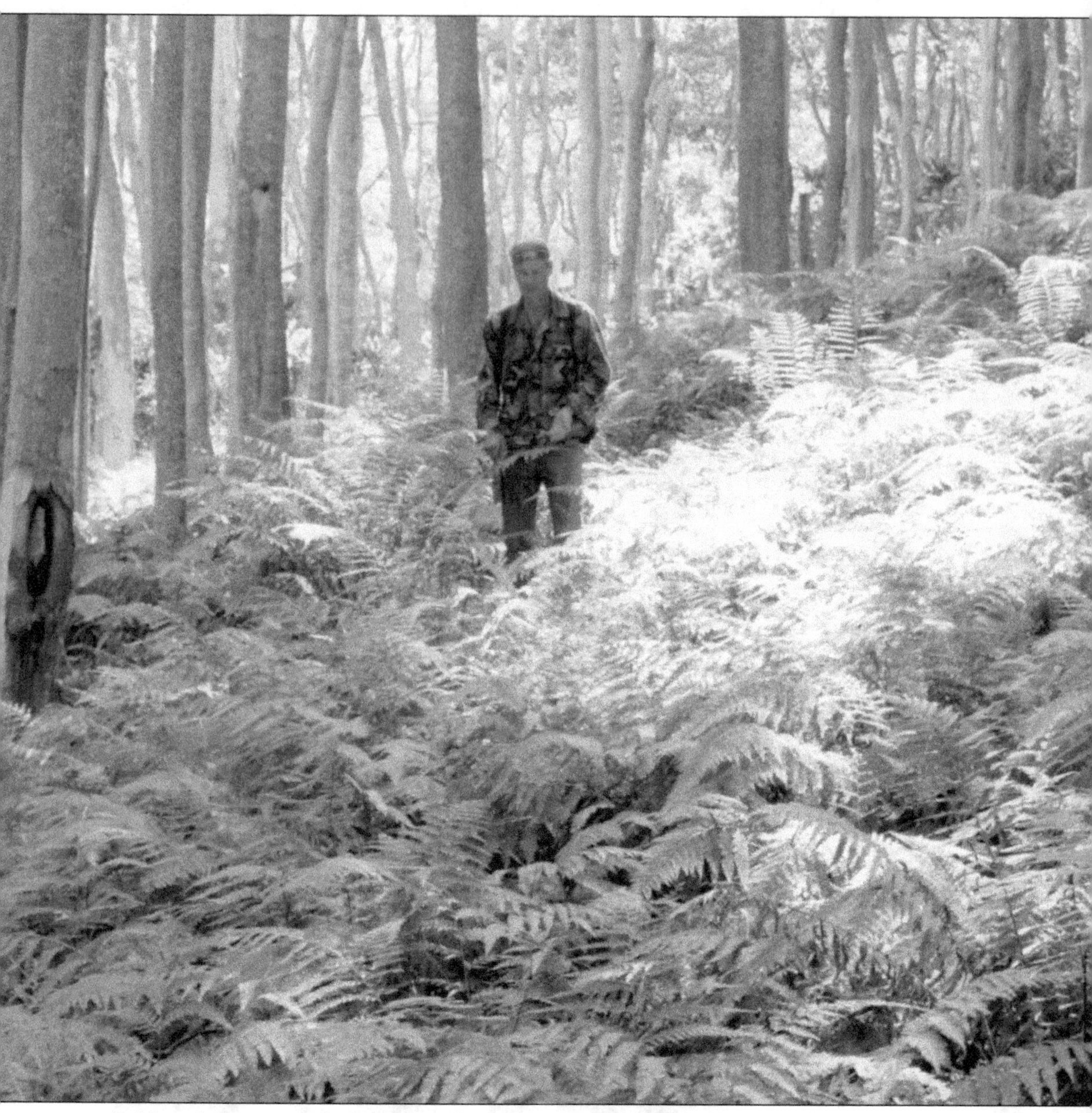

At Maunalei, ancient kukui trees have flourished throughout the changes in the island's history. Native Hawaiians collected the trees' nuts and used the oil to fuel torches they made. Albert Morita, president of the Lāna'i Culture and Heritage Center, stands within the grove. Like the ancient Hawaiians torches, the cultural center will continue to light a pathway to preserve Lāna'i's history for generations to come. (Kepā Maly collection.)

Seven

Looking Back and Moving Forward

It would have been a wonderful adventure to accompany Dr. Kenneth Emory when he surveyed Lānaʻi for the Bernice Puahi Bishop Museum and his book *The Island of Lānaʻi, A Survey of Native Culture*. Born on November 23, 1897, in Fitchburg, Massachusetts, Kenneth Pike Emory died peacefully on January 2, 1992, on Oʻahu. A frequent visitor to Lānaʻi, Emory graciously signed his book at a reception on February 2, 1982.

To sit in a circle gathered around Walter Murray Gibson and hear him tell legends of Lānaʻi would have been enchanting. Born on March 6, 1822, he became legendary himself. A confidant of King David Kalākaua, he lived in a grass hale in Pālāwai until he moved his ranch to Kōʻele. He died alone in San Francisco on January 21, 1888.

Throughout Lānaʻi's history, times of growth were followed by a decline in population. Lānaʻi became the property of one man when Charles Gay consolidated all the government-owned lands under his ownership. Later, he was forced to sell all of it except for 600 acres to settle mortgage obligations.

Each change of ownership brought new ways and ideas. James D. Dole changed Lānaʻi the most when he started the Hawaiian Pineapple Company and provided thousands of immigrants with jobs and homes. George C. Munro came to Lānaʻi to manage Lānaʻi Ranch and created the watershed on Lānaʻihale. His book *The Story of Lānaʻi* takes readers into the daily lives of the people of Kōʻele and the inner workings of Lānaʻi Ranch.

The memories of David H. Murdock's ownership of Lānaʻi between 1985 and 2012 are still fresh in the minds of many residents. Feisty and fearless, he dragged an aging community through the pineapple fields and emerged with a new economy based on tourism. His vision for Lānaʻi ended in 2012; faced with a worldwide recession, he was forced to sell the island he loved beyond reason to multibillionaire Larry Ellison. Residents look backward fondly and move forward with courage.

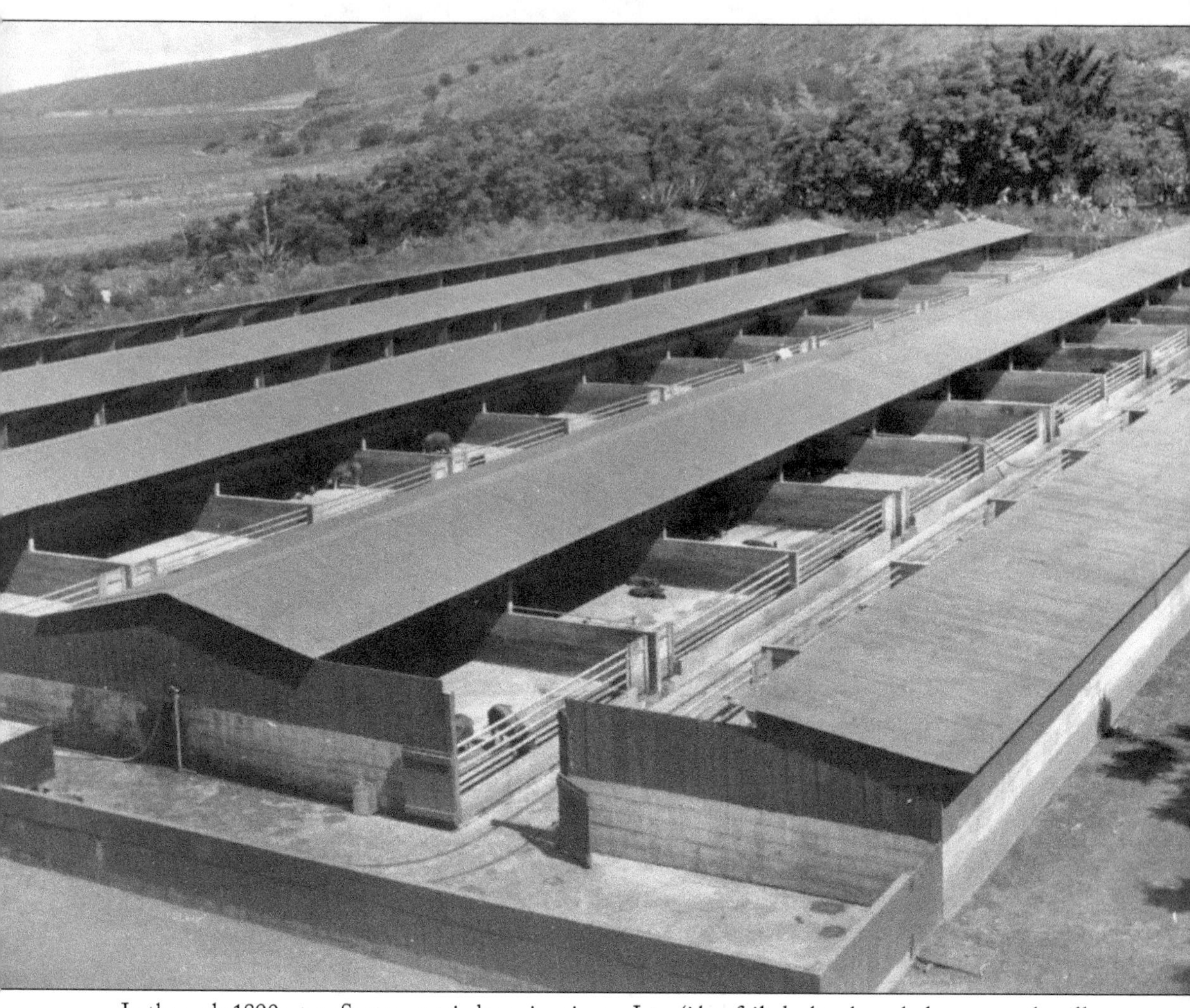

In the early 1890s, two Scotsmen tried to raise pigs on Lāna'i but failed when hog cholera or another illness killed their stock. When George Munro arrived in 1911, Captain Soule was raising pigs at Waiapa'a Flats and a Mr. Paulsen was growing beets. Both ventures failed. However, Lāna'i Company did well with a Pālāwai hog farm, which eventually closed in the 1950s. (HAPCo collection.)

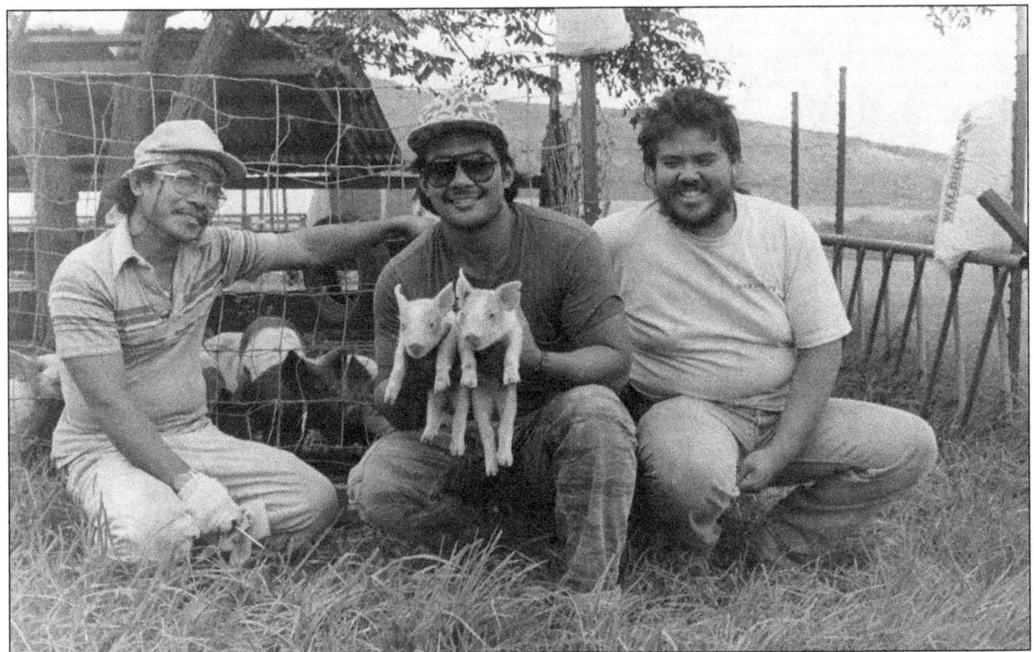

In 1986, Castle & Cooke began a diversified agricultural program on the island and started to raise hogs again at the Pālāwai facility. From left to right, Boyat Balcaso, Ed Magaoay, and Curtis Pacada inspect some arriving piglets. Other residents also raised hogs in small operations at different locations, but they all closed over time. (Joana Varawa collection.)

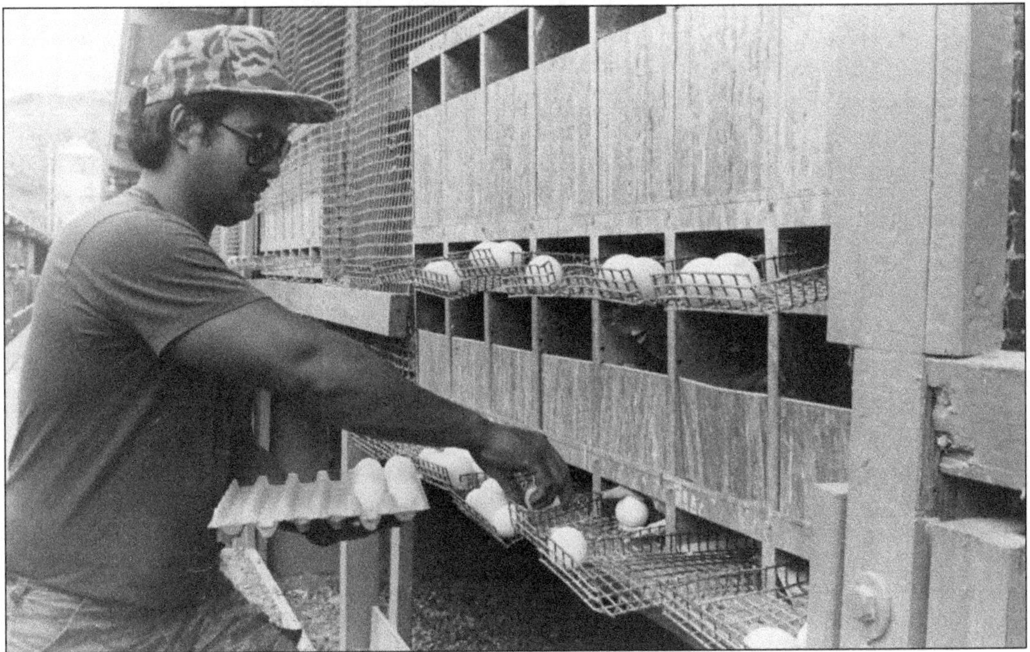

Ed Magaoay gathers fresh eggs at the Diversified Agriculture Division. Although the hens laid well, the poultry farm was not able to meet its expenses and closed. In later years, a resident started raising free-range hens and sold their eggs within the community. Although he was selling live chickens to residents too, the business was not economically viable and closed. (Joana Varawa collection.)

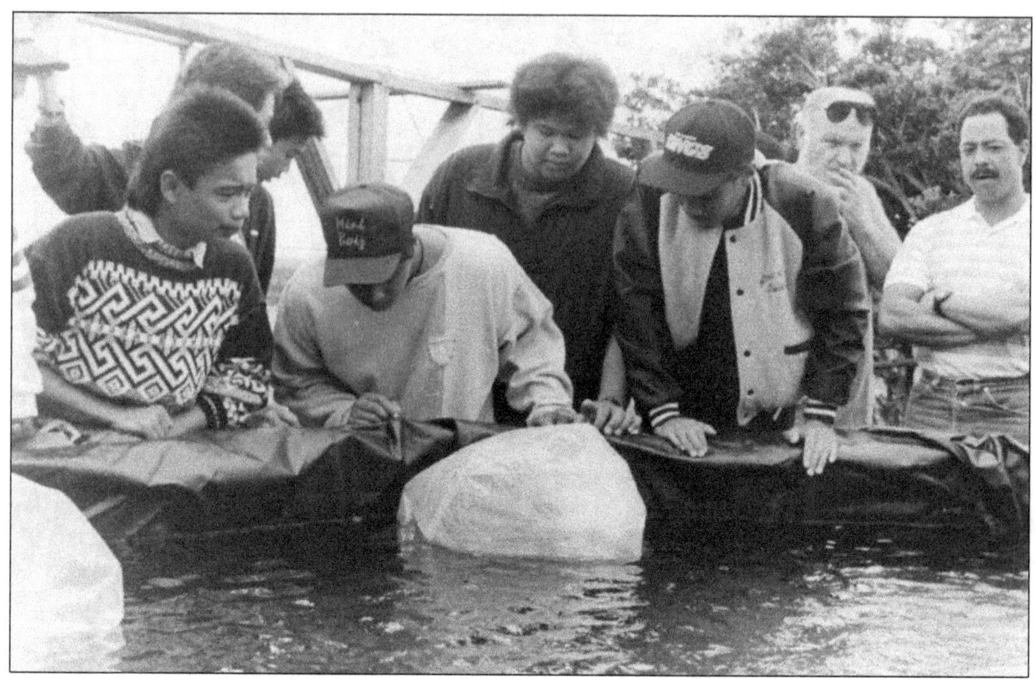

Raising fish such as tilapia became very popular but never grew into a viable business for Lāna'i residents or Castle & Cooke. Although a few residents continue to raise tilapia and catfish in backyard above-ground ponds, it is for their own consumption, and they do not sell their fish to the general public. For a short time, residents also experimented with growing snails, which were sold to the resorts. (Joana Varawa collection.)

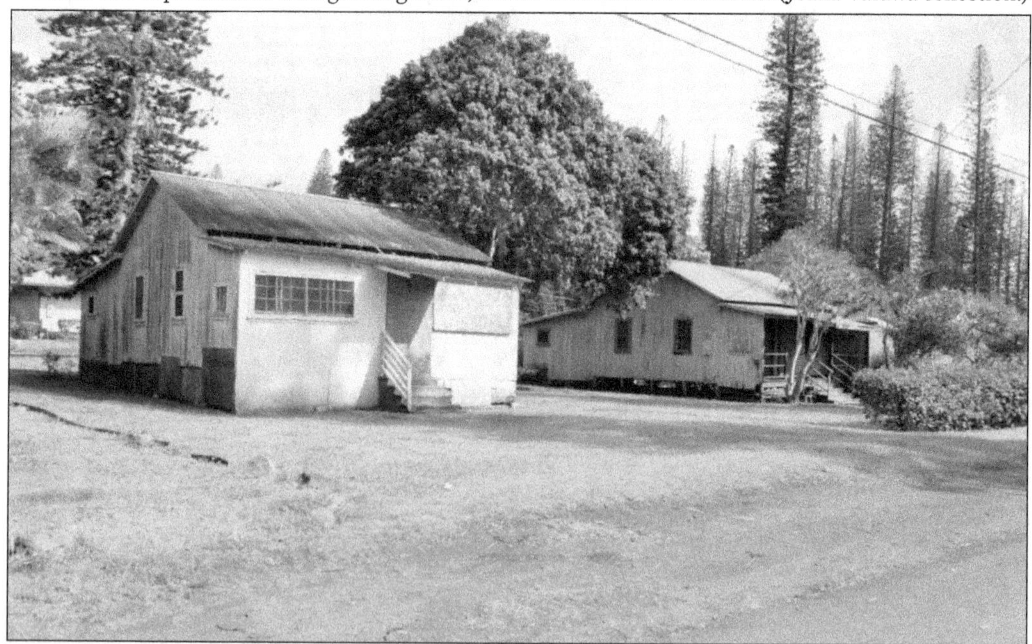

Two plantation era houses are being renovated to meet the community's current needs. Hospice Lāna'i will have two hospice care beds in the building on the left. The building on the right will be a physical therapy facility. Many of the community's older buildings are being renovated instead of demolished. (Author's collection.)

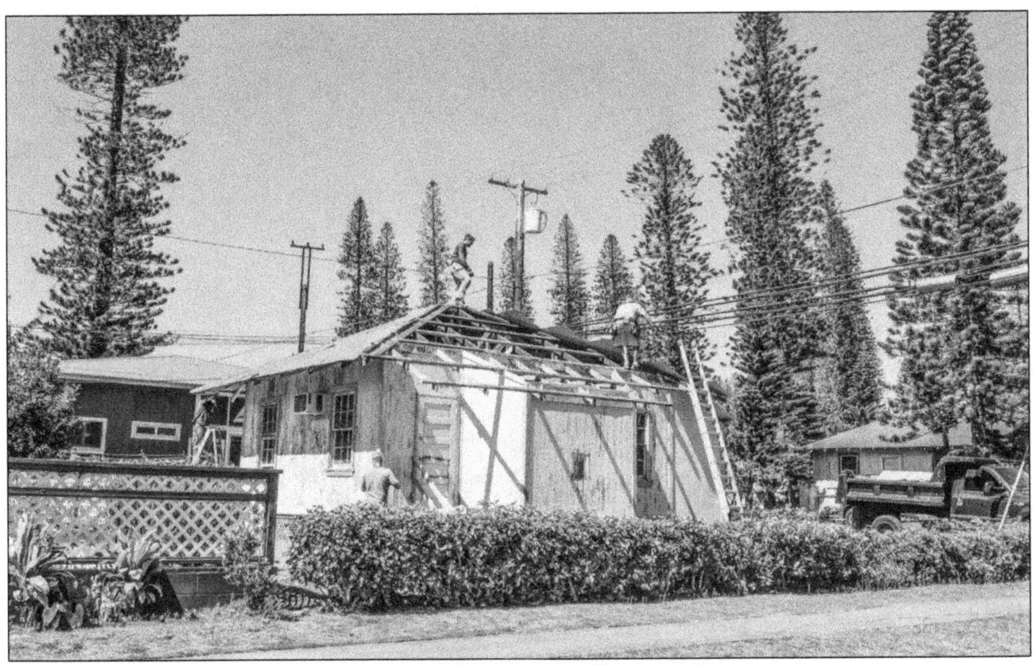

This plantation house has been repurposed several times since it was originally built during the plantation days. It has served as a kingdom hall for Jehovah Witnesses, a thrift shop for the Lāna'i Cancer Fund, and is now a hula *halau* (dance school) to teach the island's keiki their heritage through dance and music. (Author's collection.)

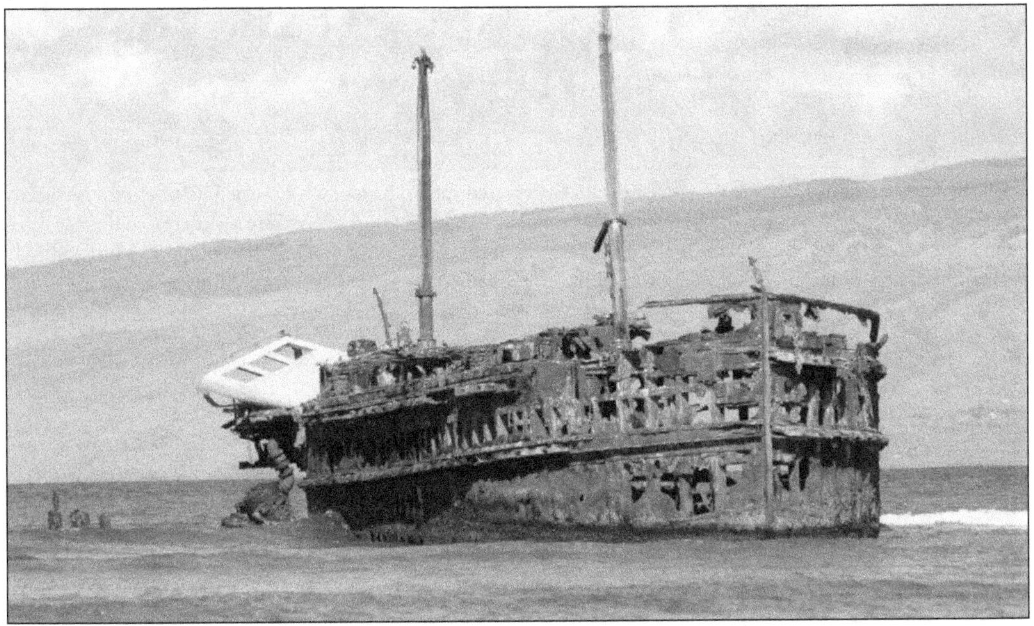

Shipwrecks abound on the island's north shore, where winds gusting in the ocean channel between Lāna'i and Moloka'i can change direction and funnel unsuspecting mariners directly onto the shore. Fourteen sites have been marked with the remains of unfortunate vessels. A Navy oil tanker, Y0-21, was intentionally abandoned in the 1950s and defied nature by refusing to rust into its watery grave beneath the sea. (Simon Tajiri collection.)

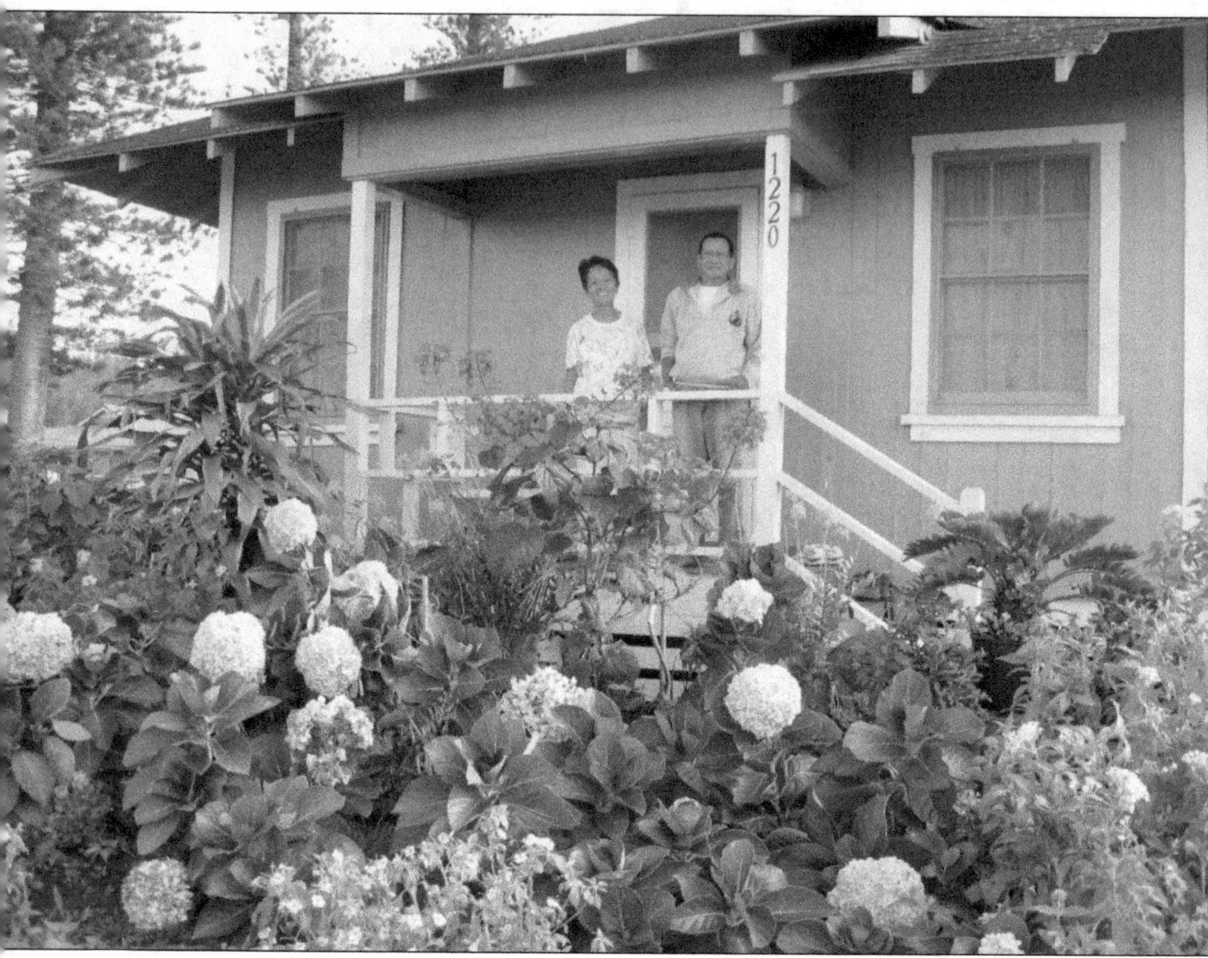

Barbara and Tony Guillen stand on the porch of their plantation home, which was built by the Hawaiian Pineapple Company in the period between 1923 and 1927. Although many of the city's original houses have been remodeled to suit the needs of their present owners, the Guillens' home has remained unchanged. Its flower-filled garden makes it a favorite of photographers and artists. (Author's collection.)

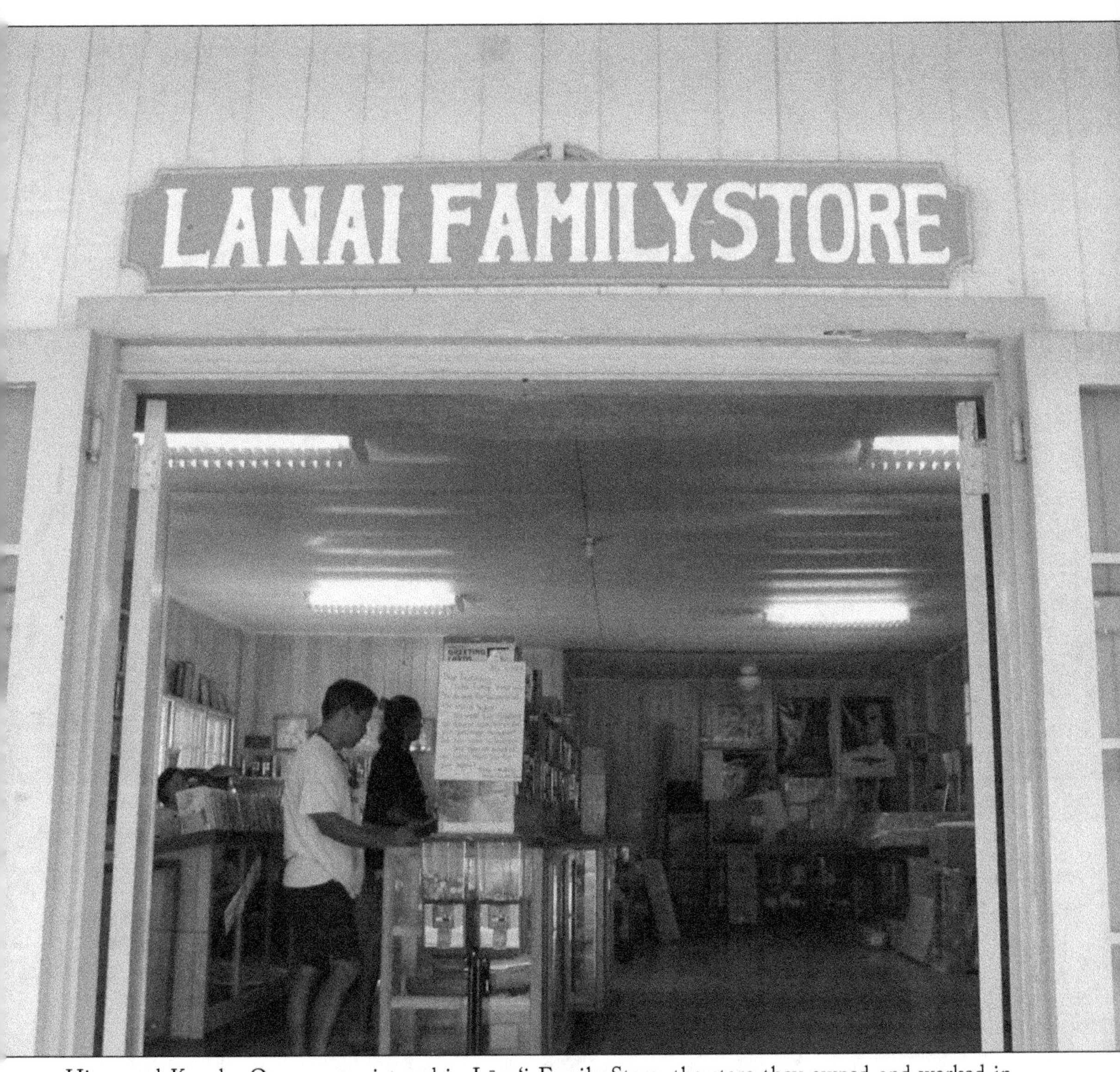

Hirao and Kazuko Oyama are pictured in Lāna'i Family Store, the store they owned and worked in together from 1951 until it closed in 2004. Hirao's family moved to Lāna'i in 1924 and worked with the plantation mules to plow its fields. In high school, Hirao was athletic and played tennis, basketball, and baseball. After he graduated in 1946, he became a carpenter but left to become a police officer for Maui County. In 1949, he resumed his carpentry position, and in 1951, he built his own store. Hirao was active in the Boy Scouts of America and was honored for his 72 years of scouting with the Lāna'i District Boy Scouts District Award of Merit and the Silver Beaver Award from the Boy Scouts Maui County Council. In addition to being a carpenter, store owner, and scout leader, he was a television repairman and a great storyteller. (Joana Varawa collection.)

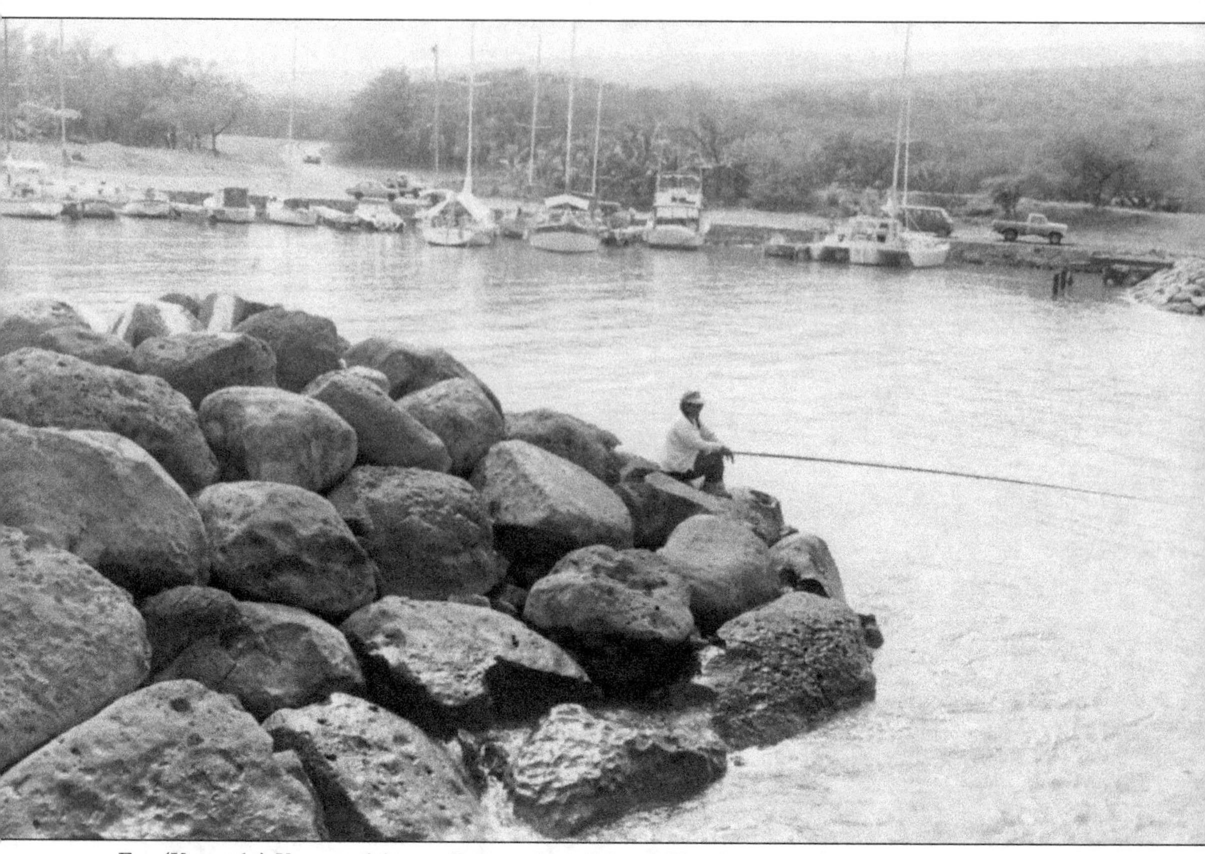

Eva (Kaopuiki) Kwon is fishing off the rocks at Mānele Bay for *halalū* (young mackerel). When schools of the fish enter the bay, fishers line the breakwater to pole fish and can quickly fill their pails with the fingerlings, which are from three to five inches long. Eva was the youngest child of Daniel and Hattie Kaopuiki and was raised in Keōmoku. (Author's collection.)

Rebecca (Kaopuiki) Richardson (seated) is pictured here with her daughters Mary Ellen "Suki" Nakoa (left) and Charlotte Holsomback. After they graduated, both daughters made their homes on O'ahu. Charlotte's daughter Michele Holsomback is currently Lāna'i High and Elementary's vice principal. Rebecca and her husband, Ernest, a ranch paniolo, lived at Kō'ele for most of their lives. (Kepā Maly collection.)

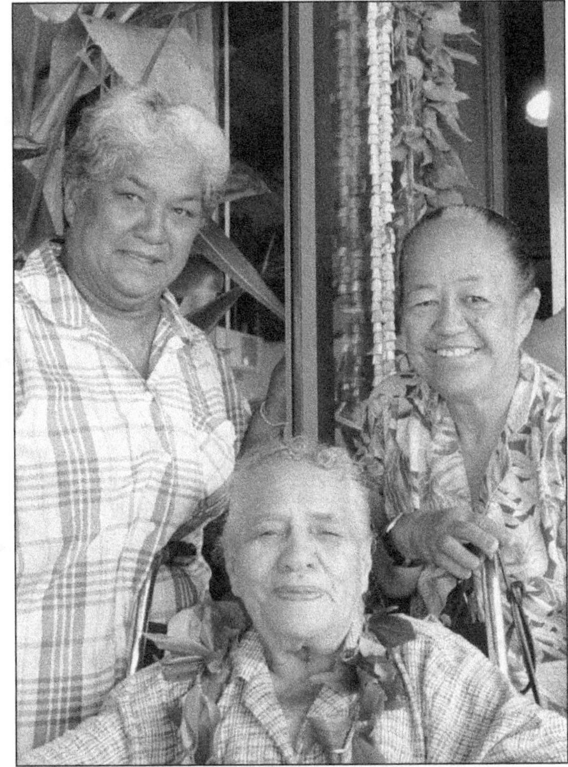

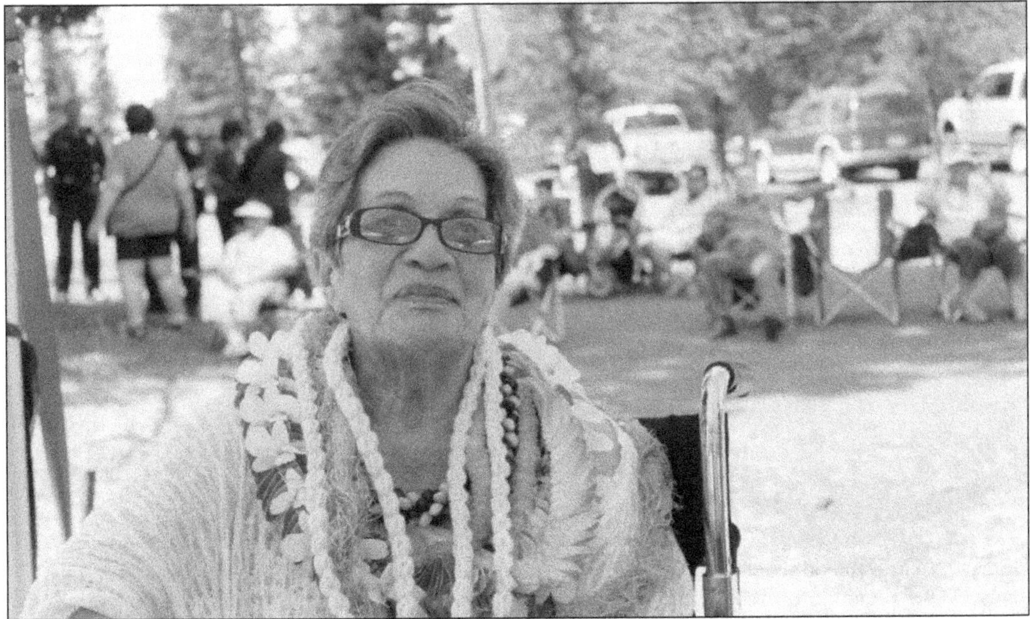

Harriet (Kaopuiki) Catiel's parents were Daniel and Hattie Kaopuiki. After her family moved to Lāna'i City, Harriet met her husband, Raymond S. "Scoop" Catiel, at a baseball game and married him. She was famous for her yellow cake with peach frosting and frequently baked it for her extended *ohana* (family) and friends. Although she resides at Hale Makua, a long-term care facility in Kahului, Maui, she is pictured here at the Festival of Aloha parade on Lāna'i in 2012. (Author's collection.)

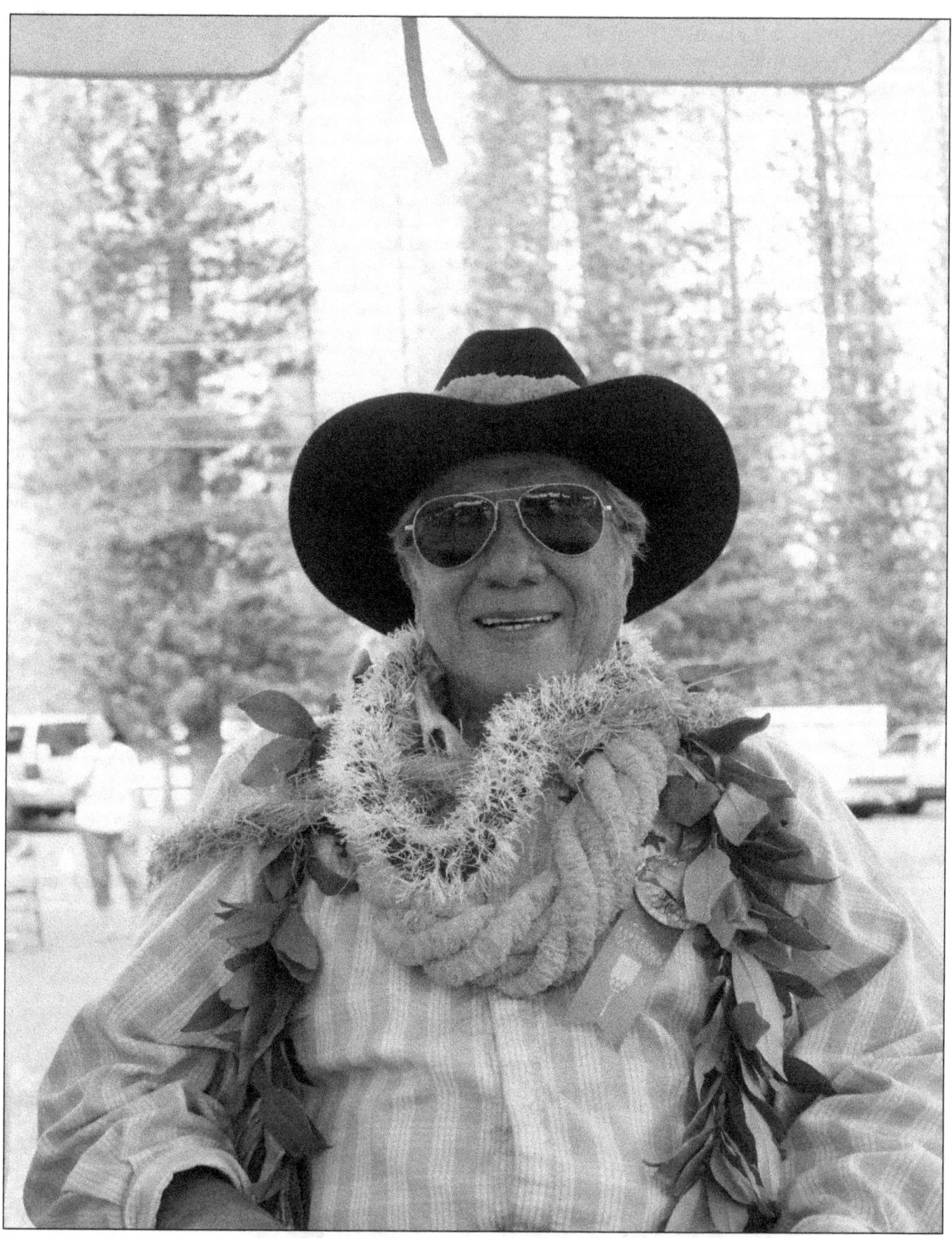

Henry Ah Yin Kau Aki lived in Lāhainā Maui with his family and frequently traveled to Lāna'i with his uncle Daniel Kaopuiki on Lāna'i Ranch's mail boat, *Nunu Lawe Leka*. During the summer months, he stayed at Keōmoku with them. As an adult, he worked at Kaumālapa'u Harbor and lived in the village above it. He was born on November 25, 1924, and died on May 6, 2015. (Author's collection.)

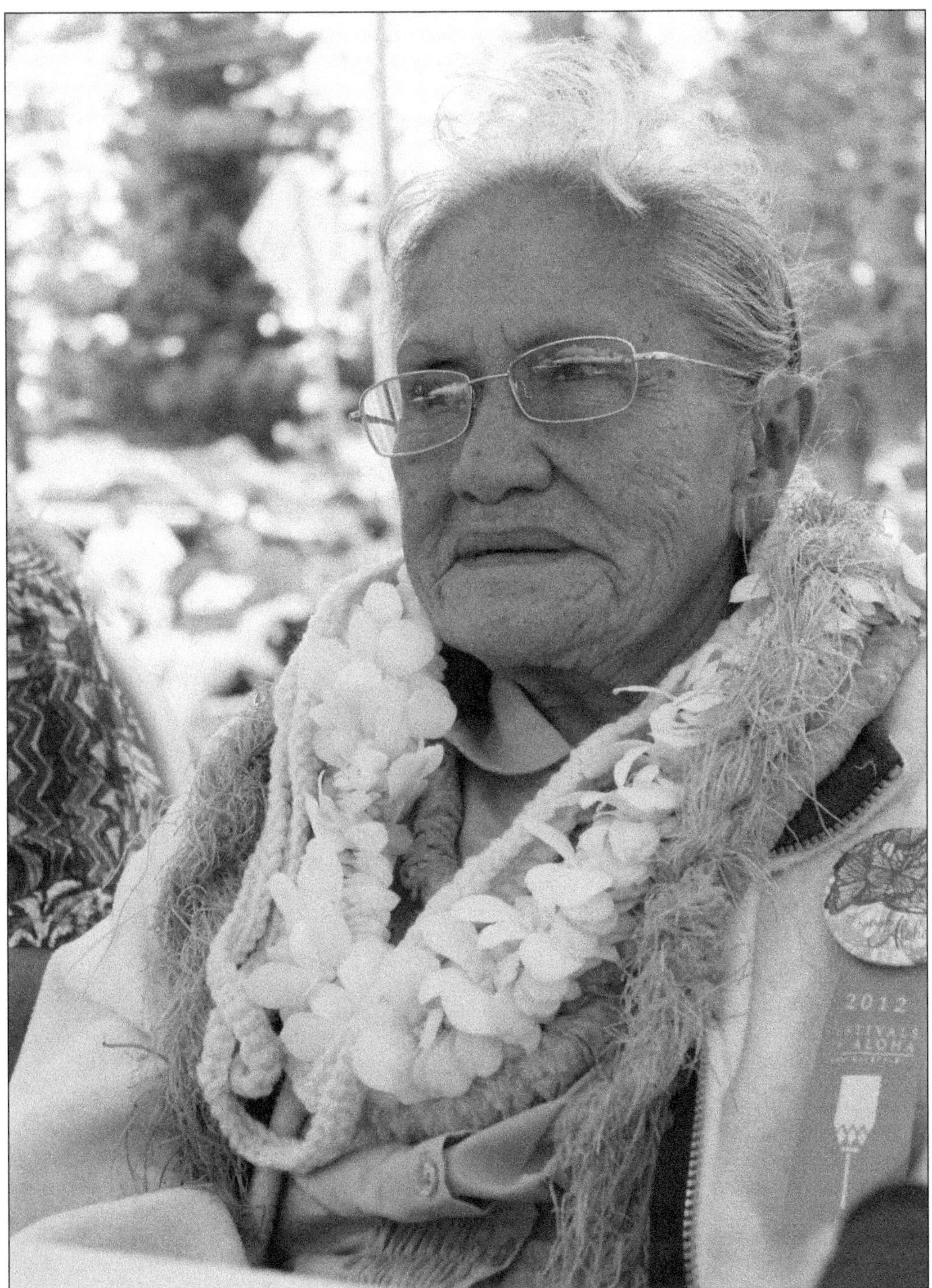

The Rev. Lei (Kaopuiki) Kanipae is the oldest living resident on Lāna'i from Keōmoku village. She has fond memories of helping her father harvest watermelons and carrying them to his boat to take to Lāhainā to sell. His young helpers made sure they dropped at least one or two watermelons every time they helped him so they could eat them themselves. (Author's collection.)

Glossary of Hawaiian Words and Names

Ahi	Isleways tugboat operated by Hawaiian Pineapple Company
ahupua'a	land divisions to assure resources for sustainable living were available for natives
'aina	land, earth
ākulikuli	succulent plant with bright pink flowers used in lei-making
ali'i	chief, ruler, monarch
'Au'au	ocean channel between Lāna'i and Maui
Ha'ikū	land division in East Maui
hale	house, building
Hale Keaka	name of Lāna'i theater
hānai	adopted, either legally or informally
Hawai'i	name of Big Island and of state
Hawaiian	native-born person of Polynesian ancestry
hoe-hana	to work with a hoe, plantation slang
honu	turtle
Ho'okio	fortified ridge in upper Maunalei Gulch, translates to "spread out"
'ili	parcel of land in a section of an ahupua'a
Iosepa	Mormon settlement in Pālāwai, translates to "City of Joseph"
Iwi'ole	apartment complex in Lāna'i City, translates to "adze"
Ka'a	Ahupua'a on western end of Lāna'i, translates to "roll, turn, or twist"
Kahalepalaoa	pier and landing site for boats near Keōmoku village across from Lāhainā, Maui
Kahalu'u	village in windward O'ahu, translates to "diving place"
Kahekili	last independent king of Maui (1710–1794)
Ka Hoku Paa Kea	the North Star, or fixed star
Kaho'olawe	uninhabited island in Maui County formerly used as a bombing range
Kainoahou	middle name of Lawrence Gay and Gay family ancestor, son of last king of Kaua'i and Ni'ihau, translates to "the sea is free"
Kalaehī	white coral knoll on northeastern coast of Lāna'i, translates to "white rock/stone"
Ka maka o Pahulu	translates to "the eye of Pahulu" from legendary story of Kaululā'au
Kalākaua	King David, last reigning monarch of Kingdom of Hawai'i (November 16, 1836–January 20, 1891)
Kalaniana'ole	Prince Kūhiō, crown prince during Kalākaua's reign, known as the Prince of People
Kalani'ōpu'u	king of Hawai'i island, killed almost every native on Lāna'i in 1778
Kamehameha	founded Kingdom of Hawai'i and dynasty lasting almost a century, died May 8, 1819
Kamoku	ahupua'a that goes across Lāna'i from north to south coasts
kāne	male gender
Kānepu'u	site of native dry land forest preserve
kaukau	eat, food: plantation slang used by field laborers, "come kaukau," come eat.

Kaumālapa'u	deep-water harbor on Lāna'i's south coast
Kaululā'au	legendary boy/man who rid Lāna'i of evil spirits, making it safe for human inhabitants
Kaunolū	land area on south coast, site of Kamehameha's summer fishing grounds/village
Kaupō	land area on East Maui coast and name of gap into Haleakalā Crater
Kawānānākoa	Nephew of King David Kalākaua, declared heir to the throne of the Hawaiian kingdom when Princess Kaiulani died. (February 19, 1868–June 2, 1908.)
Ke Alii Maka'āinana	chief/king of the common people
keiki	child, either gender
Keōmoku	village on northeastern coast of Lāna'i, translates to "white ship"
kiawe	mesquite tree
Kihamāniania	ruins of a stone church and school built by missionaries in 1840s, located next to Cavendish Golf Course
Kō 'ele	land division in central Lāna'i, translates to "dark sugar cane"
konohiki	land overseer
Kūhiō	Prince Jonah Kūhiō Kalaniana'ole
kuleana	small parcel of land assigned to natives for farm or house site; right, privilege
kumu	teacher, tutor
kūpuna	elder persons, ancestors, plural of either gender (kupuna is singular)
kukui	candlenut tree, bears oily nuts used for lights
Lāhaina	Maui village, former capital of Hawaiian kingdom, located across from Keōmoku
La'ie	village on windward O'ahu coast where Mormon settlers relocated
Lālākoa	Name of Charles Gay family home and Lāna'i subdivision; translates to "strong limbs"
Lāna'i	translates to "day of conquest"
Lāna'ihale	mountain range 3,366–3,370 feet above sea level
limu	seaweed
Luahiwa	site of petroglyph field in Pā'lā'wai
luna	foreman, overseer, field boss
Māhele	"Great Māhele" is the name of the government act that divided land in the Kingdom of Hawai'i
Mai'ōku'u	disease, possibly cholera, that killed Keōmoku villagers in 1900s
makai	toward the ocean, seaward
Maka'āinana	natives, common people
mō'i	king, chief, ruler
Moloka'i	fifth largest island in the state, part of County of Maui
Naia	inter-island steam ship that carried passengers and freight to Lāna'i
Ni'ihau	smallest inhabited island in state, privately owned by descendants of Gay family
Nininiwai	site where pineapple was first planted on island
Nunu Lawe Leke	Keōmoku mail boat, translates to "pigeon transport letter"
O'ahu	second largest island in state, capital of Hawai'i
'ōpihi	edible limpet collected from rocks along coast
Pahulu	chief/king of the evil spirits who are said to have inhabited Lāna'i
Pālāwai	land division in central Lāna'i, site of Mormon settlement 1854–1858
paniolo	cowboy
pānini	prickly pear cactus plants used as cattle feed
pili	native grass, translates to "cling together"
Pu'upehe	rocky islet in Mānele district, legendary burial site of two lovers
wahine	girl, woman
Waikapū	village on island of Maui
weke	red goatfish; evil spirits entered bodies of weke in legendary tale of Kaululā'au

www.ingramcontent.com/pod-product-compliance
Lightning Source LLC
LaVergne TN
LVHW081546100826
845153LV00004B/319

* 9 7 8 1 5 3 1 6 7 8 3 1 9 *